# PRETTYGOODHOUSE

## A GUIDE TO CREATING BETTER HOMES

DAN KOLBERT    EMILY MOTTRAM    MICHAEL MAINES    CHRISTOPHER BRILEY

The Taunton Press

The Taunton Press
Inspiration for hands-on living®

The Taunton Press, Inc.
63 South Main Street
Newtown, CT 06470-2344
Email: tp@taunton.com

Publisher: Mark Peterson
Editor: Peter Chapman
Illustrations: Mario Ferro, except as noted on p. 248
Cover/Interior design: Lynne Phillips
Layout: Lynne Phillips
Front cover photo: Robert Swinburne
Back cover photos: top, Kat Alves; bottom left, François Gagné; bottom right, Irvin Serrano
Title page photo: François Gagné

Library of Congress Control Number: 2022906240
ISBN 9781641551656

Printed in the United States of America
10 9 8 7 6 5 4 3 2

# DEDICATION

*Thanks to our families for resigning themselves to us all being overcommitted. Again.*

# ACKNOWLEDGMENTS

NOT MANY BOOKS HAVE FOUR AUTHORS, so this was a team effort by definition. But we also had the help and support of many others.

First, we need to thank our "fifth Beatle," Robert Swinburne, architect at Bluetime Collaborative in southern Vermont. Bob reviewed drafts of everything we wrote and was the driving force behind our website, PrettyGoodHouse.org.

We relied on the superior knowledge and experience of many of our friends for input and guidance. Steve Konstantino, who hosts our Building Science Discussion Group, has been central to the endeavor from the beginning, and shared his window and door expertise. Dr. Allison Bailes III, who was in the middle of writing his own book, provided critical help with the Mechanical Systems chapter. June Donenfeld helped Emily turn thoughts into intelligible sentences. David Warfel provided important content for the lighting section. David Gerstel, an inspiration for anyone writing a book, helped tighten up the introduction.

We've had plenty of people cheer on both Pretty Good House as a concept and the book in particular. Standouts include: Ben Bogie, Travis Brungardt, and Kiley Jacques, co-hosts of The BS* + Beer Show (*building science) along with Emily & Michael; Heather Chandler, editor of *Green & Healthy Maine Homes;* Brian Pontolilo, former editor of both Green Building Advisor (GBA) and *Fine Homebuilding;* and Martin Holladay, Brian's predecessor at GBA and perhaps our first booster.

Thanks to everyone who submitted a case study for the book. There wasn't room for all of them! Read more of them at PrettyGoodHouse.org.

Anyone writing about building science owes a debt of gratitude to Drs. Joe Lstiburek and John Straube; everyone's work relies on what they have done, whether consciously or not. And the community at the Northeast Sustainable Energy Association (NESEA) has been inspirational, supportive, and an essential resource.

We tried to get the book off the ground years ago, but it took the team at Taunton Press to make it happen. Working with four authors who have busy day jobs quadrupled their frustration level, but they were wonderful to work with. Peter Chapman saw to it that we covered everything important in a coherent, clear manner. Mark Peterson alternated cheerleading with well-timed kicks in the backside as needed. And Scott Gibson, another Mainer, did yeoman's service writing the case studies and reviewing the chapters for content and clarity. None of us had ever written anything lengthier than an article for *Fine Homebuilding* magazine, so if this book helps people out, the glory is theirs.

Thanks also to the wider community:

- Fellow builders and designers who have shared their knowledge at the Building Science Discussion Group or BS + Beer Show.

- Fans and practitioners of building science who, as a group, are unusually open about sharing knowledge.

- Our past, present, and future clients who inspire us to do better (and keep us grounded with their budgets).

- Anyone who has ever screwed up a building detail and shared the mistake with us!

# CONTENTS

Introduction                                                        2

CHAPTER 1    THINGS TO KNOW BEFORE YOU START            10

Case Study 1:  Seville Residence                              24

CHAPTER 2    ECONOMICS                                       30

Case Study 2:  Maquoit Bay                                   42

CHAPTER 3    DESIGN                                          48

Case Study 3:  Copper Farmhouse                              76

CHAPTER 4    BUILDING ENVELOPE BASICS                        84

Case Study 4:  Sugar Bush House                             108

CHAPTER 5    WATER/MOISTURE MANAGEMENT                      112

Case Study 5:  Jamaica Plain Legacy                         127

CHAPTER 6    WINDOWS AND EXTERIOR DOORS                     132

Case Study 6:  Timeless Barn                                149

CHAPTER 7     MATERIALS                                      154

    Case Study 7:  Low-Chem House                        178

CHAPTER 8     MECHANICAL SYSTEMS                     184

    Case Study 8:  Meadow View House                     202

CHAPTER 9     ELECTRICITY AND LIGHTING            208

    Case Study 9:  Pretty Good Renovation               218

CHAPTER 10    VERIFICATION AND
                    CLIENT EDUCATION                     224

    Case Study 10:  Pretty Good Garage                   240


In Closing          244

Glossary            245

Credits             248

Index               250

# INTRODUCTION

This book was written two decades into the new millennium, as global warming was producing record heat, storms, and floods. Houses were being built by the millions, and far too many of them were being built badly. They are unhealthy for their occupants, prone to decay and early failure, and are energy gobblers contributing massively to global warming.

None of that is inevitable. We now have the knowledge, the building science coupled with deep hands-on experience, to build much better houses. It is incumbent on those of us designing, building, or owning houses to make them better—more efficient, more resilient, and healthier—even as we strive to make them more comfortable, and beautiful. This book attempts to help us get there.

The first building scientists were presumably our hominid ancestors who figured out that a cave would keep them dry in the rain and cool in the heat. A million or so years later, we started building houses, and that's when the fun really began. If nothing else, houses represented a way to pass on accumulated wisdom about living in various climates.

For the next 15,000 years, we became more settled, and our houses got more sophisticated. We got better at keeping the weather out, letting sunlight in, and making our houses last longer. They became not just shelters but homes.

As electricity became widely available, we took a quantum leap forward in what we expected from houses. We could see at any hour of the day or night, without having to light a candle. We could heat our homes without having to start a fire. The idea that we could control the inside of the house independently from the conditions outside became commonplace.

As our societies became less agrarian, and we spent more and more time indoors, ensuring that our houses kept us healthy became more and more

A discussion group session covering the then-new PrettyGoodHouse.org website, from November 2019.

urgent. In the past hundred years, a flood of new information and ideas has transformed our understanding of homes. Indoor air quality, separate from the outdoor air quality, is predicated on our increasing technological ability to monitor and improve the conditions of our homes.

The 21st century has seen an explosion in research and information. The field of building science has reached a wider and wider audience. Sophisticated sensors, able to collect data wirelessly, have shown us conditions that previously would have been discovered only by taking the building apart. The internet has allowed us to share research and conclusions at the speed of light. Of course, it also allows misinformation to spread just as quickly. And that was part of the motivation for writing *Pretty Good House*.

The authors are two architects (Chris Briley and Emily Mottram), a designer (Michael Maines), and a building contractor (Dan Kolbert), all living and working in the southern half of Maine. We are friends and colleagues and have spent countless hours discussing how to make houses better. In 2009, Steve Konstantino (owner of Performance Building Supply in Portland, Maine, devoted to selling products at the cutting edge of building science) and I started a Building Science Discussion Group, a monthly get-together to share our successes and mistakes, and improve the knowledge base of the building community in our area. One of our sessions, in December 2011, was titled "The Pretty Good House," and the invitations explained that I'd been wondering "(W)hen does enough become enough, and what is practical for a realistic budget?"

I'd had experience with various home-rating systems by that point, and I found them all to be useful and raising important questions. But I also knew that they raised costs, and, in order to get the rating, we were often doing things we didn't think were worth it. Passive House projects required insulation under the house well beyond the point of diminishing returns. Some projects ended up with bike racks to get LEED

points, with no idea of whether anyone would use them. "Point chasing" entered the lexicon, and not as a compliment.

A couple of years prior to this, I'd built what I'd later call the Original Pretty Good House. The clients wanted a relatively simple home with high performance, and they were definitely budget-conscious. It was only my company's second new house. Building it crystallized my thoughts on new construction and helped me think about our renovations' performance as well.

---

*...a well-thought-out, carefully crafted house, designed to maximize performance and comfort within a budget.*

---

When our first Pretty Good House discussion began, I had a lot of ideas. Fortunately, so did the rest of the group. In fact, we had so many ideas that two months later we returned to the subject to try to come up with some specifics on what we thought should be in, what out. A week later, Michael wrote it up for a popular website, and the idea quickly took off. Well over 100 people chimed in on the conversation, and a movement was born! The site's editor helped keep the conversation going by soliciting input from all over the country, in dramatically different climates, on what a Pretty Good House would look like for them. In no time at all, Pretty Good House became the nonstandard building standard, and it has become shorthand in the building-science world for a well-thought-out, carefully crafted house, designed to maximize performance and comfort within a budget.

Fast-forward to December 2018. In the intervening seven years, we learned more and more about the housing industry's contribution to the climate crisis, and how essential it was that we, as concerned professionals, take steps to address it. Thus

The original Pretty Good House, with photovoltaic array installed by the owners after construction.

was born PGH 2.0–the Low Carbon Edition. With another round of online discussions, and a session at Michael's spin-off BS & Beer discussion group north of Portland, we knew we were taking the idea in a critical new direction.

When Taunton Press approached us almost a year into the pandemic, we felt it was finally time to try to set down what we'd learned for a wider audience. COVID-19 had suddenly made topics like ventilation and indoor air quality mainstream. Spending unprecedented amounts of time in their homes made people painfully aware of comfort issues. And with travel and other recreation curtailed, they had more disposable income than ever to spend on their homes. We

wanted to make sure that the new homes and renovations were built as thoughtfully and efficiently as possible, with minimal environmental impact, and this book seemed like the right way to help.

We all are professionals with decades of experience, but we're not "experts" in the way some of our friends who have provided guidance are. But we're an inquisitive bunch, and we know how to ask the right people for information. Emily and Michael are two of the hosts of the wildly successful BS + Beer Show, a monthly building-science webcast born of COVID isolation. Chris co-hosted a terrific podcast called Green Architects Lounge. Both are interview-format shows with different guests. And as moderator

# Pretty Good Renovation

Most of building-science discussion is about new construction. That's because it's easier: you're starting with a blank slate and can design all the details to work together.

We know, though, that the vast majority of people are moving into an existing house, and the number of renovations dwarfs the number of new house builds. The building science of renovation is much trickier. There are innumerable conditions you can't be sure of without demolition. Things like: How thick is the basement slab? Does it drain well? How are the walls and roof insulated? Is the framing done well? Has the house been renovated before? You are retrofitting solutions onto existing conditions.

However, there is no question that buying an existing house is much better for the planet. You are avoiding the carbon load (see p. 155) of an entire house (or at the very least what you save of the house). Some of the most carbon- and energy-intensive parts of the house are done—the site preparation and excavation, the concrete in the foundation and slab, and harvesting, milling, and transporting the framing lumber, to name a few.

It will take a long time for even a superefficient new home to save the carbon already in place in an existing home. And if there's one thing we know we don't have much of, it is time.

So why isn't this book *Pretty Good Reno?* Mostly because it's much harder to come up with general rules about renovation. Any carpenter will tell you that renovation work requires a different set of skills and judgments than new construction. Framing isn't plumb, level, or square. One part of the house might be a century older than another. The basement might have water problems. Every situation requires a judgment call. As famed building scientist Dr. Joe Lstiburek says, good judgment comes from experience and experience comes from bad judgment. It takes a lot of renovations to make enough mistakes to develop good judgment! New construction is much more predictable, controllable, designable. Any rules we made, we'd have to break almost immediately.

Nevertheless, we will try, throughout this book, to point out how the PGH framework can help with existing homes. At the end of each chapter, in our "Things to Consider" lists, we have tried to include renovation items along with the ones for new homes.

of our discussion group, I tried to know who in the room I could call on to answer a question.

*Pretty Good House* is not a "how-to" book as much as a "why-to." You will not find step-by-step instructions or prescriptions on building a Pretty Good House. Instead, you'll find a guide to thinking through the critical issues of weather protection, air leakage, insulation and comfort, and vapor control. The four authors split up authorship of the chapters, and we brought in our friends, colleagues, and men-

tors for help filling in the gaps in our knowledge. Each chapter ends with a list of issues to consider. If you don't have answers to those items, it is a sign that you haven't thought things through enough yet.

The target audience for this book is, primarily, people who wish to build or renovate a home. We have tried to make complicated topics approachable for those without a background in construction, design, or building science. We hope, however, that the book will also prove valuable for builders, architects, and others who want to improve their practices and give them tools to discuss the importance of efficient building with their clients. There are many photos of details and designs from our and others' projects, references for more information, and graphics to help explain or illustrate important points. We also have a series of case studies between chapters; we chose them to show best practices and to provide some ideas and inspiration for readers.

There is also our website, PrettyGoodHouse.org. We have more case studies, links to valuable resources, and updates to information in the book. We hope you will bookmark the site and make use of it often. We created it as a free, volunteer-curated resource before the book was even an idea, with the hopes of spreading what we'd learned as widely as possible. Perhaps most importantly, we hope the book will help create an ever-expanding circle of people interested in buildings that work better, last longer, and don't damage our planet or ourselves. We invite you to become part of it.

But before we get to the main part of the book, let's take an up-close look at that first Pretty Good House.

# The Original Pretty Good House

The first house our company built had been focused on architectural intent; we wanted to make it energy efficient, but that wasn't front and center. This second house, though, had very different priorities. The clients wanted a simple home that was very energy efficient. The architect for our first house, Phil Kaplan of Kaplan Thompson Architects, was a friend of theirs, and designed a square footprint, two full floors with a counter-gable dormer on the finished third floor.

Many of the details we worked out on this job are still the way we build houses, and, despite it not being a top priority, the house qualified for a Platinum rating from the U.S. Green Building Council's LEED for Homes.

It's easy to worry yourself to distraction thinking about building performance. I spent many nights during construction rolling details around in my head, and many nights in subsequent years worrying that we'd made bad decisions. Fortunately, we got the opportunity to open up the walls in 2015. We were asked to convert the rarely used third floor into a stained-glass studio. One part of the project was swapping out a large set of casement windows for French doors leading out to a new small balcony. The work was on the west side of the house and faced the water where the Presumpscot River empties into Casco Bay. In other words, a tough exposure, subject to high winds and heavy storms.

We were enormously relieved to find zero evidence of water penetration, mold, staining, or degradation of any of the building components. It confirmed that we were on the right track and that our details worked. In between building the house and renovating the third floor, our Building Science Discussion Group held our first Pretty Good House session. It was doubly reassuring to open up the walls and see how good they looked; I could stop worrying about the house, and I could also feel confident about relying on my experience there as a basis for thinking about PGH.

So what were the key details of this original PGH? (Don't worry if they don't make much sense now, by the end of the book they should!) Starting from the ground up:

- A well-insulated slab on grade. We poured frost walls (short foundation walls that only go down to frost depth—48 in. in southern Maine), then back-filled inside the foundation. We laid 4 in. of foam both under and around the perimeter of the slab, for about R-20. We also embedded PEX tubing in the slab for a radiant heating system and used the slab as the finished floor, dyeing the concrete during the pour to give it a rich brown color.

The original PGH shortly after completion. There is another set of evacuated-tube solar hot water tubes on the other side of the dormer.

- Double-stud walls: two 2x4 walls, for an overall depth of 11¼ in.; insulated with dense-pack cellulose for an R-value of over 40 (see Chapter 4, "Building Envelope Basics").

- Triple-glazed casement windows (see Chapter 6, "Windows and Exterior Doors").

- Rainscreen behind the siding (see Chapter 5, "Water/Moisture Management").

- Cathedral ceiling on the third floor. We gusseted down the rafters (see the efficient framing section of Chapter 7, "Materials") to provide for a thermal break and increased insulation. More cellulose, for R-52.

- Solar heat/hot water system on the south-facing roof: evacuated tubes on the roof, feeding a

storage tank, with an electric on-demand water heater as backup (see Chapter 8, "Mechanical Systems").

The solar hot water is really the only thing we haven't done again since. We built the house shortly before the huge price drop in photovoltaic (PV) solar panels of the past decade, and an evacuated tube system still made comparative economic sense. In 2012 the clients installed a 21-panel, 5.04-kw PV array on the east-facing roof of their garage. All the electricity used to heat, cool, and power both the house and studio averages $150 a month.

Otherwise, most of our current practices are refinements of what we learned here. For instance, we didn't vent the roof—the dense-pack cellulose fills the entire rafter space, to the underside of the sheath-

Radiant tubing being covered by the slab. The concrete was dyed a deep brown and serves as the finished floor.

ing. We did use a vapor barrier under the rafters, and cellulose has the benefit of being able to absorb, distribute, and subsequently release water. There have been no problems evident in the past 13 years, so I'm confident it works, but these days we would include a ventilation channel under or over the roof sheathing. Beyond being a best practice, it is also required by the building code.

We also built a big dormer facing south. It makes the roofline more complicated, harder to insulate, and more expensive to build, and makes the roof more susceptible to problems long term. But it also turns the attic from a nice spot to a truly beautiful, inviting room, so I think it was worth it. One lesson of the PGH approach is to let performance inform the design but not to dictate a narrow path.

We learned a lot about heating from this house. When completed, the only heat source (other than a rarely used gas fireplace) was the radiant slab on the first floor. It worked reasonably well, but one thing about a tight house is that the stack effect basically disappears. (Note: you'll find a definition of stack effect and many other terms used in the book in our glossary on p. 245.) Many of us have experienced blazing-hot top floors and cold, drafty first floors in old houses. That's because the more buoyant warm air is pulled up to the roof by any air leaks high in the building and is replaced by denser, colder air coming in through lower air leaks. Without those leaks, the air in the house doesn't move as much, and we discovered that each floor got 2 to 3 degrees colder than the one below. When the third floor wasn't getting used much, it wasn't a problem, but when we renovated it, we added a small heat pump system there.

While we have done a couple of radiant slabs since then, we made sure there was better distribution through the house, and we haven't done any for the past decade. As we discuss in Chapter 8, radiant slabs are usually overkill for a PGH, and we've used air-source heat pumps in new construction since then.

This was also the first project, new or renovation, where we installed a balanced ventilation system. The blower-door tests confirmed that the house was very airtight (see Chapter 10, "Verification and Client Education," for more on blower doors), and a system that wasn't bringing in fresh air to replace the exhaust air wouldn't have worked.

What are the principles we learned building the house? They are—big reveal!—most of what we will discuss in the rest of the book. I don't want to pretend that any of these were our discoveries. By the time we built this house, many other designers, builders, engineers, and researchers had done much of the hard work, and we were relying on the path they'd blazed.

Some of those principles include:

- The building envelope, or shell, is critically important. The foundation, walls, and roof need to keep weather out, keep conditioned air (either heated or cooled) in and insulated from the exterior, and allow any water vapor to disperse without damaging the building or its occupants. We talk about the four "control layers" in Chapter 4.

- Planning is key. Having the entire team—client, designer, builder—on board early, with mutual respect and comprehension of the details is essential to the success of the project (see Chapter 1, "Things to Know Before You Start"). It also makes it possible to design to a budget, rather than budget to a design. A good builder can help steer the design away from budget-busters and come up with lower-cost options to meet goals (see Chapter 2, "Economics"). Client involvement

improves the chances that the house will be well-maintained and important systems kept in operating order (see Chapter 10).

- Keep it simple, functional, and beautiful! 'Nuff said! See Chapter 3, for much more on design.

- Reducing the need for heating, cooling, and other energy consumption always comes first (see Chapter 9, "Electricity and Lighting").

We weren't thinking that much about the house's contribution to global warming back then, but in the intervening years it's become central to the work of all the authors. In retrospect, we did a reasonable job, but what you build your house from, and where, can be as important as how well insulated it is (see Chapter 7).

---

*We weren't thinking that much about the house's contribution to global warming back then, but in the intervening years it's become central to the work of all the authors.*

---

The owners of the Original PGH have remained friends, and I still lean on them occasionally for tours or pictures of the house. It (or details from it) has been featured in many articles, written by me and others, and was an inspiration for Kaplan Thompson's prefab division, BrightBuilt Home (see pp. 71, 75). I am very proud of how foundational this house has been to both my and others' careers.

With that, let's get started. Be forewarned, building science is an addiction, and once you start seeing the world through its lens, it's hard to stop! But your house, and hopefully the planet, will thank you.

—*Dan Kolbert, 2022*

# CHAPTER ONE

# THINGS TO KNOW BEFORE YOU START

While at first glance this home could be mistaken for an original, early 1800s Greek Revival, this Pretty Good House designed by architect Robert Swinburne has some very modern details and performs at a high level. A compact form and classic proportions fit the established neighborhood, the steeply pitched roof and moderate overhangs help control rain and snow, and the broad farmer's porch provides a generous entry and streetscape views for visiting friends and family.

Before we get into the specific details of designing and building your Pretty Good House, there are a few important concepts to understand. Climate, the project team, and local building regulations may not seem to have much in common with each other, but before investing in your project you should have at least some understanding of all three.

# Climate

Location, location, location. Not only is that the mantra of real estate agents, but the climate where you build also influences many of the decisions you'll make about your Pretty Good House (a.k.a. PGH). While weather is what is happening when you look out the window, climate is what happens to the weather over a longer term—months, seasons, years, or decades. Average and extreme air temperatures, precipitation types and amounts, humidity, the number of sunny days vs. cloudy days, and even the average and extreme wind speeds and direction all play a role in designing a good house. If your house will be in a place where it rains a lot but rarely gets cold enough for snow, you might prioritize windows and not worry too much about high levels of insulation. If it will be in a hot, dry environment with large temperature swings between day and night, you might make use of thermal mass, which has increasingly bigger effect where diurnal temperatures cover a wide range. Areas prone to wildfires, earthquakes, hurricanes, or heavy, wet snowfall all will have different priorities.

This Pretty Good House in Miami designed by Brillhart Architecture responds to the warm-humid climate with deep roof overhangs to block sun and rain, shutters to protect against wind, and lots of glass for natural light and indoor-outdoor connections.

**LEFT** In the Pacific Northwest (Climate Zone 4-marine), a Pretty Good House might have deep roof overhangs to protect the house from long periods of rain, generously sized windows, and covered outdoor spaces. Roof slopes don't need to be steep because there is little snow to deal with. Although exterior materials should be rot-proof, select use of natural wood is appropriate as a nod to traditional local and indigenous architecture, as in this house in British Columbia, Canada, designed by Malcolm Taylor Design.

**ABOVE** Homes in desert climates have different requirements than those in wet areas. Temperature changes between day and night can be extreme, so thermally massive walls help keep the interior comfortable without wasting energy. Little rain means roof overhangs aren't critically important, and what rain does fall is precious and might be captured for later use. Windows are modestly sized to keep heat out but big enough to allow for views of the unique landscape.

The International Code Council, an independent organization that develops building codes that most of the U.S. uses as a starting point for local codes, has divided the country into climate zones that help determine what qualities are important for homes in a given region. These zones are shown on a map used in the International Energy Conservation Code (IECC), shown on the facing page. Each numbered zone includes locations with a similar range of thermal requirements, measured in heating degree days and cooling degree days—cumulative values that describe how much above or below a baseline temperature a location experiences over the course of a year.

Climate Zones 1 through 4 use cooling-degree days as a basis; Zones 3 through 8 use heating degree days. Generally speaking, Zone 1 is hot, Zone 8 is frigid, and everywhere in between is, well, in between. The regions across the middle of the country, 3 and 4, that require significant heating *and* cooling take both factors into account.

But wait, there's more! In addition to dividing the U.S. into zones of similar temperatures, the IECC map also divides the U.S. into different regions based on how much precipitation they get. (Wetter regions often require different building details than dryer regions.) Zone A, east of the Rocky Mountain states, is "moist." Zone B, consisting of most of the western and Pacific states, is "dry." Zone C, along the Pacific coast, is "marine." This marine zone is generally not too hot, not too cold, not too wet or dry (despite the Pacific Northwest's drizzly reputation)—building scientist Dr. Allison Bailes III calls it "The Goldilocks

## IECC CLIMATE ZONE MAP

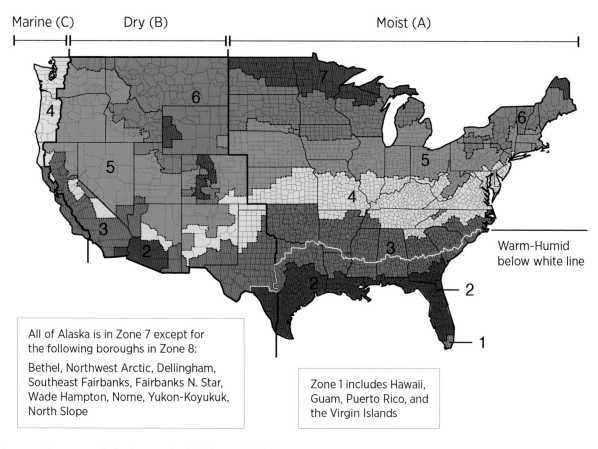

Marine (C)    Dry (B)    Moist (A)

Warm-Humid below white line

All of Alaska is in Zone 7 except for the following boroughs in Zone 8:

Bethel, Northwest Arctic, Dellingham, Southeast Fairbanks, Fairbanks N. Star, Wade Hampton, Nome, Yukon-Koyukuk, North Slope

Zone 1 includes Hawaii, Guam, Puerto Rico, and the Virgin Islands

**Knowing your climate zone is the first step in designing and building a Pretty Good House. In general, east of the Rocky Mountains is considered a moist climate and west of the Rockies is a dry climate. The west coast is mild but has more moisture than the rest of the west. Below the white line, humidity is even more of a concern than it is in the rest of the humid east.**

Zone." There is another special region that doesn't get a zone letter, just a description: "warm-humid." It includes the southeastern regions along the Atlantic and Gulf coasts and is not based on precipitation but on humidity, which creates special challenges for building design.

The IECC map is sometimes confused with the USDA Plant Hardiness Zone map, which shows the lowest average annual temperature for different locations across the U.S. (see p. 14, top). While not directly applicable to home design, a Pretty Good House should have Pretty Good Landscaping, and you should consult the plant hardiness map when selecting plants for your garden. Another map,

made by Building Science Corporation for the U.S. Department of Energy's Building America program and shown on p. 14, bottom, classifies all of North America into Hot-Humid, Mixed-Humid, Hot-Dry, Mixed-Dry, Cold, Very Cold, and Marine regions. (A map that shows what IECC zones equate to in Canada is available at https://www.ecohome.net/guides/3521/climate-zones-map-usa-canada-construction/.) U.S.-based designers and code officials use the IECC map. Except for Californians, that is—they have so many different local climates that they created their own version—the California Energy Commission's Climate Zone map.

# USDA PLANT HARDINESS ZONE MAP

### Average Annual Extreme Minimum Temperature 1976-2005

| Temp (F) | Zone | Temp (C) |
|---|---|---|
| -60 to -55 | 1a | -51.1 to -48.3 |
| -55 to -50 | 1b | -48.3 to -45.6 |
| -50 to -45 | 2a | -45.6 to -42.8 |
| -45 to -40 | 2b | -42.8 to -40 |
| -40 to -35 | 3a | -40 to -37.2 |
| -35 to -30 | 3b | -37.2 to -34.4 |
| -30 to -25 | 4a | -34.4 to -31.7 |
| -25 to -20 | 4b | -31.7 to -28.9 |
| -20 to -15 | 5a | -28.9 to -26.1 |
| -15 to -10 | 5b | -26.1 to -23.3 |
| -10 to -5 | 6a | -23.3 to -20.6 |
| -5 to 0 | 6b | -20.6 to -17.8 |
| 0 to 5 | 7a | -17.8 to -15 |
| 5 to 10 | 7b | -15 to -12.2 |
| 10 to 15 | 8a | -12.2 to -9.4 |
| 15 to 20 | 8b | -9.4 to -6.7 |
| 20 to 25 | 9a | -6.7 to -3.9 |
| 25 to 30 | 9b | -3.9 to -1.1 |
| 30 to 35 | 10a | -1.1 to 1.7 |
| 35 to 40 | 10b | 1.7 to 4.4 |
| 40 to 45 | 11a | 4.4 to 7.2 |
| 45 to 50 | 11b | 7.2 to 10 |
| 50 to 55 | 12a | 10 to 12.8 |
| 55 to 60 | | 12.8 to 15.6 |
| 60 to 65 | | 15.6 to 18.3 |
| 65 to 70 | | 18.3 to 21.1 |

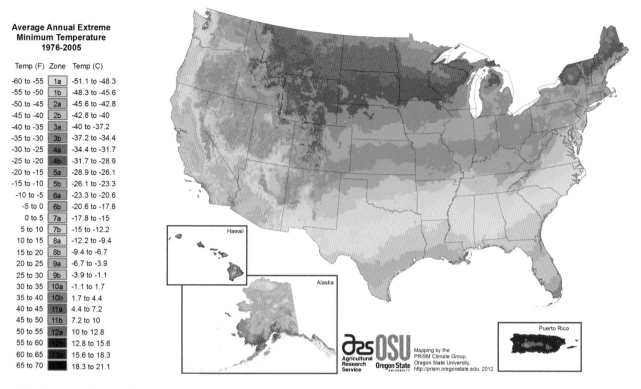

Mapping by the PRISM Climate Group, Oregon State University, http://prism.oregonstate.edu, 2012

While the USDA Plant Hardiness Zone map doesn't relate directly to how we design the building and enclosure, it does help when choosing plants for landscaping and also shows the lowest average temperature in different regions.

# BUILDING AMERICA CLIMATE MAP

DOE's Building America map is similar to the IECC map but more general and perhaps easier to read.

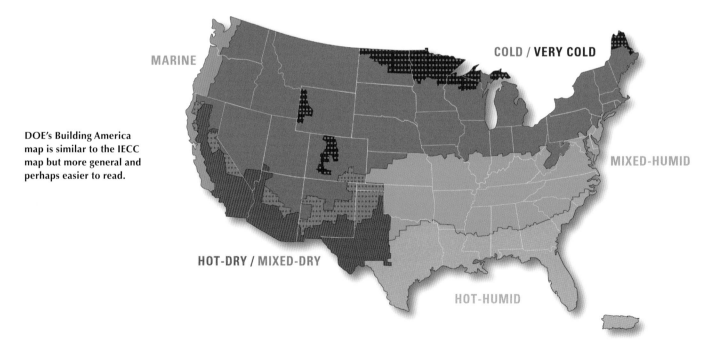

MARINE

COLD / VERY COLD

MIXED-HUMID

HOT-DRY / MIXED-DRY

HOT-HUMID

## MICROCLIMATE

Near the borders of climate zones, and sometimes within climate zones, conditions may vary. In fact, because climate zones represent an average across a large area, you will want to understand how your local climate varies from the regional average. You may be in a valley where cold air flows from hilltops; author Michael's house is on a Maine hilltop and his mother-in-law lives at the base of a hill just two miles away. She gets a hard frost—26°F, enough to kill many garden plants—two or three weeks later in spring and earlier in fall, so the growing season is as much as six weeks shorter despite being in the same climate zone.

---

*Where you intend to build makes a big difference in how the house should be designed and built.*

---

Hilltop exposure often means more wind than lower areas, but wind can also be funneled into valleys or slowed by trees. Wind blowing on a building increases its rate of heat loss by increasing the rate of infiltration of outside air into the house and exfiltration of indoor air out of the house. The tighter you make the house, the less the wind affects it. Wind also drives rain into building assemblies. While most Pretty Good Houses will do best with a roof overhang, in microclimates such as an offshore island where the rain typically approaches horizontally or upside-down, overhangs can be a liability. Other microclimate features include sunlight reflected off snow or water, or sunlight blocked by trees or buildings. Long views to the east or west can bring cheerful sunshine and solar energy, which can be either desirable or undesirable.

In short, where you intend to build makes a big difference in how the house should be designed and built. The better you and your team understand the site and how it behaves in different seasons and situations, the better your Pretty Good House will be.

# The Team Approach

Every building project is like a three-legged stool: someone needs to want it and pay for it, someone needs to design it, and someone needs to build it. Each leg is equally important. If one is shortchanged, the stool will wobble and the project won't be as

## Changing Climate

The world's climate zones are shifting due to climate change. Scientific models show that by 2050 some climate zones will have shifted as much as 500 miles to the north. By then, Maine can expect to have a climate comparable to what Virginia's climate is today. An important part of the Pretty Good House approach is to make decisions that will help slow climate change—more accurately called catastrophic climate disruption—and also to make our houses more durable and adaptable to changes that will occur.

Already, many regions are experiencing much hotter or colder temperatures than normal; storms will continue to bring more powerful wind and rain events more frequently; a weakening jet stream will create more polar vortexes that bring periods of extreme cold to typically temperate zones. Wildfires are increasing in size, intensity, and quantity, and western states are experiencing severe drought, sometimes interspersed with torrential rains. We can wish this was not the case or debate the specifics, but a Pretty Good House should be prepared to weather these and other changes.

## THE TEAM APPROACH

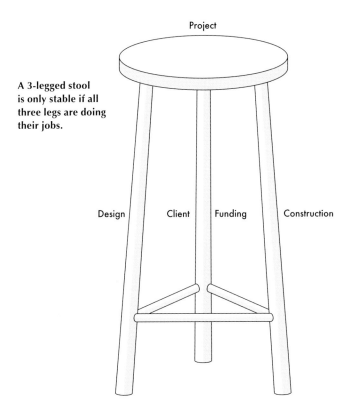

Project

A 3-legged stool is only stable if all three legs are doing their jobs.

Design    Client    Funding    Construction

good as it could be, or it won't get built at all. Sometimes one person serves more than one role, and often multiple people or entities are involved with each leg, but without the three legs there is no project.

## LEG 1: THE CLIENT

Every project starts with a client's idea or a developer with a future owner in mind. The client (or developer) is the driver of the project and is usually responsible for selecting the primary members of the design and build teams. Unless the builder offers financing, the client either funds the project directly or works with lenders for financing (see Chapter 2). Although he or she is usually the team member who knows the least about design and construction, the client is the ultimate decision-maker. Some lending institutions offer "green" mortgages, which consider the added value and reduced operating costs of a high-quality, energy-efficient PGH. Clients who self-finance projects may be more concerned with return on investment than clients who finance projects through a mortgage.

Jesse Schwartzberg, an architect in Lake Placid, New York, meets with clients to plan their new Pretty Good House.

# How to Be a Pretty Good Client

The most important member of a Pretty Good House team is not the designer or the builder, but the client, without whom there would be no project! That doesn't mean a client can or should run roughshod over other team members. In fact, on the best projects there is a high degree of trust and respect among all parties.

Builders and designers who have been in the trenches for decades can forget what it's like not to know much about design or building. But they can also be stuck in their ways, while the client is the one who wants to push the envelope. How can you, as a client, be the most effective team member?

1  **Do your homework.** As tired as that phrase is, it's accurate. Read contracts thoroughly, research different approaches, follow up on references, take your own notes during meetings, and follow through on your to-do items. While professional designers and builders will do their best to make the process clear and straightforward, there are thousands of decisions to be made along the way and you have a responsibility to do your part.

2  **Vet your team.** Having a good personality fit among team members is just as important, or possibly more important, than having the highest levels of intelligence, skills, or experience, though those are good to have as well. Take the time to interview a few designers and builders and think about who you want to spend the next year or two working with. The snazziest architect may be a terrible communicator; the most experienced builder may not be open to your Pretty Good ideas.

3  **Understand that the design process is not linear.** As much as we'd like every project to follow a straightforward path, every custom home is a prototype—you're not buying a Ford pickup truck with a choice between a few options and colors. There are always surprises, even for the most experienced builders. There can be delays in the delivery of building materials, confusion about the ideal order of operations for assembling something, dimensions that aren't quite what they should be. What may seem like a mistake may simply be part of what it takes to build any custom home. If you choose predesigned plans (see pp. 71–75), much of the design end of the process will have been completed, but there will still be plenty of decisions to make.

4  **Don't focus entirely on price.** The designer or builder with the lowest rates may not have the skills or experience of a more expensive designer, may forget or not understand things, and may be too busy to give you their full attention because their low rate keeps them up to their eyeballs in projects. That doesn't necessarily mean that the most expensive professionals will be better to work with, either. Just that how much someone charges shouldn't be the deciding factor on whether you hire him or her.

## LEG 2: THE DESIGN TEAM

The role of the design team is to guide the creative and technical planning process. The team can include licensed architects, professional engineers, landscape architects, interior designers, unlicensed building designers, consultants, and design/build contractors, or the client can do the design themselves. While it can be fun and easy to create a basic design, working with experienced design professionals will help ensure a safe, secure, and engaging home to live in.

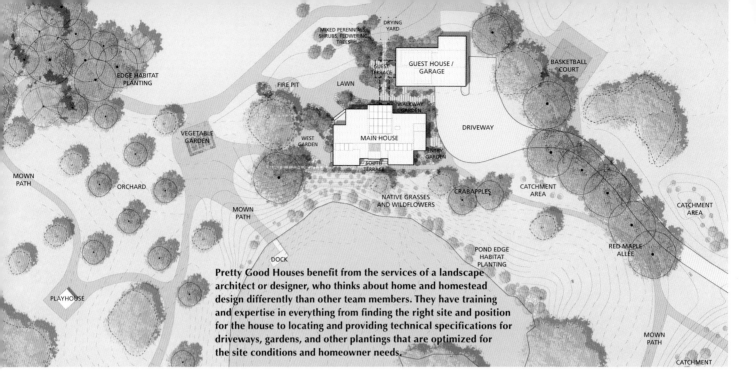

EDGE HABITAT
PLANTING

MIXED PERENNIALS,
SHRUBS, FLOWERING
TREES

DRYING
YARD

GUEST HOUSE /
GARAGE

BASKETBALL
COURT

GUEST
TERRACE

FIRE PIT

LAWN

WALKWAY
GARDEN

DRIVEWAY

VEGETABLE
GARDEN

WEST
GARDEN

MAIN HOUSE

ENTRY
GARDEN

MOWN
PATH

ORCHARD

SOUTH
TERRACE

CATCHMENT
AREA

CATCHMENT
AREA

MOWN
PATH

NATIVE GRASSES
AND WILDFLOWERS

CRABAPPLES

RED MAPLE
ALLÉE

DOCK

POND EDGE
HABITAT
PLANTING

MOWN
PATH

PLAYHOUSE

CATCHMENT

**Pretty Good Houses benefit from the services of a landscape architect or designer, who thinks about home and homestead design differently than other team members. They have training and expertise in everything from finding the right site and position for the house to locating and providing technical specifications for driveways, gardens, and other plantings that are optimized for the site conditions and homeowner needs.**

# Who Should Design a Pretty Good House?

Architects complete rigorous training to earn their title, and maintaining a license requires them to adhere to a professional standard of care and to complete continuing education. Their credentials help ensure a superior project, and in some locations homes and renovations can be designed only by architects. In most places, however, one- and two-family homes also can be designed by unlicensed building designers, sometimes called residential designers, building designers, or simply designers. Sometimes they are called drafters but that's something of a misnomer.

Even without an architect's license, a designer may have just as much or more experience and talent and may carry equivalent insurance. Don't rule them out—just do some research (i.e., check references and question them for their knowledge of the PGH approach) before committing, and make sure you feel a good personality connection.

Most PGH design is led by a licensed architect or an unlicensed building designer, who we'll call the designer. Many people outside the industry don't appreciate what a good designer brings to the table, which is more than coming up with a creative design or drafting construction drawings. They are trained in guiding clients through what is usually a complicated process, from identifying what features are important to overcoming regulatory and budget hurdles the project may face. The designer makes sure the design is aesthetically appealing and practical, and that it integrates all of the technical elements required in a PGH. Finally, the designer checks on construction at key points to make sure it is being built as planned. A PGH should be relatively simple to build, but it may not be what the builder is used to. Finding a designer who is comfortable with educating the contractor is usually helpful. In some cases, the contractor is more knowledgeable than the designer when it comes to performance-related items. If that's the case, the builder may want to be on the design team to ensure the target performance levels are achieved.

While some projects are turned over fully to the builder at the start of the construction phase, it's usually better to keep the designer involved until construction is complete. They can ensure the house is

## MECHANICAL DESIGN

Mechanical design, such as sizing and laying out a balanced ventilation system shown here, should be done by someone with training and experience, not by rules of thumb or whatever the installer did on the last project. Most mechanical contractors work with their supply house or equipment manufacturer's engineers, but those systems are almost always oversized, resulting in extra cost and short-cycling; it's best to find a designer or engineer familiar with designing systems for high-performance, low-load homes.

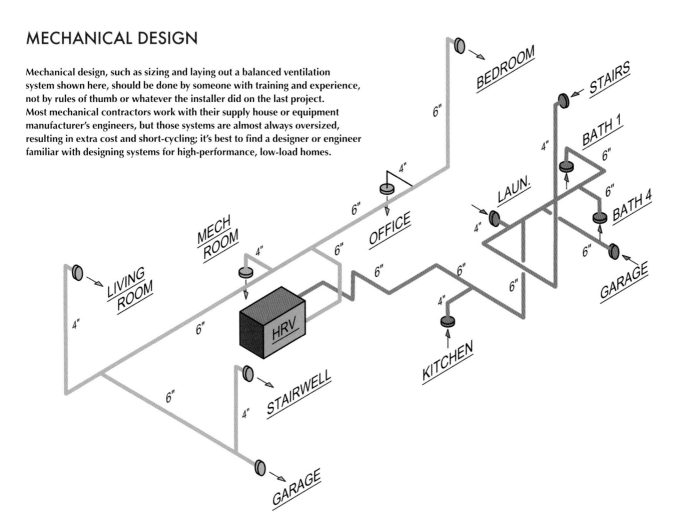

being built as designed, answer any questions, and anticipate problems.

In addition to the designer, other members of the design team may include:

- Structural engineer to ensure that the building is safe and can withstand site conditions.

- Geotechnical engineer for difficult sites.

- Mechanical engineer to design the heating, cooling, ventilation, and dehumidification systems.

- Landscape architect to help site and orient the house for accessibility, drainage, and solar gain, to take advantage of views, and to work with the native landscape.

- Energy consultants to model the home for optimal energy performance.

- Sustainability consultants to suggest materials and systems with the least environmental impact.

- Lighting designer to plan the illumination strategy.

- Kitchen designer to refine the kitchen layout (and order cabinets).

- Interior designer to select fixtures, finishes, and furnishings, and sometimes to help with the broader design.

It's rare to have all of these consultants on every project, but someone on the design team needs to complete these tasks, or else it will be left to chance or decisions will be made without adequate thought.

# How to Find Pretty Good Designers and Builders (a.k.a. Pretty Good Folks)

One of the first hurdles a client must face is putting together a Pretty Good Team. The authors have considered various ways of providing a database for PGH-literate designers, builders, and consultants. But some of the main benefits of the PGH approach—the lack of a central organization providing training, and an absence of hard-and-fast rules about what constitutes a PGH—make it difficult to vet potential providers. Here's what we tell people who ask for suggestions:

**Tap your local network.** This is a good place to start for anyone considering a renovation or construction project, Pretty Good or otherwise. Between friends, neighbors, colleagues, and family members, you likely know someone who has had a home built or renovated. Ask them about their designer and builder. If you interview potential designers and builders and find that their priorities and experiences are not in line with the PGH approach, ask them if they know anyone who specializes in net-zero, Passive House, or otherwise "green" building.

**If you find one PGH-literate potential team member, ask him or her for recommendations.** Your first contact may be with a builder or a designer. The designer will be the most important team member early in the process; getting the project off to a good start depends on having a designer who understands your needs and how to implement all of the factors that go into a PGH. You will end up spending a lot more money with the builder, and their skills and abilities will ultimately be what you live with. It can be tricky to find a designer or builder familiar with the PGH approach so if you find one, ask him or her who they like to work with.

**Check lists of Passive House, LEED, and other "green" programs:**
https://www.phius.org/
https://passivehouse-international.org/memberSearch.php
https://zeroenergyproject.org/
https://www.usgbc.org/people

While not a perfect match for PGH, these long-established programs do a good job of educating and certifying practitioners, and there is enough overlap with the PGH approach that a designer or builder who is Passive House certified, for example, will understand much of what is needed in a PGH.

**Ask for suggestions at greenbuildingadvisor.com or check the bulletin board there:** greenbuildingadvisor. com/article/bulletin-board. While not comprehensive or vetted, Green Building Advisor (and the website's former editor Martin Holladay) have been central to spreading the PGH concept.

**Check your local shelter magazines for advertisements that suggest "green" qualifications.** While anyone can pay for an advertisement, and "green" is a nearly useless term at this point, it's better than nothing. At least if someone is basing their advertising on doing green, sustainable, or net-zero work, there is a higher-than-average chance that they are aligned with PGH values.

Start or join a local discussion group. Seriously! PGH started at the Building Science Discussion Group at Performance Building Supply in Portland, Maine—a group of mostly professionals getting together monthly to share ideas, knowledge, and fabulous Greek food made by host Steve Konstantino's wife. Authors Emily and Michael run a similar program on Zoom called The BS + Beer Show, which has helped spark many local groups across the U.S. and one in Australia. It's a good way to be social, learn, share, and develop a local network. Visit thebsandbeershow.org for tips on starting your own group.

## LEG 3: THE BUILD TEAM

To state the obvious, builders and their teams are responsible for actually constructing things. "Builder" and "general contractor" have specific meanings to some people, but we will use "builder" to indicate the person mainly responsible for construction, usually a general contractor who may or may not work physically on site. The build team also includes carpenters, plumbers, electricians, insulators, drywallers, painters, excavation contractors, foundation contractors, and anyone else who contributes to the physical building. Ultimately, the project is in the hands of this key group. As with designers, building high-performance homes requires builders with a different type of knowledge, so look for one experienced or at least interested and educated in high-performance building. Most construction projects are run by a general contractor (GC), who hires specialty contractors, or subcontractors ("subs"), and often has his or her own employees to build the project.

Sometimes a client with some construction experience (and sometimes simply with chutzpah) takes on the GC role, with the idea of saving the GC's markup on subcontractor invoices. While this can be an effective strategy, and many are owner-contracted, most clients underestimate what an experienced GC brings to a project. They organize the flow of construction activities, provide access to qualified subcontractors, anticipate potential problems before they affect the project, ensure quality and completion of construction tasks, and perhaps most importantly, provide pricing information. For the vast majority of new homes and renovations, cost is one of the most important factors and one only the builder can address accurately. The earlier in the process you start getting pricing information, the greater the chances that you will know and be able to afford the ultimate cost.

A traditional approach to building can create an antagonistic environment. The client hires an architect to design the building. Once the design is complete, the architect invites bids from contractors and the lowest qualified bid wins the project. While this approach can be helpful on large commercial and institutional projects, on residential projects it may leave one or more parties unhappy because each leg of the stool is its own team. Another common scenario is for a client to hire a builder directly, and to use a generic house design from a plan book, or to buy a prebuilt home in a development (see Chapter 3). In both cases, an architect or professional designer is minimally involved, if at all.

The PGH approach is to consider all three legs of the team as a whole and to work toward the common goal of building a successful project. Working with a design professional or professionals will help ensure an optimized and attractive design; bringing a builder into the design process early to get their input on details and pricing gets them invested in the project.

Designing and building a PGH does take a high level of planning and preparation. This is not the time to go with the lowest bidder but rather the team with the highest level of expertise and communication skills. Getting these professionals together during the design

## Design/Build

One approach to get the designer and builder on the same team is to find a design/build firm that provides both services. There are often efficiencies to this approach. The designer and builder may be a single person, or two people who have worked together closely on other projects. Drawing time may be reduced because less work needs to be done purely for legal purposes.

Don't, however, automatically assume that design/build is necessarily the best approach. While some design/build teams have staff who are skilled in both the artistic and scientific aspects of home design, in other cases the quality of design is not up to par with an independent design professional.

stage is a good way to make sure everyone is rowing in the same direction and to address any issues well before they become problems. Since the builder, who will figure out the cost, is in the room, it also allows you to design to a budget, rather than budget to a design.

# Regulatory and Infrastructure Constraints

Before getting into the fun parts of design, it's important to understand what you will and will not be allowed to do, due to laws, regulations, and building codes, and also what resources are available on your site. Every designer has experienced the disappointment of having a nice design rejected by a municipality because some aspect does not meet local requirements, and that's no fun.

## BUILDING CODES AND OTHER REGULATIONS

Building codes are the regulations your state or municipality uses to ensure that housing is reasonably safe and comfortable for its occupants. Some places don't use building codes, or may have minimal codes, which may appeal to the more independently minded population. But building codes have developed over many years to represent a baseline building standard and can be used to help design any house or renovation. Most building codes for homes in the U.S. are based on the International Residential Code (IRC), a publication from an independent company called the International Code Council (ICC). The ICC also publishes code books for commercial buildings, energy efficiency, existing buildings, electrical and plumbing codes, and others. The codes are updated on a three-year cycle, with changes based on input from many parties. Most places that use the IRC adopt local amendments to tailor the code to local needs.

Building code compliance is overseen by local building departments, through a code enforcement officer (CEO) or building inspector. Because every department does things a little differently, the blanket term for the person or entity who enforces these rules is the Authority Having Jurisdiction, or AHJ. Where building codes are enforced, you will need to submit a building permit application that includes information about the site, building owner, applicant (owner, designer, or builder), and drawings and specifications that show that the building will meet code requirements. Costs for permitting vary widely.

The same department that administers the building code also administers the zoning ordinance. While the building code is specific to the structure, the zoning ordinance describes what is allowed on the site. The zoning ordinance may include a land-use ordinance, shoreland zoning ordinance, nonconforming building ordinance, and other sections. Most municipalities divide towns and cities into different zones, such as Commercial, Residential High Density, Residential Low Density, and Resource Protection Zones, as well as historic districts. Different zones have different requirements for building setbacks from property lines, lot coverage, building size, and height and other restrictions. In locations prone to flooding or wildfires the zoning ordinance will have additional requirements.

In addition to building code and zoning regulations, you may have to deal with a homeowner's association (HOA). HOAs are often set up by developers of new neighborhoods, with rules that can be mild, such as minimum house sizes, or more involved, such as limiting what siding colors or roofing types are allowed or whether residents can have gardens or playsets. Developers often administer the rules until enough homes in the development are sold that residents can take over.

In places where regulations are complicated, or where natural features such as soil type can influence design, the AHJ may require a survey or involvement of a geotechnical engineer. Surveys range from what is sometimes called a Class D survey, used when buying and selling houses, to a full boundary survey with site features identified and elevation contours mapped. If the site is amply sized and without complicated restrictions, involving a licensed surveyor may not be necessary. But on tighter or more complicated sites it can be smart to include a licensed surveyor on your team even if the AHJ does not require it. No one wants to find out that his neighbor owns a corner of their house, or that they have to move a deck.

## INFRASTRUCTURE CONSTRAINTS

In addition to these regulatory requirements, you will need to know what is available, allowed, or required on site for utility connections. Rural homes usually have a drilled well for fresh water and a septic system (septic tank and leach field, sometimes with a pump station) that have to meet state rules for size and for separation from each other and from structures and neighbors. In more heavily populated areas, municipal water and/or sewer may be available. For sewer connections the elevation of the sewer line can influence the house design—it's always best not to pump effluent uphill because it uses energy and could potentially fail. In some locations, stormwater systems are also available at the street; in older communities the stormwater system may be combined with the sewer system, which leads to pollution in heavy rain. When they are separate, your home's foundation drains may tie into storm drains. (Those in arid or drought-prone areas may wonder why those of us in wet areas worry so much about water. While water is the stuff of life, it's our homes' number one enemy!)

Other utilities to consider are power and fuel, which we'll cover in more detail in the chapters on mechanical systems and electricity and lighting. Most homes are connected to the electrical grid, and PGHers are encouraged to be grid-tied. As romantically appealing as off-grid living may be, it's a relatively expensive way to get electricity and usually involves higher carbon emissions than on-grid living. Batteries are expensive, and unless you have a very unconventional lifestyle, you will need a petroleum-fueled, polluting generator for backup power. Grid-tied homes may still generate some or all of their own power. Electrical service may be overhead or underground, depending on your location and preferences.

As for fuels for heating and cooling, in most cases a PGH should not burn any on site. Heat pump technology makes electrically derived heating and cooling clean, safe, and affordable. In some cases, it makes sense to take advantage of natural gas provided at the street or have a propane tank on site. If you are considering using firewood for heat or ambiance, be sure it's not a violation of clean air laws—and read the chapter on mechanical systems to make sure that's really the approach you want to take.

## THINGS TO CONSIDER

- Know your climate zone and what it means for your project.

- Understand how the details of your microclimate might affect your design.

- Consider that climates are changing around the globe, more drastically in some places than others, and ask yourself what that means for you before building and renovating.

- Take care in choosing your project team: who will make up the three legs of the stool?

- Learn what regulatory and infrastructure constraints you will face.

- If you're renovating, are you taking steps to make your home more resilient, able to survive changing climates?

# Seville Residence

It blends right in with a neighborhood of late 19th- and early 20th-century homes, but Carl Seville's house is a thoroughly modern, net-zero ready structure with very little air leakage and low energy use.

CARL SEVILLE IS NO STRANGER to high-performance building. The Decatur, Georgia, contractor, consultant, and principal at SK Collaborative is a master verifier for the National Green Building Standard, and when he built this house in 2017, he was thinking of something far beyond simple code compliance.

Seville relied on high-performance building concepts and with the help of his friend, architect Tom Bateman

Hood, adapted them to a home that fits comfortably into a neighborhood of mixed architectural styles from the late 19th and early 20th century. Core design features include a layer of continuous exterior insulation, airtight construction, an uncomplicated house shape, and an energy-recovery ventilator for high indoor air quality. Three-foot roof overhangs and a vented rainscreen for the composite siding are features that should increase durability for the house exterior.

Building in a mixed-humid climate prompted Seville to pay particular attention to air sealing as a way of minimizing moisture infiltration. The floor of the attic, installed before any drywall went into the house, is a layer of sealed ZIP sheathing. This feature allowed Seville to locate a mechanical chase below the attic insulation so lights and fans in the ceiling needed no special air sealing. These steps paid off with a blower-door reading of less than 1 ach50—very tight by any standard and approaching the Passive House benchmark of 0.6 ach50. (For an explanation of blower-door testing, see p. 226.)

In developing plans for the mechanical systems, Seville tried to minimize HVAC ductwork. To that end, he settled on ductless mini-splits for heating and cooling. There are two heads upstairs and one down, and while they have performed adequately, they have required more maintenance and repairs than Seville would have liked. In retrospect, he says he might have used ducted mini-splits, which he suspects would have been less expensive to maintain.

**ABOVE** Located at the front of the lot, the house completes a small compound that includes a renovated guest house and an open carport.

**LEFT** The kitchen opens to a private, screened porch on the south side of the house.

An open floor plan on the first floor includes connected living and dining rooms on either side of the main entry.

High humidity is a fact of life in this part of the country. In the shoulder seasons, humidity can be high even when temperatures are not. Seville experimented with a dehumidifier to make indoor conditions more comfortable, but he discovered these appliances can produce a lot of heat, which must then be countered with air conditioning. Eventually, Seville removed the dehumidifier and these days simply knocks the thermostat back a couple of degrees on especially muggy days.

The house was the first to be certified under the 2015 National Green Building Standard, qualifying for its top Emerald efficiency rating. It's also a LEED Platinum, Earthcraft Platinum, and Net-Zero Energy Ready Home. Although Seville did not seek Passive House certification because of the cost of a Passive House consultant, the energy use intensity of his house is lower than most Passive Houses he's seen posted online and about one-third that of a standard new home.

Despite Seville's decades-long association with green building certification programs, he did not go into this project with a Pretty Good House playbook. But he could have, and what he would have emphasized is the importance of early planning on high-performance building details. "The best way to think about this is that so many buildings are overly complicated," he says. "If you just think simply, it's really easy to build a high-performance house. When I do certification and consulting for people, they usually call me after the house is designed and they say, 'Let's make it green.' It's too late. All I can do is make it less crappy."

Three-foot-wide roof overhangs and composite siding should mean long-term durability on the exterior.
Brick veneer masks the concrete stemwalls of the slab-on-grade foundation.

# How Integrated Design Worked

Integrated design is a process in which all the principal players work together from the start. In this case, Seville's background as a builder and consultant gave him many of the tools he needed to plan technical features for the house. But while Seville had the box shape and mechanical systems laid out in his mind, he did not have any of the particulars of a finished design. Then he called on a friend, architect Thomas Hood, who flew in from California. Together, they roughed out the architectural basics over the course of a weekend. Hood, with a background of working on historic buildings,

was able to take Seville's fundamentals and weave them into plans that matched the neighborhood and met strict historic district requirements. Seville had bought the lot some 20 years earlier, and it came with an 800-sq.-ft. guest house built in the 1920s. Seville lived there for more than a decade before building the new house. "We worked really hard to make it fit in," he says of his work with Hood. "I finally got around to building the house in front. Now that I've filled in the neighborhood, people really can't tell it's a new house."

A storage cubby and coatrack found a home on the first floor between the back door and the kitchen.

## TYPICAL WALL SECTION

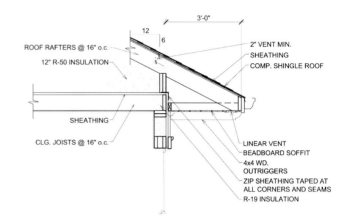

ROOF RAFTERS @ 16" o.c.
12" R-50 INSULATION
SHEATHING
CLG. JOISTS @ 16" o.c.

3'-0"
12
6
2" VENT MIN.
SHEATHING
COMP. SHINGLE ROOF
LINEAR VENT
BEADBOARD SOFFIT
4x4 WD. OUTRIGGERS
ZIP SHEATHING TAPED AT ALL CORNERS AND SEAMS
R-19 INSULATION

LOCATION: Decatur, Georgia; Climate Zone 3A

ARCHITECT: Thomas Bateman Hood, AIA

BUILDER: Carl Seville

LIVING AREA: 2,646 sq. ft.

NUMBER OF BEDROOMS/BATHROOMS: 3/3

FOUNDATION: Concrete slab on stem walls

SUBSLAB INSULATION:
1-in. XPS (R-5) under first 2 ft. of perimeter

WALL CONSTRUCTION:
2x6 with ZIP sheathing (R-3)

ABOVE-GRADE WALL INSULATION:
R-22 blown fiberglass with R-3 continuous on exterior

ATTIC FLOOR INSULATION:
Loose-fill fiberglass R-50

AIR LEAKAGE: 0.88 ach50

SPACE HEAT: Ductless mini-splits (3 heads)

DOMESTIC HOT WATER:
Rheem Marathon electric tank

MECHANICAL VENTILATION: ERV

PV SYSTEM CAPACITY: None (shaded lot)

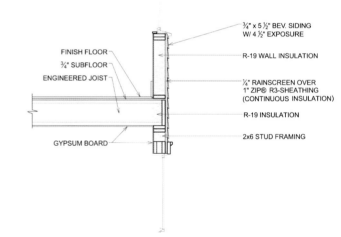

FINISH FLOOR
¾" SUBFLOOR
ENGINEERED JOIST
GYPSUM BOARD

¾" x 5 ½" BEV. SIDING W/ 4 ½" EXPOSURE
R-19 WALL INSULATION
¼" RAINSCREEN OVER 1" ZIP® R3-SHEATHING (CONTINUOUS INSULATION)
R-19 INSULATION
2x6 STUD FRAMING

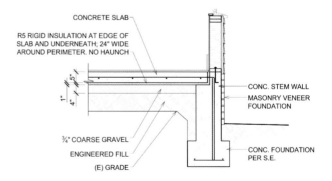

CONCRETE SLAB
R5 RIGID INSULATION AT EDGE OF SLAB AND UNDERNEATH; 24" WIDE AROUND PERIMETER. NO HAUNCH
¾" COARSE GRAVEL
ENGINEERED FILL
(E) GRADE
CONC. STEM WALL
MASONRY VENEER FOUNDATION
CONC. FOUNDATION PER S.E.

# FLOOR PLANS

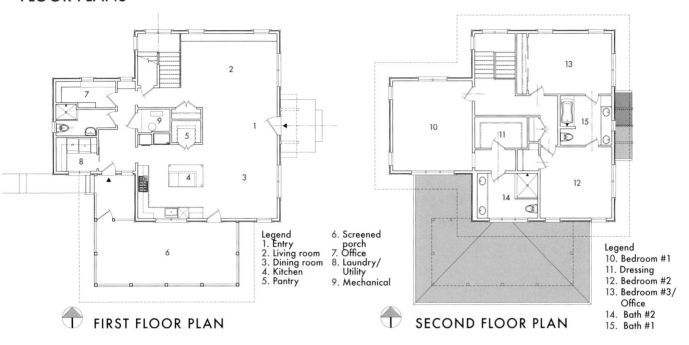

**Legend**
1. Entry
2. Living room
3. Dining room
4. Kitchen
5. Pantry
6. Screened porch
7. Office
8. Laundry/ Utility
9. Mechanical

**FIRST FLOOR PLAN**

**Legend**
10. Bedroom #1
11. Dressing
12. Bedroom #2
13. Bedroom #3/ Office
14. Bath #2
15. Bath #1

**SECOND FLOOR PLAN**

## WHAT MAKES THIS A PRETTY GOOD HOUSE?

- Simple house shape.

- Recycled and composite material for virtually all of the exterior.

- Building in high-performance features from the start.

- Camouflaged slab foundation meant minimal disruption to lot while remaining compatible with other houses in the neighborhood.

- Careful site work with vegetated swale for surface runoff.

- Emphasis on airtightness to minimize moisture infiltration.

- Uncomplicated mechanical systems with no ductwork.

- LED lighting throughout and WaterSense plumbing fixtures.

Historic district constraints helped guide the design of Seville's new home. He and architect Thomas Hood worked hard to make the house compatible with older homes around it.

# CHAPTER TWO

# ECONOMICS

Money is always hiding in the corner in any construction project, just waiting to jump out and say "Boo!" You can either resent the constraints that money places on your project or embrace them. Central to the Pretty Good House concept is an exploration of the trade-offs that a finite budget places on choices. Money is one of the dials we have to turn to get a project right; it helps us home in on essentials.

## Size Matters

Pretty Good House began as a reaction to several trends in residential construction. The chase to maximize square footage is one of them. Most of us are aware of the incredible growth in the average size of homes since World War II, from about 1,000 sq. ft. in 1950 to double that in 2000 (since then, they grew another 25% before peaking in 2014, and have bounced up and down to the present). At the same time, family size has shrunk, so the rise in square feet per person has been even more dramatic.

Jokes about poorly built, mass-produced McMansions, with their three-story "lawyer foyers," abound. These homes are often compared to junk food—empty calories, high in fat, low in health, and so on.

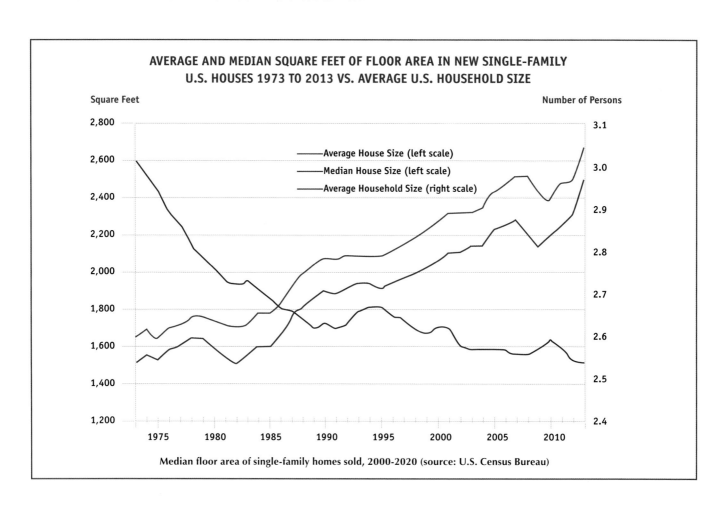

**AVERAGE AND MEDIAN SQUARE FEET OF FLOOR AREA IN NEW SINGLE-FAMILY U.S. HOUSES 1973 TO 2013 VS. AVERAGE U.S. HOUSEHOLD SIZE**

Square Feet

Number of Persons

— Average House Size (left scale)
— Median House Size (left scale)
— Average Household Size (right scale)

Median floor area of single-family homes sold, 2000-2020 (source: U.S. Census Bureau)

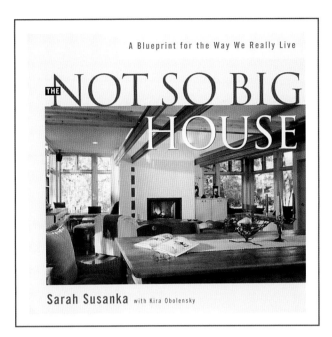

A Blueprint for the Way We Really Live

# NOT SO BIG HOUSE

Sarah Susanka with Kira Obolensky

Sarah Susanka's *Not So Big House* series had a huge impact on home design, helping pare back the excess square footage and wasted space.

But it's the story that much of the housing industry is telling: the highest square footage for the lowest price is the only thing that matters.

Fortunately, there always have been people pushing back against that narrative, arguing that making a house functional and comfortable means avoiding large, sterile spaces that are rarely, if ever, used. Perhaps the best-known practitioner is Sarah Susanka, architect and author of the influential *Not So Big House* series. She helped move the conversation away from quantity to quality.

# First vs. On-going Costs

The first question for a potential PGH owner is: Where is the money coming from? Do you have the money saved or will you have a mortgage? Most people finance through a mortgage, and the options for better-built homes are improving. In the U.S., the Federal Housing Administration (FHA) has a program called the Energy Efficient Mortgage (EEM). It allows homeowners (whether building new or renovating) to borrow more than a standard mortgage would allow, with the understanding that ongoing operating costs will be lower. Private banks are following suit, and property appraisers are increasingly realizing the added value of high-performance homes. In all these cases, the assumption is that your monthly out-of-pocket costs (mortgage plus utilities) will be the same or less than those for a house that doesn't perform as well.

If you're paying for the house from savings, the calculation is more about upfront vs. long-term costs. You are essentially banking money in the form of reduced expenses over the life of the home. A decent energy model (see the sidebar on p. 34) can calculate how much energy you will save using different variables (triple-glazed vs. double-glazed windows, R-40 walls vs. R-30, etc.), and from there you can plug in what the cost savings might be, depending on your heating and cooling equipment, the current cost of fuel or electricity, the average temperatures in your location, and so on. We don't know what fuel or electricity will cost in the future, of course, and we've seen dramatic peaks and valleys in energy costs this century, but it seems likely that the overall trend will be toward higher prices, making the improvements more valuable over time.

With renewables, especially photovoltaics (PV), the financial equation is simple. The amount of electricity produced by a PV system, at a specific latitude and angle, is predictably calculated by any competent installer (or you can use https://pvwatts.nrel.gov/ to find a good approximation). So, essentially, you are pre-paying for whatever electricity is produced for the life of the equipment. Depending on the cost of grid electricity, tax incentives, and the ever-decreasing cost of the equipment, the electricity produced can pay off the equipment in as little as 3 to 5 years.

# Calculating Payback

Back in 2011, Martin Holladay wrote a very good article for Green Building Advisor (GBA) called "Payback Calculations for Energy-Efficiency Improvements." He starts with a general list of questions that may help frame the question, including:

- How soon do you expect to move?
- Will the improvement increase the value of your home?
- Can you finance the work with a low-interest loan?
- What is the expected lifetime of the improvements you are contemplating?
- Do you value the environmental benefits associated with reduced energy use, even if the cost of achieving that goal is high?
- Do you value the peace of mind that comes from lower energy bills?
- Do you value the increased comfort that may result?

As he writes, "Some of the items on this list—for example, the interest rate on a loan—are quantifiable. Others—for example, the rate of energy cost inflation—can only be estimated. And some—for example, how much one values having a reduced carbon footprint—can't be quantified at all."

Holladay goes on to detail a few ways to calculate payback. For a simple payback analysis, divide the cost of the work by the projected savings per year. In his example, a $5,000 project that saves $350 a year will have a payback of 14.3 years (5,000/350). Insulation or PV panels should provide savings long after the 14.3 years elapse. An air-source heat pump might not.

Another method is a cash-flow analysis. If you're borrowing for the project, you can compare monthly expenses. In Holladay's example, the same $5,000 project rolled into a 20-year, 6% mortgage adds $35.82 per month to the mortgage. That's $430 per year, more than the $350 savings, so borrowing for it doesn't work out financially.

You can add in variables like inflation, future energy costs, and so on. These are predicated on predictions (a.k.a. guesses) of what those costs will be, so take them with a grain of salt.

Finally, there's Return on Investment (ROI). By thinking of the improvement as an investment, you can compare the ROI with that of other investments, like stocks, bonds, and real estate. It is a useful tool, with one major caveat: "If you invest $5,000…the equipment will wear out in 20 years and be carted off to the dump. On the other hand, if your money is invested in a government bond, you might earn 2% interest per year—and you'll still have the $5,000 of capital at the end of 20 years."

You also need to include things like maintenance and repairs in your project costs; it's easy to gloss over some potentially significant items.

The end of Holladay's article provides the most valuable framing: "Since the continued burning of fossil fuels at current rates is likely to lead to catastrophic environmental disruptions whose effects could linger for thousands of years, it's fundamentally impossible to choose an appropriate price for fossil fuel. Seen from this perspective, efforts to reduce our use of fossil fuels are a moral imperative, and the actual payback periods for energy-efficiency measures are irrelevant. We still need to make some simple calculations, however, so that we invest our money wisely. Efforts to reduce energy use should always start with the low-hanging fruit."

## CARBON ACCOUNTING

There is an entire area of accounting we have not talked about yet, what is called "carbon accounting" in the environmental and building-science community. It refers to a calculation of how much "carbon" (really $CO_2$ equivalent) results from the production, transport, and use of various materials and machinery vs. how much is saved through lower energy or material consumption. Is the payoff fast enough to ensure that it's worth the environmental cost? Or will it take so long that the damage in the short term outweighs the benefit over time? We will return to this question in Chapter 7.

Related to carbon accounting is the question of *resilience.* In the building-science community, it refers to a building's ability to survive intact the various challenges nature, and a rapidly changing world, can throw at it. Will a flood destroy it? Is it fire-resistant? Will it remain above freezing during a prolonged

power failure? Will it be comfortable in a hotter world?

As we are unfortunately learning, making predictions about precisely how and how fast global warming will impact our lives is imprecise at best. But we know we will see more severe weather events, and a house that isn't built with that in mind is not a good investment of time, money, or carbon.

# Costs vs. Benefits

Let's look at some of the specific areas where cost is typically a limiting factor.

**Insulation and air sealing** You obviously need to meet code minimums in a new house. But is it worth it to go beyond? If you look at the graph below of the amount of insulation (R-value) vs. the amount of heat flow blocked, you'll see that the initial insulation does a tremendous amount, but it drops off precipitously from there, until the difference approaches zero.

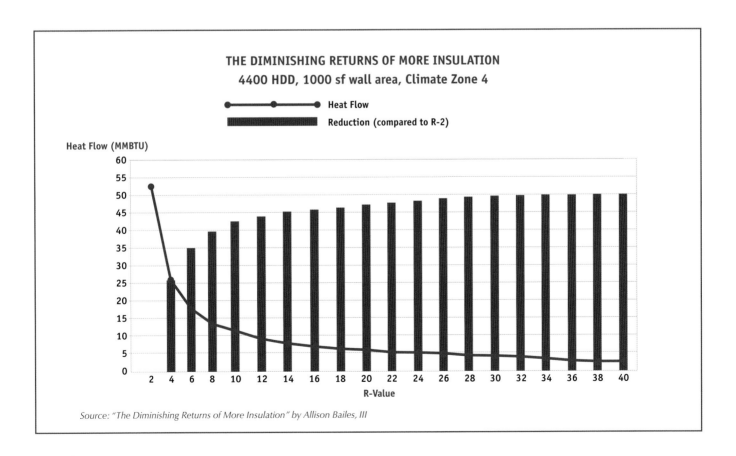

THE DIMINISHING RETURNS OF MORE INSULATION
4400 HDD, 1000 sf wall area, Climate Zone 4

*Source: "The Diminishing Returns of More Insulation" by Allison Bailes, III*

# Energy Modeling

We can't predict precisely how a building will perform, but based on studies of existing housing and the basic physics of heat loss, we can form educated opinions. Energy modeling consists of computer software or a spreadsheet with varying degrees of detail and complexity. An energy model is an upfront cost that can save considerable money both in design and in operating costs. It allows the designer, builder, and client to make informed decisions about where the budget is best spent.

The usual inputs are things like insulation, the size and type of windows and doors, the efficiency of heating and cooling equipment, house size, geographical location and orientation to the sun, and so forth. The output can be a variety of things: how much energy will be required to keep the house heated or cooled in a typical year, how the house compares to other similar houses, whether the house meet the standards for various rating systems, and whether it meets the energy code.

There are some free energy models, like BEopt, from the U.S. National Renewable Energy Laboratory (NREL), that are simple enough for homeowners to use. The Passive House Planning Package, on the other hand, is proprietary, complex, and requires training to use. A professional energy modeler and rater can give you an accurate sense of the options and help monitor the quality of the work.

Since models are only approximations, they are most useful as a tool for comparing options. In most modeling software, it is fairly simple to make substitutions and see the difference they make. For instance, you can see the expected energy savings by using triple-glazed instead of double-glazed windows, or decide whether you can use a smaller heating or cooling system if you increase the insulation.

Energy models can only model the house itself, of course. It can't tell you what will happen if your children don't close the door, if you like to take half-hour showers, or if your TV stays on 24 hours a day. We call these factors "occupancy" and discuss this further in Chapter 10. Builders often joke that our houses are perfect and then the clients ruin them by moving in, but the truth is that a house can only perform to the model if those living in it understand how the house was designed to operate.

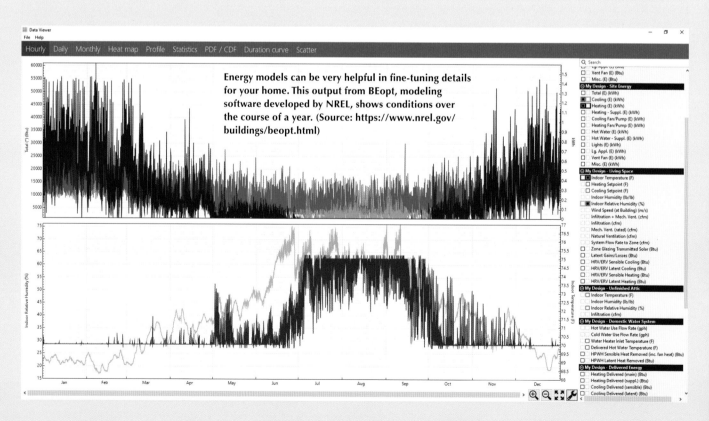

Energy models can be very helpful in fine-tuning details for your home. This output from BEopt, modeling software developed by NREL, shows conditions over the course of a year. (Source: https://www.nrel.gov/buildings/beopt.html)

Where to stop adding insulation is one of the first questions we looked at in our discussion group. As with much else, the answer is "it depends," and this issue is explored in more detail in Chapter 7. But the essential goals for a PGH should be to keep condensation from forming inside your walls or roof, and to be well enough insulated that you can dramatically reduce your heating and cooling needs (and thus the size of the equipment). Much of this is dependent on local climate, orientation, ambient humidity levels, and other factors specific to your project.

*The more your house looks like one a kindergartener would draw (minus the smoking chimney), the better off you are, at least in the north.*

**Structure/Shape** Complexity adds cost. Dormers, overhangs, and jogs in walls all require more labor and materials, and more work to air-seal, insulate, and waterproof. In addition, anywhere that requires a beam or a post is a place where you will have a hard time insulating. Simple roof lines are easier to build, easier to insulate, and will be much less prone to leaking. Similarly, lots of jogs, connections, overhanging rooms, or ells will maximize the exterior surface area of the building, exposing more of it to heat loss (or gain, in a hot climate), be harder on materials, and will, of course, be more expensive to build. The more your house looks like one a kindergartener would draw (minus the smoking chimney), the better off you are, at least in the north.

This is not to minimize the importance of good, or interesting, design. You don't want a generic house with poorly thought-out details. But one advantage of a PGH is that it should be relatively easy, and thus cheaper, to build.

Two simple rooflines (a steeply pitched gable roof and a shallow shed roof) combine to create a classic New England form.

This house (design by Joe Waltman, construction by Ben Morton) is a stunning modern take on Maine Shingle Style. It is also expensive to build and, with its complicated roofline, very hard to air-seal and insulate well.

Proximity to the water and multiple grade changes from one side of the home to the other make this a particularly challenging site, adding to the construction cost.

**Size** Any space inside your shell needs to be heated, cooled, lit, and protected from the elements. A dining room you use six times per year costs the same per square foot as the eat-in kitchen that gets used six times per day. If you use your bedroom for sleeping and getting dressed, a smaller bedroom will probably meet your needs as well as, if not better than, a large one with either open floor space or furniture whose purpose is mostly to hang clothes on. A basement whose only purpose is to store items that won't get touched until your children sell the house may be better left out.

More square footage should always be a last resort in a PGH. Size allows you to ignore design problems, add unnecessary cost, and can easily take a house from cozy to sterile. We'll talk more about house size in Chapter 3.

**Site** If you're trying to build a new house, typically the first thing that happens is finding land and deciding where on the property to put the house. It can often cost as much as the construction itself, so it's important to get it right. Does it have good exposure for active or passive solar? Do you have access to municipal sewer and water or will you have to dig a well and install a septic system? Will you need hundreds of feet of driveway, which will have to be plowed and maintained? Can you keep water away from the house site? Can you dig a basement or is there ledge you will have to blast?

Many of the issues a homeowner must consider and budget for will be discussed in more detail in later chapters. Let's now take a look at some of the considerations the other two parts of the team need to balance.

# The Builder's Perspective

An idea that emerged from one of our discussion group sessions was to make the building shell non-negotiable. The contractor, perhaps in conjunction with the designer, comes up with a wall section, roof section, air-sealing details, minimum window performance, rainscreen details, and so on. These are presented as a package. They are based on the contractor's experience, research, and expertise and are not up for negotiation when the budget gets tight.

This route places a lot of responsibility on the contractor. He or she must know costs early in the process, needs to have complete confidence in the package presented, and needs to be able to articulate its value.

The hardest part is usually the wall section. If there's one thing building-science enthusiasts like to obsess over, it's debating the pros and cons of various wall assemblies (see Chapter 4). Many of us prefer double-wall (or double-stud) construction, both for performance and ease of construction. Others prefer using Larsen trusses, where all or most of the insulation goes outside the building shell by attaching I-joists or home-made trusses to the exterior of the building and filling the bays with insulation. With the advent of wood-fiber insulating sheathing, builders are coming up with even more assemblies.

They all can work very well, but for the sake of this discussion, the important thing is comparative costs. Different crews, based on experience, access to different materials, skill level, and so forth, can produce some wall assemblies at a lower cost than others, or get better performance for the same budget. If you, as the contractor, are going to present a package to the client, it's important that you've done your homework.

The contractor or their subcontractors and suppliers should have sufficient expertise in HVAC-D, lighting design and equipment, nontoxic materials and

Double-stud wall construction minimizes thermal bridging and uses conventional materials and techniques, making it a popular choice in high-performance houses.

While tricky the first time, the Larsen truss wall is a system that gets easier and more efficient through repetition.

finishes, doors and windows, and insulation to make informed recommendations to the client and designer about the performance and cost implications of various choices.

While the contractor is the party with the least financial incentive to rein in costs, he or she ironically has the greatest responsibility to do so in a PGH. Contractors ultimately are the ones who have to figure out a way to balance budget and outcome.

# The Designer's Perspective

If it's important for the contractor to have a handle on the shell of the building, it's equally so for the designer. First, the designer needs to be on the same page, literally, as the builder. Plans need to be something the builder can both understand and build. Otherwise, the design budget will be sacrificed on redoing drawings later, or even worse, the plans will be ignored by the builder.

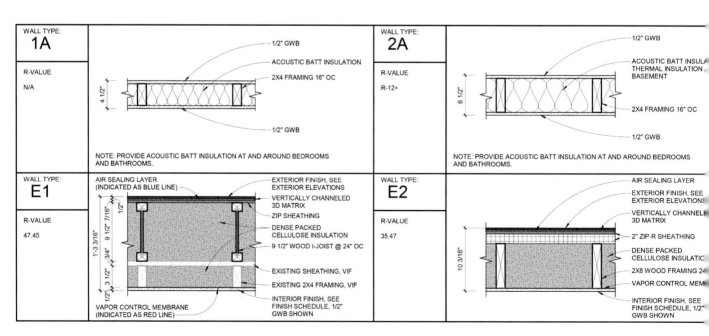

Wall-section details, by Briburn Architecture for Life, show the acoustic (1A and 2A) and thermal (E1 and E2) insulation construction of interior and exterior walls in a project combining renovation (E1) and new construction (E2).

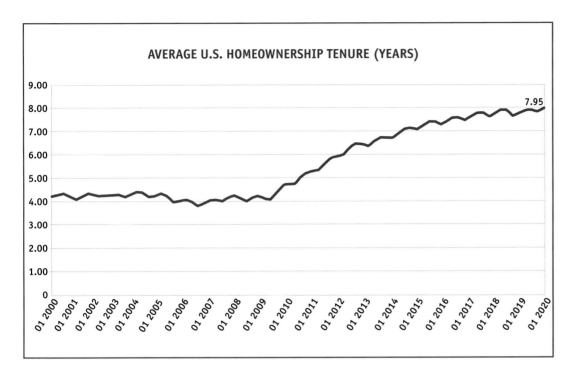

**AVERAGE U.S. HOMEOWNERSHIP TENURE (YEARS)**

7.95

Adapted from ATTOM
Data Solutions

Integrating critical drainage, air sealing, ventilation, and other details into the design is also much easier (and cheaper) if done during design rather than after construction has started. Simple things like thickening an interior wall for ductwork, making sure window and door trim or roof overhangs can accommodate a rainscreen, or designing a roof to maximize PV panels are very difficult to shoehorn in after construction has started.

> *Every house is, ultimately, a study in compromise. How many of your priorities can you fit into your budget? What are you willing to sacrifice?*

While a project is typically designed for a specific client, no one, as far as we know, lives forever. And the average length of home ownership, while lengthening, is still shamefully short in the U.S. (just under 8 years in 2020, according to U.S. Census data). Will the current owners stay and want to remodel? Will new owners want to make more substantial changes?

Designing for an unknown future requires some flexibility in design. Could interior walls be moved to change the floor plan? Could a photovoltaic system be installed later? Can plumbing and wiring be accessed, either through a ceiling or through a centralized layout? A Pretty Good House should be designed so that it can be modified without significant destruction. This means that the structural, water management, and insulation details are clear enough to be understood by future designers and builders and are well documented, with the information stored in a retrievable way (see the discussion of the owner's manual in Chapter 10). Water and air management details should meet the same test.

Every house is, ultimately, a study in compromise. How many of your priorities can you fit into your budget? What are you willing to sacrifice? Which expenses could get delayed (like a garage), and which would be very hard, and much more expensive, to do later (like insulation)?

We can't predict future needs and uses. How we live later will not be exactly the same as how we live today. Costs fluctuate: at the time of writing, lumber prices have skyrocketed after many years of stability. After a spike in energy costs following Hurricane Katrina, the fracking revolution and other developments made a mockery of "peak oil" predictions. The climate is changing, and we don't know how long our design assumptions will hold up. But with a thoughtful, humble approach, we can hopefully leave room to account for the uncertainties.

## THINGS TO CONSIDER

- Think long term: don't build for your maximum needs. Smaller homes are easier to build, easier to maintain, easier to age in.

- Think long term: spending more up front can pay off, sometimes very quickly.

- Think long term: we need to think about both energy efficiency *and* resource efficiency. Spend our "carbon account" very cautiously.

- Think long term: the climate is changing. Can your house function under changing conditions?

- And remember, renovating an existing house is almost always cheaper than building new.

# Tedd Benson and Open Building

Tedd Benson of New Hampshire-based Bensonwood is one of the smartest and most passionate people in residential construction. In a career dedicated to developing a better way to build, Tedd has helped bring high performance to both timberframe and prefab construction. More recently, Bensonwood, along with some partners, have been making homes more adaptable for the long term.

The Open Built model "disentangles" a building into multiple layers, separating components into their expected longevity and making sure one can be adapted or replaced independent of the longer-term layers.

In conversation with us, Tedd writes: "In our collective effort to create buildings that provide the longest possible service with the lowest possible impact, Open Built disentanglement strategies may be one of the most important attributes. It's how embodied energy is accounted for and it's how our good work today pays forward for centuries not decades."

The houses are built so that the structure is on the exterior insulated, airtight walls as much as possible, leaving the entire interior open for future renovations. Spaces for electrical wiring, plumbing, and so on are built to be easily accessible and are clustered in areas that won't be affected by later modifications.

We know that houses change, in ways we can't predict. As Stewart Brand, an early inspiration for Open Built, writes in *How Buildings Learn*, "(A)ll design is prediction, and all predictions are wrong." The genius of the Open Built model is seeing that inevitable unpredictability as inspiration, as an opportunity for innovation.

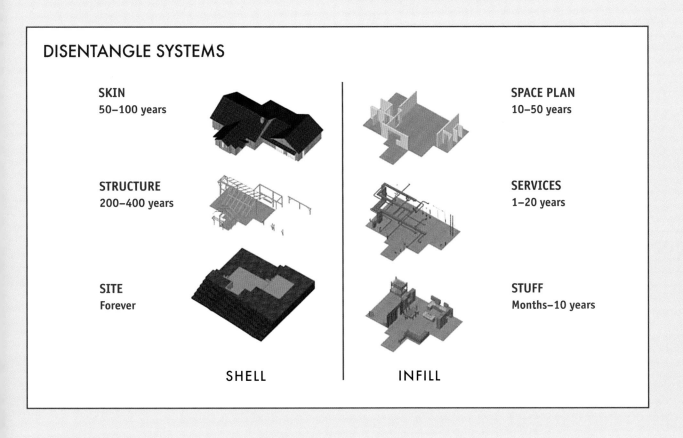

## DISENTANGLE SYSTEMS

**SKIN**
50–100 years

**SPACE PLAN**
10–50 years

**STRUCTURE**
200–400 years

**SERVICES**
1–20 years

**SITE**
Forever

**STUFF**
Months–10 years

SHELL

INFILL

# Maquoit Bay

The house overlooking Maquoit Bay in Maine's Midcoast borrows architectural themes from the region, including simple shapes and an attached barn, in a style the architect calls "regional modernism." A kink in the floor plan helps separate the house from the barn visually.

THE COUPLE RELOCATING from suburban Washington, D.C., to Midcoast Maine with two children and a big dog were clear on a couple of points, recalls architect Harry Hepburn of Briburn. Chief among them was that their new home should be highly efficient and let them live comfortably for a week without grid electricity and without resorting to fossil fuels.

Their building lot was on family-owned property on the shores of Maquoit Bay, close to where the husband's parents lived, and a place that had special memories. One of the owners once had a treehouse and enjoyed bonfires on the site. "He had grown up going to this spot," Hepburn says. So Hepburn designed them a net-zero home with a robust building enclosure, photovoltaic panels on the roof, and battery storage for those off-grid stretches. But he did it in a way that also satisfied clear aesthetic aims.

"They were open to modern," Hepburn says, "but they wanted regional forms and shapes. They really liked the idea of a farmhouse, a meandering barn attached to a house. We were looking at what we call regional modernism, regional forms with modern interpretations of window sizes and groups, and materials. There's some memory here of what was next door or down the street, what they grew up with, traditional house shapes and materials that you'd find in Maine or on the coast."

Briburn, the firm founded by Hepburn and Chris Briley, is committed to the AIA 2030 Challenge, which seeks to reduce carbon emissions and energy use. That requires every project the firm does to go through energy modeling. The family didn't have any interest in seeking Passive House certification, but that would have been within sight had they chosen to do so. In addition to very low air leakage (nearly

**ABOVE** A wood stove, along with rooftop solar panels with battery backup, will help the family live comfortably without fossil fuels should the power go out.

**LEFT** A screened porch next to the entry faces southwest, offering water views as well as shelter. It's on the same level as the adjacent open deck.

The heated tile floor in combination with triple-glazed windows and a very tight building enclosure will keep the great room on the first floor warm through long Maine winters.

LOCATION: Freeport, Maine; Climate Zone 6A

ARCHITECT: Harry Hepburn of Briburn

BUILDER: Benjamin & Co.

LIVING AREA: 3,000 sq. ft.

NUMBER OF BEDROOMS/BATHROOMS: 4/3

FOUNDATION: Partial slab on grade, partial full concrete foundation

FOUNDATION INSULATION: 2-in. FRP-faced polyiso on interior, R-13

SUBSLAB INSULATION: 4-in. rigid foam

WALL CONSTRUCTION: Double-stud wall, 11¼ in. thick

ABOVE-GRADE WALL INSULATION: Dense-pack cellulose, R-42

ATTIC FLOOR INSULATION: 18-in. loose-fill cellulose, R-61

CATHEDRAL CEILING INSULATION: R-25 closed-cell spray foam and R-35 dense-packed cellulose

AIR LEAKAGE: 0.67 ach50

SPACE HEAT: York water-to-water ground-source heat pump supplies hydronic radiant floor on first floor and ducted forced air on second floor for both heating and cooling.

DOMESTIC HOT WATER: York heat pump

MECHANICAL VENTILATION: Imperial Air ERV

PV SYSTEM CAPACITY: 8.64 kW; 10,083 kWh expected annually

# FLOOR PLANS

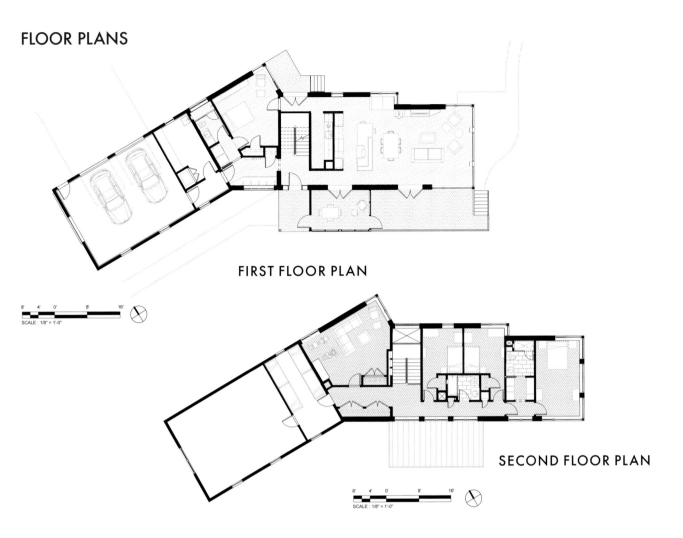

FIRST FLOOR PLAN

8' 4' 0' 8' 16'
SCALE : 1/8" = 1'-0"

SECOND FLOOR PLAN

8' 4' 0' 8' 16'
SCALE : 1/8" = 1'-0"

but not quite at Passive House levels), the double-stud enclosure includes triple-glazed windows and a lot of cellulose insulation.

The house is a simple shape with the second floor stacked directly over the first and no double-height spaces inside except for the stair. That, Hepburn says, maximizes the envelope and floor area. There is a kink in the building plan, a sort of "knuckle" as Hepburn puts it, that creates an aesthetic break between the barn and the house while providing rooms with a view of the water. Other than that, the house and barn are simple rectangles.

While energy performance was key, the owners were interested in materials and detailing inside that had what Hepburn calls an "Old World" charm, more of a European feel with lots of stone, tile, and wood.

## WHAT MAKES THIS A PRETTY GOOD HOUSE?

- Simple shape without unnecessary architectural flourishes.

- Superinsulated building enclosure with high-performance windows.

- Cellulose insulation has a low carbon impact and is high in recycled content.

- Net-zero design powered by photovoltaic panels with battery storage for extended periods off-grid.

- All-electric mechanicals without the need for fossil fuels.

**ABOVE** Walnut kitchen cabinets, stone countertops, and a tile floor are part of a materials palette that helps give the house an Old World flavor.

**RIGHT** The double-stud wall house is conventionally framed for the most part, but the design also includes a timbered ceiling on the first floor. A service cavity between the first and second floors houses ductwork and other utilities.

The floor of the great room is a terracotta tile (over a radiant floor), and kitchen cabinets are made from a dark walnut. And while the house is mostly framed with dimensional lumber, the first-floor ceilings in the great room and kitchen incorporate heavy timbers. To keep mechanicals hidden, Hepburn worked in a 2x6 service cavity over the ceiling where ERV ducts, wiring, and plumbing could be run.

To Hepburn, the notion of a Pretty Good House leaves room for interpretation. Owners and designers are pursuing many of the same performance standards as Passive House, but without a rigid framework for certification. "You're doing your best within your means to make the best house possible," he says, "and that could mean different things to different people. This house could have been Passive House if we wanted it to be. The client didn't have an interest in pursuing certification. I think that's one of the fine lines—not interested in certification but interested in a lot of the benefits you receive from it."

## The Everyman Path to High Performance

The house on Maquoit Bay is neither small nor inexpensive, but the double-stud construction on exterior walls is a relatively simple feature that can enhance energy performance of houses of any size and most any budget. Two framed walls are separated by a gap and the entire assembly filled with dense-pack cellulose, making for a highly insulated wall and very little thermal bridging. "It's really easy for builders to understand," says architect Harry Hepburn. "It's really easy to execute, and the cost of the lumber is generally less because the members are smaller. Anyone can do this, and you can do this at any scale."

An attached barn is a trademark of New England architecture, but in this instance provides room for two vehicles instead of cows.

# CHAPTER THREE

# DESIGN

Design encompasses many steps, from general construction planning to specific decisions that determine how the house will look, perform, and feel. When designing a Pretty Good House, the key elements to consider are: location, orientation, size, function, form, beauty, comfort, security, emotion, integration of trades, and, last but not least, budget.

**In the country: Birch farmhouse, by Mottram Architecture, in Maine is built on a 1.5-acre lot on the outskirts of the city of Portland. It's not uncommon to find PGH homes in rural locations connected to nature and their surroundings.**

## Location: The Critical Role of the Site

Is the house in an urban, suburban, or rural area? Close to neighbors or secluded on acres of land? Are shops, services, and work opportunities nearby, or do they require travel? Is public transportation, cycling, or walking an option for some, all, or none of daily-life activities? These are just some of the many things to consider when choosing a location for your PGH.

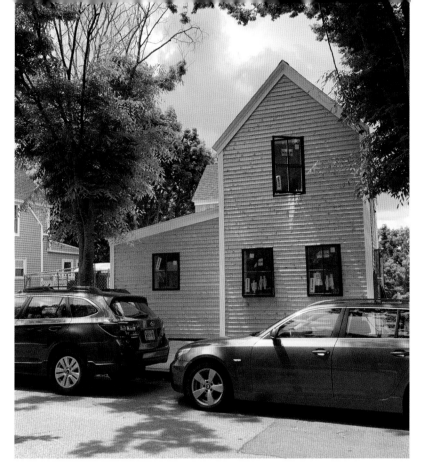

ABOVE  Building in town can be challenging. Access to parking, deliveries, dumpsters, and scheduling become important logistical challenges when improving structures in dense areas of the city, as with this PGH renovation in Portland, Maine. Walkable access to the amenities that cities provide can be key to the success of a project.

ABOVE RIGHT  Blending in: This new PGH built by Kinsey Construction is respectful of the surrounding architecture with its classic New England style. Despite its secluded look the house is in town and visible to neighbors nearby.

RIGHT  In a subdivision: The Artemis Way neighborhood, built by Progressive Path Building, provides PGH-level rental properties for aging in place less than a mile from the center of Freeport, Maine. The rental market was nonexistent for this older demographic, and controlled utility costs for fixed income is a great incentive for building and living in a community like this.

Once you've chosen the location, a PGH should be designed to maximize the strong points of the site and minimize the weak ones. Steep, north-facing, water-view sites, for example, can be difficult to work with. While they may not present insurmountable challenges, they do call for a disciplined design team to ensure that the choices made in the planning stage result in a home that's a dream to live in—not a disaster.

Building close to the water presents challenges in terms of water management in the structure and foundation; potential state, local, and town regulations; and access to the site for construction. Shown here is the Dragonfly Pond House, by Briburn.

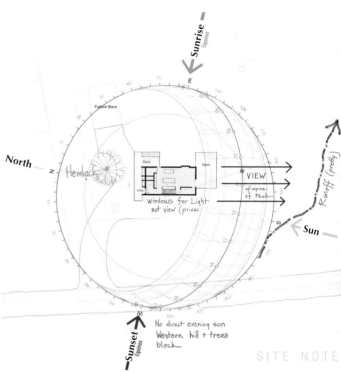

Building orientation can significantly influence the cost and performance of a home. Good orientation can enhance daylighting, maximize the warming effects of the sun during winter months, and promote cooling during the summer. In colder climates, positioning a garage or trees to the north can protect the home from cold winds.

# Orientation

Careful site planning is the most cost-effective thing you can do when building a PGH, and one of the most common site challenges in designing a new house is building orientation. Do not leave it up to the excavator. Get it right and you can, for example, take advantage of a stunning view, minimize poor site drainage, and maximize the sunlight in all the right spaces, turning a seemingly basic home into a PGH. Get it wrong and, unlike poor paint-color choices, you'll be stuck with a result that you won't be able to fix.

From an energy standpoint, in cold climates in the northern hemisphere, the ideal PGH should face south, with some windows (but not too many) on the east and west sides, and few or no windows or doors on the north (see Chapter 6). And though windows, doors, and solar panels keep getting better, it's still best to keep the house oriented within 30 degrees of due south, if possible. This ideal PGH would also have a south-facing roof to support photovoltaic pan-

els, unless there is a possibility of installing panels on the ground next to the home (see Chapter 9).

*Careful site planning is the most cost-effective thing you can do when building a PGH.*

What might happen if you don't orient the house in the most advantageous way? Plenty. If you put the driveway on the north side of the building in a cold climate, for example, you might end up with an icy surface that will make it hard to get in and out of the garage. In warmer climates, if you have too many west-facing windows and little or no shading, you'll have trouble keeping your home cool.

Flat sites like this one are easy to access, easy to work on, and present few challenges when coordinating equipment and deliveries. This home was built by Kolbert Building.

A landscape architect can provide vital guidance on water management, house orientation, site access, and selection of native vegetation.

During the design phase, we highly recommend that you have your lot surveyed. This could help avert a potential disaster, like siting the house in the only logical location for a septic field. And we strongly recommend hiring a landscape architect during this phase, too, as they do a whole lot more than choose pretty plants. Among other things, a landscape architect can determine grading for proper drainage, identify the best access for a driveway, and locate and preserve native vegetation on your site.

## LET THERE BE (THE RIGHT KIND OF) LIGHT

To maximize sunlight in all the right spaces, the first task is to understand how the sun would track through the building over the course of the day throughout the year and understand what this would mean for interior temperatures. In colder climates (a.k.a. heating climates, or ones that require indoor heating), for example, if you orient the building correctly, you'll create the right conditions for passive solar heat in the winter, which can both lower your heating costs and boost your spirits. If you're in a warm climate (i.e., a cooling-dominated one), you can help keep your home cool and comfortable by

including a wraparound porch or exterior shading devices. That may mean building a house with a smaller footprint.

Think about light in relation to your daily habits. If you're an early riser, say, an east-facing bedroom might be wonderful, but if you're a night owl, having your bedroom on the east side of the house will be a major annoyance, unless you install blackout window coverings—which can then cause major moisture issues. But that's another story.

Planning for daylighting in different spaces throughout your home also helps to reduce the amount of electricity you need to light the interiors. If there is too much daytime glare in your living room, you might not be able to see the TV screen, for example, or it might be too hot in your home office during the day. But if there is too little daylight, you might end up using electric lights all day and still be unhappy with your workspace. (For more information see Chapter 6 and Chapter 9.)

Because of site restrictions, you may be forced to make compromises on the orientation of the house. But once that's done, you'll be able to make judicious

The Sparrow, designed by Mottram Architecture, has a deep wraparound porch to shade a 12-ft. sliding-glass door from summer sun.

A less traditional solution, seen here in the Tula by Mottram Architecture, is to provide some form of exterior shading device, like this trellis, that shelters windows or doors.

Designer Michael Maines and the homeowner collaborated to transform an existing garage into a family room. By opening the wall between the new family room and kitchen beyond, they were able to let light and views travel across the two spaces.

# DESIGN CHARACTERISTICS OF DAYLIGHTING STRATEGIES

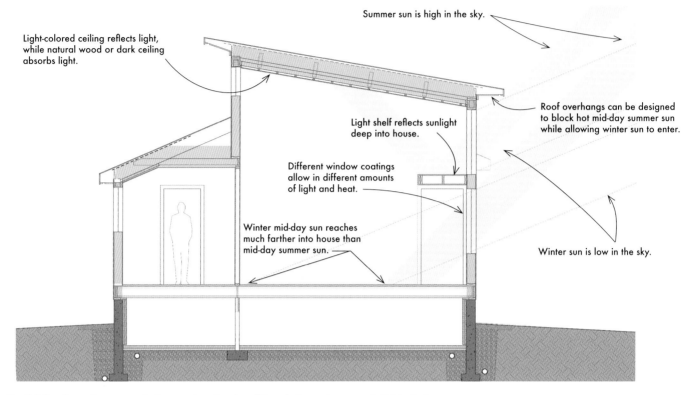

Summer sun is high in the sky.

Light-colored ceiling reflects light, while natural wood or dark ceiling absorbs light.

Light shelf reflects sunlight deep into house.

Roof overhangs can be designed to block hot mid-day summer sun while allowing winter sun to enter.

Different window coatings allow in different amounts of light and heat.

Winter mid-day sun reaches much farther into house than mid-day summer sun.

Winter sun is low in the sky.

Daylighting depends on many factors, such as the size of the windows, doors, or skylights, their location and orientation, the site's access to daylight, room geometry, the visible transmittance of the glazing, reflectance of room surfaces, the contents of the room, enhancements such as light shelves or shading devices, and the reflectance of the exterior surfaces surrounding your home.

Slate Farmhouse, by Mottram Architecture, has a particularly cozy living room in December. Low windowsills and south-facing orientation allow the maximum amount of warm winter sunlight to stream across the room. This brightens the space during the coldest months of the year and creates a space where people love to gather.

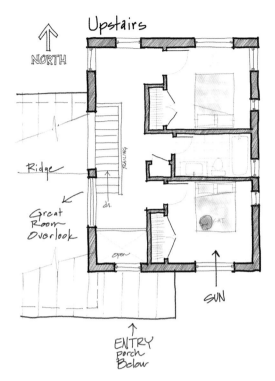

Upstairs

NORTH

Ridge

Great Room Overlook

ENTRY Porch Below

SUN

**Although the view is to the north, southern sunlight is captured by the front bedroom, while additional south-facing windows filter light to the lower level through the open section of flooring at the upper stair landing. This concept sketch of Blueberry Woods House drawn by Robert Swinburne.**

choices about window placement, the use of interior windows to transfer light between spaces, and adding windows to take advantage of important sight lines and views.

# Size Matters

In terms of resource use and cost, the PGH philosophy favors structures that are as small as possible and budget-conscious. When the PGH guidelines were first developed in 2011, the following targets for building size were recommended: up to 1,000 sq. ft. for one occupant; 1,500 sq. ft. for two occupants; 1,750 sq. ft. for three occupants, and 1,875 sq. ft. for four or more occupants. The national average is much higher (see the sidebar below), but the important thing is to think carefully about how much space you really need and how flexible interior spaces can be. Clever storage solutions can reduce the amount of square footage that's truly needed.

## Average Home Sizes Are Growing

In 1975, the average American single-family home was 1,660 sq. ft. Now, new houses measure about 2,500 sq. ft. As the size of the average household has shrunk since 1975, this doesn't seem to make much sense. But you don't have to look far for two big reasons: the concentration of wealth in the U.S. and the deeply entrenched car culture, which means that cheaper land outside city centers is easily accessible. Other factors are the American consumer culture and marketing designed to persuade prospective buyers that 2,500 sq. ft. and "luxury" features like opulent marble bathrooms are must-haves. Unfortunately, the current appraisal and real estate markets seem to place a premium on these eye-candy elements instead of solar panels, better insulation, and improved interior air quality. So "fancy" features and size (regardless of our true needs) too often win out over the pocketbooks, comfort, and health of the occupants.

And even if you are able to hire a qualified builder, designer, or architect, you can't assume that you will get a house that runs on renewable energy, is well insulated, and has efficient mechanical systems. Alas, this is rarely the case, which is all the more reason for homeowners to choose their team wisely and be clear about what they want.

More space doesn't necessarily make our homes more valuable, even though it certainly might make them cost more. But what's the secret to building smaller? Unfortunately, it's not as simple as putting a floor plan on a copier, hitting 90%, and expecting the finished product to function perfectly or cost 90% of the original estimate. Building smaller doesn't always mean it will cost less. No matter how small you go, you still have to pay tradespeople to dig a foundation, run electrical lines, and install plumbing. And even if you've got world-class DIY skills, you still need to install bathrooms and a kitchen, and that equipment and cabinetry doesn't come cheap.

In terms of deciding how to spend your hard-earned money, remember that kitchens and baths also are the two spaces in a home that get renovated most often. Don't be tempted to put in a luxury kitchen and skimp on basics like wall insulation. Insulation is complicated and costly to upgrade. Your kitchen will most likely get renovated in 10 or 20 years anyway.

Remember, too, that the PGH is a flexible framework, so if your house has to be 2,500 sq. ft. (or more) to work well for you, so be it. Build a mudroom that's 15 ft. x 15 ft. instead of 10 ft. x 10 ft. if that's the amount of space you need. You'll be happy you did.

Bottom line: When you design a PGH, you may not necessarily build as big a home as you originally envisioned, but you *will* build smarter. How? By focusing on the site, but also on functionality, comfort, security, and the ways in which our home can support us mentally, physically, and emotionally. Let's take each of these in turn.

# Designing for Functionality

A well-designed home focuses on how the occupants use the space and store their belongings, not on square footage. More space doesn't equal more func-

**This small living room design by Michael Maines uses large windows to open up the space to the outdoors. A wood stove makes this a cozy spot to curl up with a book.**

Large windows and a vaulted ceiling help to increase the feeling of spaciousness in this flexible yet functional living room without overwhelming the space with cavernous volume. The cozy arrangement of furniture allows for a great gathering space but also takes advantage of the views provided by the double-height windows.

tionality. To determine how a home can best meet your needs, a great design team will start by asking questions that lay the foundation for a beautiful, comfortable, healthy, durable home.

If we consider the spaces in our homes in terms of function, not size, we are in for some happy surprises. One could be a beautifully designed, smaller living room able to handle a wide range of activities, from cocktails to quiet reading, or furniture arrangements that allow one or two people to feel cozy on a snowy winter night but also enable a smooth flow of guests for brunch on a balmy summer day.

The PGH guidelines will make you rethink, say, that grand staircase you initially thought you wanted and focus on the activities you do for much of the time. Once you've had this reality check, you may be ready to give up spaces you use only a tiny fraction of the time.

## SPACES THAT SERVE LITTLE FUNCTION

**Guest rooms**  Let's rethink spare rooms that serve only one purpose for limited amounts of time. If you have lots of visitors or lots of children, you do need bedrooms for them, of course. But a guest room for the few visitors that stay with you only once a year will cost you more than you might think, if you calculate the square footage of the room itself, plus the possible addition of an attached bathroom. And then there's the cost of heating and maintaining that extra square footage. But what if that room can double as a home office that you use eight hours a day, five days a week? This would give it a dual, valuable purpose—and value for the next owner, who may have a bigger household or also work from a home office.

**Basements**  Basements can be tricky. In some parts of the country a basement provides life-saving shelter during tornadoes or other extreme weather events.

# PGH Guidelines for Design

Think of these questions as jumping off points, not an exhaustive list:

- **Where do you spend most of your time at home?** Do you hang out in the living room or need a separate cozy space for watching TV?

- **Getting things from the outside in**: Coming home with groceries or other purchases—where do you come in and where do you want to put things down?

- **Meal preparation:** Do you or other people who share your home love cooking? Do you need a kitchen for one, two, or even more cooks? Is cooking just not your thing? If not, then there's no need for a restaurant-grade kitchen.

- **Working from home:** Do you spend all day on the phone? Do you need a quiet space to write and think?

- **Leisure activities**: What do you and other household members do and what's the ideal place for them? That may mean playing an instrument, knitting up a storm, or quietly reading.

- **Seasonal considerations**: Do you have seasonal interests? Are you a gardener with a need for a potting station? Are you a fisherman and need a place to clean fish? Are you an avid skier and need a place to dry your winter gear?

- **Outside spaces**: How do you use (or want to use) your outside spaces?

- **Entertaining**: Do you usually have small gatherings or big ones—or both? What kind and where (sit-down dinners, lawn game parties, relaxed tea for two)? How much gardening do you want to do? How much yard maintenance are you willing to do?

Even in regions that are prone to tornadoes, a storm shelter could be a cheaper option. In other locations, a basement is a convenient place to put the water heater and electric service panel, although it can be hard to keep it warm and dry. Too often, basements wind up as catchalls for storing anything from broken toys to dated clothing that will never come back into style.

And then there is the role that basements can play in the health of our homes—and of ourselves. Which is why we need to make more deliberate choices about what we keep and where we store it—for instance, storing toxic material, like paints, sealants, and adhesives inside our homes. Or whether we really need spaces, like basements, that complicate water management (think leaks) that affects our health and the health of the structures we live in.

**Formal spaces** Unless you frequently entertain on a grand scale (and some people do), formal living rooms and dining rooms usually don't have roles to play in the PGH. Nor do home offices that aren't separate enough from the rest of the house to function well, or large, formal entries that are difficult to heat and cool and take up valuable space.

The moral of this part of the story? Build a home that meets all your needs for function and comfort, as large as you truly need it—but not one bit larger.

Basements have a tendency to collect toxic materials like paints, stains, glues, and pesticides, as well items that should be recycled, donated, or thrown away. They can also be wet, contributing to poor indoor air quality.

## Long-Term Thinking

Though you are building a new house—or making it "new" through renovation—keep in mind that it will someday be an old house. It should be flexible enough to work for a wide range of occupants, including people with physical disabilities who might one day live there. Although we do not suggest you build your dream home for future homeowners, we do suggest thinking about universal design, which focuses on creating environments that are safe and comfortable for people of any age. This reduces the need for adaptation down the road but does not impede how you use the space today. These considerations do add another layer to the planning process, but it's better to consider these things now rather than later.

# Form Follows Function: Shape and Complexity

The larger the surface area of exterior walls and roof for a given floor area, the less efficient the building is to build, heat, and cool. The most efficient surface-to-area shape is a sphere, but that's impractical to build. The next most efficient shape is a cube, so boxy two-story homes are common for PGHs and other high-performance homes. Single-story homes, especially ones with many corners, will generally cost more to build, as they call for more foundation and more roofing, two expensive parts to build, and also will use more energy than a two-story home with com-

Simple but classic New England forms, like the one above by design/build team Michael Maines Design and Kolbert Building, bring character and charm and are efficient to build, heat, and cool.

parable square footage. Complex rooflines are more expensive than simple ones and more difficult to insulate. They're also more prone to leaking over time and provide less area for photovoltaic arrays.

# Beauty

Current concepts of what constitutes a beautiful home too often result in extraneous bumps, jogs, and other unnecessary embellishments. Though these architectural frills add interest, they also add cost, often create wasted space, and are the hardest features to manage well in terms of water leakage, air sealing, and insulation. Every transition, such as where a dormer pops out of the roof, is a building failure waiting to happen. And making a house more architecturally complex does not necessarily make it more interesting or attractive. The clean lines and utilitarian designs that follow the Shaker philosophy of simplicity, utility, and honesty are still considered fresh and beautiful. Whether modern or traditional, these designs are rightly celebrated for their clarity of form, elegant proportions, human scale, and attention to detail.

**Barns, like this one renovated by Briburn and Emerald Builders, are naturally boxy and can be great PGH conversions. With few jogs and bumps, they are simple and efficient to build and insulate.**

**This Shaker-style home is an excellent example of a boxy structure that is easy to heat and insulate and makes a great PGH. The simple roof form and proper orientation allow this home to have a full solar array and generate all its power right on site.**

Vermont Classic: In the hands of a skilled designer, it's amazing what can be done with a simple box, like this home by architect Robert Swinburne and builder Dylan Kinsey. It's a Pretty Good House twist on a classic New England Cape.

Vermont Contemporary: Sugar Bush House, by Robert Swinburne, is a great example of contemporary architecture with simple forms that create an ideal PGH for owners with more modern tastes. Check out the Case Study on this house on p. 108.

When it comes to homes, there is a dizzying array of architectural styles, from the traditional New England Cape to the sprawling ranch, intensely modern structures to timber-frame barns. Preservationists argue for traditional hand-crafted details, while some architects

*The PGH philosophy is to use functional shapes to create interesting forms, because if the form doesn't have a function, it just means an extra cost that doesn't provide true value.*

long to prove that modern design is neither cold nor forbidding. Some homes have elaborate, purely decorative details, while others have details that serve real functions. Each of us has different design preferences, and PGH principles are flexible enough to accommodate them, but regardless of the visual design of a home, form needs to follow function. The

PGH philosophy is to use functional shapes to create interesting forms, because if the form doesn't have a function, it just means an extra cost that doesn't provide true value. If the function of a particular room is to provide a space for family and friends to gather, for example, but the form is an octagon with no place to put the furniture or the TV, then it fails. This guideline goes for outside elements, too: a porch, overhang, or window shading each serves a purpose—and adds character to a home as well.

# Comfort

Comfort and performance are closely linked. A big part of what makes a high-performance house successful is that it's comfortable to live in. It's a big design challenge to create a comfortable home. Human beings are like Goldilocks: We want our dwellings not too hot, not too cool, but just right. And this seems to have been the case for thousands of years. Romans built south-facing structures that took advantage of the sun for warmth. In the 1980s, we built houses with oversized mechanical systems because oil was cheap. But energy isn't cheap any-

**This sketch by Robert Swinburne maps out the cozy locations in a design— the places to sit, eat, and relax.**

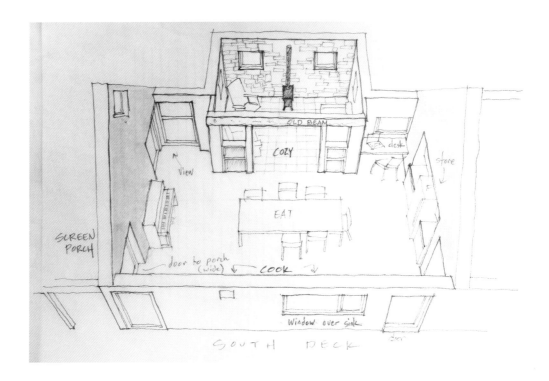

In the Crescent Lake House, designed by Briburn, a combination of warm wood floors with bright white walls and large windows makes the space light and bright without too much glare and reflection. The soft sofa and rugs help absorb sound reflected off hard surfaces.

more, either financially or environmentally. We are no longer comfortable in our under-insulated, drafty homes. Few people can or want to cut 10 cords of wood to heat their homes. As temperatures and energy costs continue to rise, we can't afford to air-condition rooms with broad expanses of single-pane glass and no exterior shading.

*We can build the most efficient house in the world, but if it's not beautiful or comfortable, the occupants will sell it and move on.*

We are comfortable only in a narrow range of temperature and humidity. Turning down the air conditioning doesn't necessarily make our spaces more comfortable because we haven't dealt with the prob-lem of interior humidity. No matter how beautiful your kitchen countertops or how stunning your hardwoods floors may be, if the house isn't comfortable you won't want to live there.

Humidity and temperature are not the only factors that contribute to comfort in a carefully planned PGH. Others include hard and soft surfaces that affect sound transmission and noise vibration, as well as materials that reflect sunlight.

This brings us to the essential reason so many of us are part of the PGH movement: We are driven to learn all we can to make the homes that we design and build function as well as they look and feel. Every element that we add can have a direct effect on comfort, from windows and their placement to dehumidification and heating systems to sound insulation and mechanical systems. And a whole lot more. We can build the most efficient house in the world, but if it's not beautiful or comfortable, the occupants will sell it and move on.

# Security

We all want to feel secure in our homes. In a PGH that goes beyond typical security-related features, like door locks, fire and carbon monoxide detectors, and security alarms. Security in a PGH also means security from non-human intruders, like insects, mice, and other pests. It means protecting our homes against increasingly unstable weather conditions and dealing with large amounts of rain, ice storms, or smoke from wildfires. It considers hurricanes and floods and allows you to leave on vacation and feel confident that you will not return to frozen pipes.

Security lies in a home that won't make us sick, whether from allergens, VOCs, wildfire smoke, or mold, which means using proper ventilation systems, materials, and building techniques. Security also includes lighting that prevents tripping and falling, or task lighting that aids cleanup in the kitchen and reduces stress on tired or aging eyes. Feeling secure in our homes means being able to pay the utility bills on retirement incomes or having a home that functions beautifully for individuals with disabilities, with lever handles instead of door knobs, for instance, wide hallways, or lower light switches. When we embark on creating a PGH house, these are some of the most important considerations of all.

# I Second That Emotion

The way you feel physically in a home is directly related to how the house performs in terms of temperature, humidity, and air quality. But designing a home that is emotionally uplifting is vital, too. A key to accomplishing this is to consider how the house helps us maintain a strong relationship with the natural world. This may include placing windows to take full advantage of views, or treating exterior spaces as part of the floor plan to create smooth patterns of movement from inside to outside.

We've been conditioned to have emotional attachments to things we can see, but what about the design elements that we can't, ones that affect key areas of our well-being, whether physical, emotional, or psychological? The PGH philosophy factors in how we may live in relation to others, including household members, guests, or friends who've dropped by. And though they may not realize it, the reason they all love being in your home—other than the pleasure of your company, of course—is that it's been designed as part of a deeply thoughtful process that looked at how to achieve those successes as effortlessly as possible.

# The Integrated Design Approach

In conventional homes, tradespeople who come through during construction do what they need to do, sometimes without a lot of thought as to how it will affect the work of other trades. It's better to plan ahead, so everyone knows what to expect and there are no conflicts. A good general contractor (and design professionals) should be familiar enough with all trades so that they can collaborate effectively and direct traffic as efficiently as possible. This is often a

ABOVE This second-floor space, washed with sunlight and overlooking fields beyond, makes you yearn to sit down and gaze out the window. Special spaces like these are what make a house feel like home.

LEFT Many architects are proponents of biophilic design, like architect Emily Mottram and landscape architect Kerry Lewis, who designed the Copper Farmhouse. A great PGH will strive to create maximum connectivity to the natural environment from the inside and outside. It is carefully sited to share the land with the native species (plant and animal), capture the sun, and "play well" with the neighbors.

The team at Kolbert Building spends time all through construction reviewing the project details with the owners, subcontractors, and design team.

downside to owner-built homes. Although it's possible to build a very good house without a lot of experience, there is a lot to know and anticipate, and we should recognize the important things a general contractor brings to a project: relationships with subcontractors and suppliers, and, most importantly, experience—preferably with other high-performance homes.

As we saw in Chapter 1, an important part of a carefully planned home is the integration of every discipline while you're working through how to build the home. Yes, people often build homes without using any design professionals, and though contractors are rarely involved in the design for smaller residential structures, their input really adds value when designing to a budget and for mechanical, electrical, and plumbing systems.

A truly integrated design approach would include the following people: the subcontractors responsible for designing the systems, the design team that will coordinate the drawing and systems, and the contractor who will build the home. If you can limit the amount of "figuring it out in the field," you can significantly improve the efficiency of the build. And, as ever, time is money—money that the homeowner will have to pay. If there is no coordination between the trades, you often end up with unplanned and undesirable outcomes to problems that pop up.

# Designing for Your Budget: Spending Wisely vs. Spending Less

Now comes the part of the chapter that everyone tuned in to read: budget. You've read most of the design guidelines that take a home from four walls and a roof to a Pretty Good House. Now let's talk about designing to your budget. As you can tell from the principles listed in this chapter, you make decisions based on emotions, the knowledge of your team, and your performance goals. These decisions should be built into every PGH, but that doesn't mean you need to start from scratch. Sometimes, the best way to achieve a PGH new build is to start with something that has already been designed. In the lengthy "Predesigned with PGH Principles" sidebar on pp. 71–75, we talk about alternative options to fully custom design.

*From a design standpoint, the whole point of PGH is to provide the best possible house for the available budget.*

Whether your project is predesigned with PGH principles or custom designed for your specific needs, performance goals are important metrics. PGH adherents will typically use an energy model during the design phase to guide decisions on windows, insulation, and other features (see Chapter 2 for more on energy modeling). Energy performance is a critical part of designing a PGH, but if you need to cut costs, never do it by skimping on the building envelope unless you want to build a really uncomfortable house. That's why it's critical to understand your performance goals as you design, so they become a seamless part of your PGH.

Rely on your team to help you build the most comfortable, durable, and healthy home possible. And stop value-engineering out the part of your home that keeps you safe and comfortable. **Do not** put your health in jeopardy by eliminating the ventilation system and building a house that "breathes." Houses don't need to breathe; people need to breathe, houses need to dry. From a design standpoint, the whole point of PGH is to provide the best possible house for the available budget. But what cannot be sacrificed is durability, structural integrity, and occupant health and comfort.

**Lessons learned: During the design phase, the architect suggested that the owner/builder eliminate a complicated and costly dormer. The stovepipe sticking through the roof was never connected to a wood stove and could have been eliminated, along with the never-used bulkhead.**

So where can we realistically make compromises that will still give owners the best PGH that they can afford? Can we afford to sacrifice the comfort of better windows for their less costly cousins? Can an R-30 wall save enough to make it an acceptable substitute for an R-40 one? We never suggest starting the cost-savings discussion with cutting corners on the building envelope, but when is "pretty good" good enough?

Pretty Good might be good enough after you've looked at eliminating extra windows and unnecessary spaces. Pretty Good might be good enough after you've replaced the high-end kitchen cabinetry and appliances with more modest versions. Pretty Good might be good enough once you've gotten the orientation of the home just right and ready for future solar. Pretty Good might be good enough when you've improved your air-sealing details.

**Eliminating the dormer and not putting in the wood stove that was originally planned left room in the budget for a dream kitchen and triple-pane tilt-and-turn windows.**

A good design team can often use its experience and expertise to save on cost when detailing the energy-saving upgrades. Trust your team, and let them tell you what you can't afford to do right away and what you can't afford *not* to do now.

It's complicated to design and build a house. It might be the most money you spend on any single purchase in your life. As you may have gathered, the performance of a PGH is directly tied to every design decision you make. How you construct your walls and the materials you choose to use can directly

affect your comfort and security. The lot you chose to build on can impact your social life, the ability to get public transportation to and from work, or your ability to retire and stay in your home longer. Design covers a wide range of topics. On one hand, it's simply the planning stage of a construction project. On the other, it's where all the critical decisions are made. Every chapter in this book is about how to design a PGH; this chapter covered what is most commonly understood as design. But you need the information in all the chapters to get the design right.

The Royal River House, designed by Briburn, is a contemporary example of a Pretty Good House. The single-level home encompasses many, if not all, of the design guidelines of PGH. Its net-zero design incorporates natural daylight and solar heat gain from the south-facing façade. Exterior finishes were selected for both their aesthetics and low maintenance. To pull all of these elements together, while meeting the clients' vision and budget, and create a low-carbon, high-performance structure, is the true meaning of PGH.

## THINGS TO CONSIDER

- The location of your site and how you place the home on it can be critical to achieving your PGH goals.

- Only build the amount of home you need and not a bit more.

- Making your home beautiful doesn't have to make it more complicated.

- Comfort and performance are closely linked, so pay attention to performance so you can be comfortable for years to come.

- Security means so much more than an alarm system.

- Our homes have a direct impact on our physical, mental, emotional, and psychological well-being.

- Integration is a collaborative effort among everyone, owner through subcontractor, that relies on great planning and a healthy dose of respect for everyone involved.

- Spend wisely; a great PGH team will tell you how.

- Consider reworking your existing layout. It may provide you with the space you need without a costly addition or building a whole new home.

# Predesigned with PGH Principles

As much as every homebuyer might dream about having a home that is individually designed, custom tailored, and built from scratch, it's not financially feasible for everyone. If that's the case, the next best way to create a new Pretty Good House is to opt for something that already exists and was created with PGH principles in mind.

Start with a plan that someone else has already paid to design and engineer (predesigned). Make as few changes as possible, and make sure you pick a design that is appropriate for your site. This doesn't mean architectural style, but a design that is appropriate for your geographic location and one that doesn't need engineering alterations to make it work.

**ABOVE** The plans for Mottram Architecture's Birch Farmhouse are available for purchase. The home is designed with PGH principles and is appropriate for Climate Zones 6 and 7.

**LEFT** The Vinalhaven, by BrightBuilt Home, is full modular construction, constructed almost completely off-site and shipped in boxes to the site, with minimal finish work to be done after assembly.

The Zum, by Unity Homes, is a hybrid off-site/on-site construction, panelized in Unity's factory in New Hampshire. The exterior envelope arrives on site in panels to be assembled, and all finish work from plumbing and electrical to siding and flooring is finished on site.

# Predesigned with PGH Principles *continued*

## THREE WAYS TO TAKE ADVANTAGE OF PREDESIGNED PLANS

**Predesigned plans** (i.e., stock plans, plan sets, or house plans) are a set of floor plans, often with construction drawings and specifications for a builder, that have been created by an architect or designer and are available for purchase. They are not custom homes and are often built several times by developers or individual homeowners in many locations.

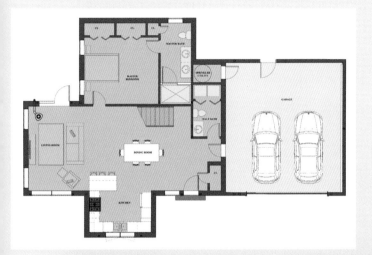

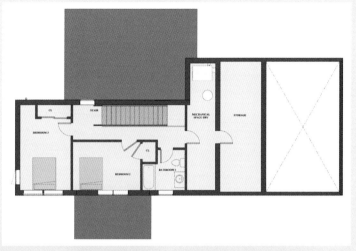

Tula Modern is an example of a predesigned set of plans available from Mottram Architecture, specifically for cold Climate Zones 6 and 7. It's a 3-bedroom, 2.5-bathroom, 2,200-sq.-ft. home that is intended to be stick-built on site.

**Panelized construction** A panelized PGH would have a predesigned plan that you can choose from a manufacturer's catalog. The home is partially built in the factory in several panels and shipped to the site to be assembled on site. Panels can be as simple as framing, sheathing, and openings for windows and doors to fully insulated, windows and doors installed, and utility chases ready for site installation. Depending on the size of the manufacturer, there may be several home styles to choose from, wall-construction choices to meet your budget or climate zone, and upgrades that can be made to your windows, doors, or layout.

LEFT Panelized houses are typically assembled with a crane due to the weight of the panels. Fully insulated panels with windows and doors can weigh upward of 10,000 lb.

BELOW The Varm, by Unity Homes, is a two-story, 3- to 4-bedroom, 2- to 3-bath home that can be modified from 1,520 sq. ft. to 2,940 sq. ft. Several versions of the Varm and other Unity designs are available.

# Predesigned with PGH Principles *continued*

**BELOW** Panels are shipped flat or stacked upright on a large truck and delivered to the site, where a crane or lift offloads and installs them like a kit.

**BELOW RIGHT** Panels are installed by skilled carpenters who are familiar with how to connect the panels properly and work safely with a crane operator.

**Modular construction** A modular home is built in a factory. Houses are shipped to the site as boxes that are assembled with a crane. Finishes have already been completed in the factory prior to their arrival on site; only minor details such as finish flooring, siding trim, and plumbing connections remain.

## THE RULES FOR USING PREDESIGNED PLANS

Predesigned plans vary, not only in terms of architectural style and size, but also in how they're built. Remember, tweaking the design adds cost and also increases the amount of time it takes to produce your home.

Panelization and modular construction are faster than building on site. The more that can be done in the factory, the lower the cost of production. The controlled environment of a factory eliminates weather delays. Detailed drawings of every component have already been produced and can be used over and over again. Trades that work in-house, such as plumbers and electricians, can save time and money by not traveling to each individual jobsite.

Keep in mind, however, that panelized or modular construction is not always cheaper, especially if you customize a design. Factories must pay for overhead, staffing, and machinery, along with transporting their product to the building site where heavy-equipment will be needed. Don't be fooled into thinking it's a simpler method, it's just a different way to build with its own challenges and complexities.

And last, but not least, consider hiring a consultant to help you evaluate the predesigned plans you have just purchased or are going to purchase. A consultant can do an energy evaluation to make sure the plans meet your goals (energy savings, carbon offsetting, healthy indoor air quality, etc.) and advocate for you during construction when you don't feel confident on your own.

TOP **The Cushing, by BrightBuilt Home, is a 3- to 4-bedroom, 2.5-bath home that is 1,970 sq. ft. and fully constructed off-site. BrightBuilt can construct, deliver, and fully complete their homes in New England and the Mid-Atlantic regions of the U.S.**

BOTTOM **Modular boxes are typically set and installed within a day. Shown here are modules by EcoCraft Homes being installed with a crane on a site in Pittsburgh, Penn.**

# Copper Farmhouse

Copper Farmhouse is one of five high-performance houses in a small development in Cumberland, Maine. The architect and developer set out to create a community, not just five energy-efficient homes.

ON ITS OWN MERITS, the house has plenty to offer, including a tight, superinsulated building enclosure, a light-filled interior, and carefully framed views of the outside. But it's best understood in the context of the houses and people around it.

"We wanted to create a community of like-minded individuals," says architect Emily Mottram. "It wasn't just about building efficient houses that were solar ready or net zero. It was about creating a community of people who were connected to the land."

The 1,700-sq.-ft. house, with an attached garage and another 700 sq. ft. in office space above it, is one of five homes in Cumberland, Maine, designed by Mottram and developed by Patrice Cappelletti on land that Cappelletti bought in 2014. The first house was something of an experiment, giving the partners the chance to test their theories of design and develop stock plans that could be replicated by others. If it didn't work out, Mottram said, they would not have gone on to build others. But the first house was a success.

**TOP** Outdoor spaces are just as important as what's going on inside. The owner of Copper Farmhouse is a landscape architect who sought to create inviting areas around the house with native plantings.

**LEFT** Adjoining the house is a 700-sq.-ft. garage with office space on the second floor. Cedar shingles on the garage exterior are expensive and time-consuming to install, but also highly durable.

The Copper Farmhouse, named for the copper fixtures and antique pieces the owner brought to the project, is the fourth in the series. Local land-use regulations will limit the small subdivision to five homes. The property includes hiking trails, a community yurt and fire pit, and a sense of shared purpose among homeowners.

"It's not so much a subdivision," Mottram says. "It has more to do with how people relate to one another. It's not a place where you drive in your garage door, go into your house, and never see your neighbors."

**TOP** Mottram chose wood flooring for the first floor but used engineered flooring in the office space. Material selection often balanced one relatively expensive choice against a less costly option elsewhere in the house.

**LEFT** This custom built-in is new, but painted to match an antique sewing desk that the homeowner uses as a kitchen island. The cabinet's upper doors feature copper screen that the solar installer had salvaged some 40 years earlier.

Tall windows are instrumental in connecting indoor and outdoor spaces. The architect specified double-pane windows but has since started using triple-pane units for added performance.

The Copper Farmhouse's double-stud exterior walls are insulated with dense-pack cellulose and a vaulted scissor-truss ceiling with enough room for R-60 worth of blown cellulose. Air leakage is low, with fresh air provided by an energy-recovery ventilator. Its all-electric design is powered by a 7.9-kW grid-tied solar array.

Mottram based design decisions on what she calls "high-low-salvaged" material choices, meaning the house is a mix of high-end and relatively inexpensive materials and fixtures with a few salvaged components added to the mix. Windows, for example, are builder-grade, double-paned wood units (she's since switched to triple-glazed windows), and window returns are drywall rather than more expensive wood trim. The garage is clad with wood shingles, a time-consuming and relatively expensive choice, but that's balanced by vertical wood siding on the con-

nector between house and garage. Salvaged materials show up in the form of single-pane windows used in interior walls to help distribute light and add some character.

The interior's connection to the outdoors is key. The owner is a landscape architect who carefully developed the area immediately around the house with plants that naturally flourish in the environment rather than what Mottram calls a "sea of monoculture grass." Window placement was important, too, along with orienting the house on the lot so it enjoyed the best views possible and related well to other houses in the development. Lots of upgrades will be possible as needs change, but Mottram only got one chance to position the house correctly.

"The one thing you're never going to do," she says, "is move the location of the house."

# Developing a House Around a Theme

**A**ll of the net-zero energy houses in the Live Solar Maine development are designed around a theme. First was the Birch Farmhouse, named for a birch-themed Angela Adams rug belonging to developer Patrice Cappelletti. When Mottram and Cappelletti got to work on the fourth house in the series, they learned that its new owner had inherited copper fixtures and antiques from her parents. "Having a design theme helps guide the process," Mottram says.

The Copper Farmhouse gets its name from the copper fixtures and antiques the owner brought with her, including a range hood (above) and copper bathroom fixtures (right).

LOCATION (AND CLIMATE ZONE):
Cumberland, Maine; Climate Zone 6

ARCHITECT: Emily Mottram

BUILDER: Patrice Cappelletti

LIVING AREA:
1,700 sq. ft. with 700-sq.-ft. office over garage

NUMBER OF BEDROOMS/BATHROOMS: 2/2.5

FOUNDATION: Full basement, poured concrete

FOUNDATION INSULATION: R-15 foam

SUBSLAB INSULATION: R-20 EPS foam

WALL CONSTRUCTION: Double-stud

ABOVE-GRADE WALL INSULATION:
Dense-pack cellulose, R-32

ATTIC FLOOR INSULATION:
Vaulted scissor truss with R-60 blown cellulose

AIR LEAKAGE: 1.5 ach50

SPACE HEAT: Ductless mini-split heat pumps,
supplemental wood stove

DOMESTIC HOT WATER: Heat-pump water heater

MECHANICAL VENTILATION: Broan ERV

PV SYSTEM CAPACITY: 7.9 kW

## WHAT MAKES THIS A PRETTY GOOD HOUSE?

- Design process involved the owner, architect, and builder.

- Careful attention to the connection between the house and its neighbors, enhancing the sense of community.

- Landscaping that includes a variety of native plants and materials rather than a monoculture of grass lawn.

- House mixes relatively low-cost and salvaged materials with more expensive components.

- High-performance building enclosure with all-electric mechanical systems and a 7.9-kW photovoltaic system.

**Although ductless mini-splits provide the bulk of the heat, a wood stove will be a welcome addition come winter. This Shaker-inspired Wittus stove is small and doesn't overwhelm the room.**

The house
is part of a
neighborhood,
not an island unto
itself. Property
owners have
banded together
to build a yurt,
a fire pit, and
hiking trails.

## FLOOR PLANS

### FIRST FLOOR

### SECOND FLOOR

# CHAPTER FOUR

# BUILDING ENVELOPE BASICS

You'd look pretty ridiculous showing up in a cotton hoodie and jeans for an extended winter camping adventure in Maine. Yet so many not-so-good houses are doing the architectural equivalent with their poorly insulated foundations and slabs, fiberglass-insulated 2x6 walls, and minimal attic insulation. They are basically admitting to the rest of the group, "I plan on staying by the fire the whole time, or in my heated car, or in the heated cabin," essentially dependent on an external source of energy to remain comfortable. They're not serious about being outside.

A Pretty Good House should have an exterior building envelope appropriate for its climate. In a cold climate, such as in New England, the home needs to be wearing the equivalent of a winter parka. In Virginia, it needs a sturdy fall jacket; in Oregon, a well-insulated raincoat. A PGH is going to do its best to stay comfortable and not depend so much on that external energy source. It will be more resilient, comfortable, and efficient.

The term *building envelope* refers to the building assemblies that separate conditioned interior space from the exterior of the home. It is important to visualize the continuity of all of these assemblies to ensure that there are no gaps or weak spots and to make sure they are of equal integrity throughout. A robust, R-40 double-stud wall sitting on top of an uninsulated foundation wall or slab is a silly thing (like wearing sandals with your winter parka). Equally silly would be to install single-pane windows.

We need to think about more than just exterior walls and roof assemblies, but also about foundation walls, basement slabs, the wall between an unconditioned garage and living space, dormer knee-walls, doors and windows, and all the many connections between all of these components. In this chapter we'll discuss how to approach each of these major components.

## Heat Transfer

Heat always travels from hot to cold (high energy to low energy), and it does so in three basic ways: conduction, convection, and radiation. Conduction is heat energy traveling directly through a material, like from your warm body through your parka to the sub-freezing air. Insulation in a house functions the same way, combatting heat loss by conduction.

Convection is heat transfer via another media, such as air. Imagine that your parka had holes in it. It almost wouldn't matter how insulative the rest of the jacket is. You fight convective heat loss in your house by air sealing and establishing an effective air control layer to seal the building envelope as tightly as possible. If by some chance you read that last bit and just thought to yourself, "Yeah, but houses have to breathe," then this chapter (and the following chapter about water/moisture management) is for you!

Radiation typically has a smaller impact on the efficiencies of our buildings than conduction or convection. If your home is in the sunny south, however, radiation might play a bigger role in your preparedness for your climate than the others. Radiation is the electromagnetic energy emitting from a heat source—like from a campfire, for example—to a cooler object. When that fire is roaring and you feel the heat on your face, all you have to do is place something, anything really, between your face and the fire and the

## THE BUILDING ENVELOPE

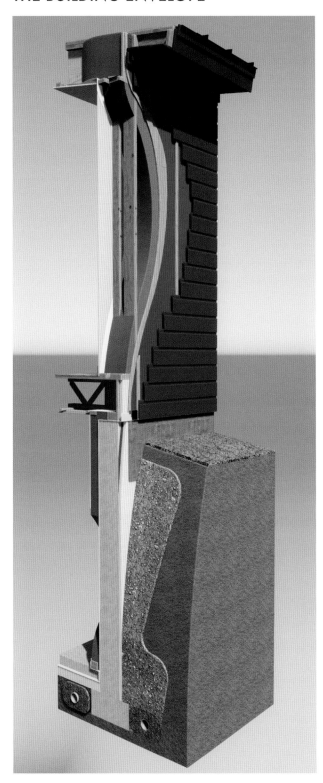

The building envelope is comprised of all the assemblies that contain the conditioned space within. Shown here is a cutaway view of a double-stud wall on a basement foundation; later in the chapter, we'll zoom in on some of its components.

heat transfer stops immediately. A warm object will radiate its energy toward a colder one, but it's far less noticeable with moderately temperate objects—that is, until *you* become the warm object and all the surfaces around you are cold. Your home will combat heat loss (and gain) from radiation through shading, radiant barriers, and coatings on glass (the latter will be covered mostly in Chapter 6, on windows and exterior doors).

# Insulation

Extra insulation is probably one of the first things people think of when they visualize an energy-efficient house. And rightly so. Increasing the amount of insulation in the building envelope is one of the most effective ways of reducing a building's energy demand, especially in colder climates. It should come as no surprise, then, that a PGH will have relatively high insulation values.

But how much insulation do you need? When this question was first discussed by the Building Science Discussion Group in Portland, Maine, as the

Dense-packed cellulose is a favorite insulation among PGH builders and designers. Made from recycled paper and pulp fibers, it is an excellent, nontoxic draft-stopper for wall and roof cavities.

# Understanding R-Value

Long ago, the insulation industry needed to come up with a way to quantify insulation values. More accurately, they needed a way to convey insulation values to the general public.

In calculating heat loss, engineers use U-factors (values that represent "resistance") in their heat-loss calculations. The lower the factor, the greater the resistance to heat flow and the smaller the transfer of heat. For example, a material with a U-factor of 0.125 is a better insulator than one with a U-factor of 0.25.

But using numbers where smaller equaled better wasn't the best way of describing heat flow to the general public. So, the industry simply used the reciprocal of the U-factor (1/U) to get an R-value. Thus, U-0.125 became R-8, and a U-0.25 was R-4. Clearly, the R-8 should be twice as insulative as the R-4. And it is! R-value was much easier to understand and it stays with us today.

Glazing and window companies still use U-factors, not R-values (there's more about this in Chapter 6). Also, note that it's R-*value* and U-*factor*.

Pretty Good House concept was being developed, building codes were *way* behind the times. This group of builders, architects, and engineers debated, studied data and anecdotal evidence, and generally concluded that the Building Science Corp.'s 10-20-40-60 rule fit the bill in Climate Zone 6 rather well. Generally, that means slabs would have an R-value of 10, basement walls 20, exterior walls 40, and roof enclosures 60. The formula also is easy to remember.

To the lay person or "traditional builder" at the time, these numbers seemed high and were well above code minimums. To those executing some of the state's first Passive Houses (which had walls of R-75 and roofs of R-95) they seemed less than aspirational. But these numbers seemed just right to those who had worked on net-zero homes in Maine's climate. Likewise, the engineers and energy modelers of the group agreed that at these insulation levels the heating load was greatly reduced, to the point where meaningful reductions could be made to the size and cost of mechanical systems.

Great, but what about other climate zones? Luckily for all of us, many professionals have researched this question exhaustively. For example, the Building America Program, in partnership with the Building

---

## HOW MUCH INSULATION DO YOU REALLY NEED?*

| Climate Zone | R-Value | | | | | |
| --- | --- | --- | --- | --- | --- | --- |
| | Slab | Basement Walls | Exposed Floor | Walls | Compact or Cathedral Roof | Vented Attic |
| 1 | 0 | 5 | 10 | 10 | 35 | 40 |
| 2 | 0 | 10 | 20 | 15 | 40 | 50 |
| 3 | 5 | 40 | 20 | 20 | 45 | 50 |
| 4 | 8 | 15 | 30 | 25 | 45 | 60 |
| 5 | 8 | 15 | 30 | 35 | 50 | 65 |
| 6 | 10 | 20 | 40 | 40 | 60 | 70 |
| 7 | 15 | 25 | 45 | 40 | 65 | 90 |
| 8 | 20 | 35 | 50 | 50 | 75 | 100 |

*Based largely on "Building America Special Research Project: High R-Value Enclosures for High Performance Residential Buildings in All Climate Zones"

True R-Value numbers       <- - - differing values from BSC

These whole-wall R-values are good guidelines for a Pretty Good House. Energy modeling will provide more precise recommendations by taking into account the shape, size, solar orientation, and fenestration of the building.

# Building Science Corporation

A rite of passage for budding building-science enthusiasts is learning how to pronounce "Lstiburek." That is, Dr. Joe Lstiburek, Principal at Building Science Corporation (BSC), a building science consulting and full-service architecture firm near Boston, Mass. BSC has had an enormous influence on the industry, from providing the studies and language that make up large portions of the U.S. building codes, to research and education on how and why to create high-performance assemblies, to pointing out the BS in building science.

Dr. Joe's persistent, sharp wit infuses his writing and lectures, making them both approachable and entertaining. BSC has particular expertise, according to its website, "in moisture dynamics, indoor air quality, and building failure forensic investigation." They provide a wealth of free information on their website, buildingscience.com. The PGH authors try to read and understand everything BSC publishes, including Dr. Joe's latest book, *Moisture Control for Residential Buildings (2021),* and it's a lot of information.

"Friends of PGH" at BSC include former employee, architect Steven Baczek, well known for his prolific design work and an unrelenting desire to educate, with his tagline "long live our buildings." And Kohta Ueno, a long-time researcher there, can frequently be spotted on Green Building Advisor (GBA), BS + Beer, and elsewhere, sharing essential building science facts in an enthusiastic way. The Pretty Good House team is indebted to Dr. Joe and his illustrious team.

Oh, and for the record, it's pronounced "STEE-brek."

---

Science Corp., published a great report back in 2010-2011 entitled "High R-Value Enclosures for High Performance Residential Buildings in All Climate Zones," which makes recommendations for insulation values in all climates (https://www.buildingscience.com/sites/default/files/migrate/pdf/BA-1005_High%20R-Value_Walls_Case_Study.pdf).

The report has stood the test of time, and its recommendations remain a good set of targets for "whole assembly R-values" for various climate zones. We have based our PGH recommended R-values largely on the report's findings and highly recommend downloading the report. You'll find many similarities between their chart and ours.

# Thermal Bridging

You might have noticed the term *whole assembly R-values* in the previous section. This refers to the R-value of the entire assembly. In an exterior wall it would include framing and sheathing as well as the insulation. Bear in mind that with most homes more than 20% of the material in the walls is not insulation. It's the stuff holding up the house and keeping it together. A 2x6 wall with R-21 insulation in the stud cavities is not really an R-21 wall; it's actually more like R-19. It's important to keep that distinction in mind.

This introduces the concept that building envelope assemblies have weak spots in their thermal integrity, spots where the insulation is missing or can't be placed. If steps aren't taken to deal with these weak spots, then you have thermal bridges.

A classic example of thermal bridging can be seen on a typical drive through an old New England town in winter. The snow has fallen evenly across all the roofs but there will be that poorly insulated roof where the snow has melted a little faster, where the rafters are creating bare stripes in the snow. These stripes reveal exactly where the rafters are because heat is flowing faster through the wood of the rafters than through the insulation. These are the weak spots, the thermal bridges that allow heat to bypass the better-insulated cavities. In typical "traditional" construction, thermal bridges are everywhere and they have a significant negative impact on the building envelope.

Handling the thermal bridging of assemblies is relatively easy. What's trickier is handling the connections between the assemblies. In this chapter, we'll show you some classic thermal bridges and some solutions that PGH builders and designers are implementing to address them.

## WALLS

Let's say you're in Climate Zone 4. From the previous section you know you should be aiming for a whole-wall R-value of about 25. A typical 2x6 wall with fiberglass batt insulation doesn't get you there (see the top left drawing, p. 89), so additional insulation will be required. Let's look at two ways to increase insulation and compare the effects of thermal bridging.

You could easily change the depth of the studs from 2x6 to 2x8, increasing the depth for insulation by 1¼ in. and thereby increasing its insulation value to R-27.5. But once we account for the thermal bridging at each stud every 24 in., the whole R-value increases by only 4.9.

Now what if we decided to add a similar amount of insulation, not in the stud cavity but continuously on the outside of the building in the form of sheathing bonded to a layer of rigid polyiso insulation? The polyiso has an R-value of 6, giving the insulation a

## 2X6 WALL ASSEMBLY

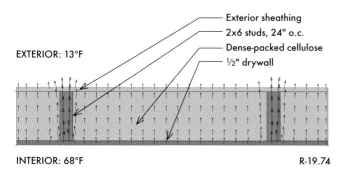

EXTERIOR: 13°F

Exterior sheathing
2x6 studs, 24" o.c.
Dense-packed cellulose
½" drywall

INTERIOR: 68°F

R-19.74

The insulation in this 2x6 wall has an R-value of 21. The R-value of the whole wall assembly is 19.74.

## 2X8 WALL ASSEMBLY

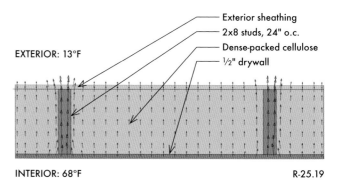

EXTERIOR: 13°F

Exterior sheathing
2x8 studs, 24" o.c.
Dense-packed cellulose
½" drywall

INTERIOR: 68°F

R-25.19

In a 2x8 wall, the R-value of insulation is 27.5; R-value of whole wall is 25.19.

## 2X6 WALL ASSEMBLY WITH CONTINUOUS INSULATION

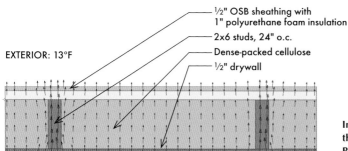

EXTERIOR: 13°F

½" OSB sheathing with
1" polyurethane foam insulation
2x6 studs, 24" o.c.
Dense-packed cellulose
½" drywall

INTERIOR: 68°F

R-26.05

In a 2x6 wall with insulated ZIP-R sheathing, the R-value of the insulation is 27, while the R-value of the whole wall assembly is 26.05.

total value of R-27. In this case, however, the insulation is unbroken across the assembly, so it acts as a thermal break at each stud. While less than the increased depth in the previous example, the added insulation is actually more effective at slowing the flow of heat through the weaker, less insulative studs.

Now let's say you're in Climate Zone 6. We'd be shooting for a whole wall R-value of 40. That's quite a bit more insulation and more opportunity for some serious thermal bridge reduction. Let's look at three common methods of reducing thermal bridging in Pretty Good wall assemblies.

**"Outsulation"** Similar to the example above, one common method of reducing thermal bridging in walls is by wrapping the exterior surface with a continuous layer of insulation (see the drawing on

p. 90). At the time of this writing, the types of insulation commonly used are mineral wool board, rigid polyisocyanurate, rigid polystyrene (extruded or expanded), and wood fiberboard (the latter is currently gaining in popularity for its low carbon footprint). The advantage of this method is that it's relatively easy to install and detail, and the primary air barrier and vapor barrier are located at the sheathing where the assembly is warm enough to prevent condensation.

**Larsen truss** A Larsen truss is made by attaching a truss to the outside of a fairly typical stud wall (see the drawing on p. 91). These trusses are wood I-joists, open web trusses, or custom site-built trusses. The cavity made by the trusses is filled with a dense-packed cellulose and usually held in place by an advanced weather-resistant membrane.

## "OUTSULATION" WALL ASSEMBLY

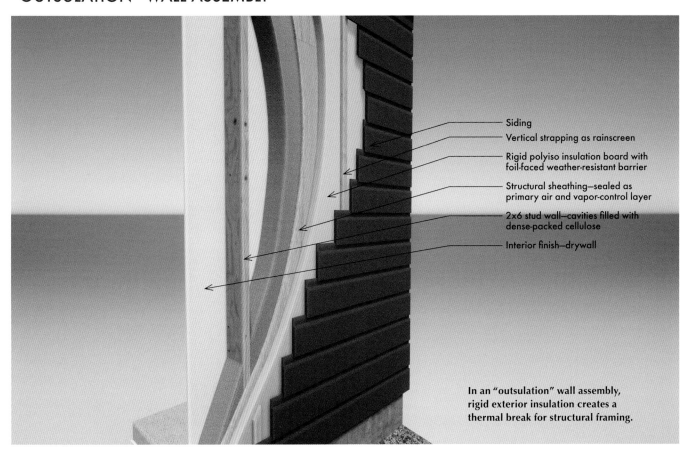

- Siding
- Vertical strapping as rainscreen
- Rigid polyiso insulation board with foil-faced weather-resistant barrier
- Structural sheathing—sealed as primary air and vapor-control layer
- 2x6 stud wall—cavities filled with dense-packed cellulose
- Interior finish—drywall

In an "outsulation" wall assembly, rigid exterior insulation creates a thermal break for structural framing.

This renovation in progress shows the outsulation layers. The existing sheathing boards were sheathed with ZIP system OSB and air-sealed, followed by 2 in. of recycled polyiso insulation board, 2 in. of polyiso with a foil-faced weather barrier, vertical strapping, then hemlock siding.

# LARSEN TRUSS WALL ASSEMBLY

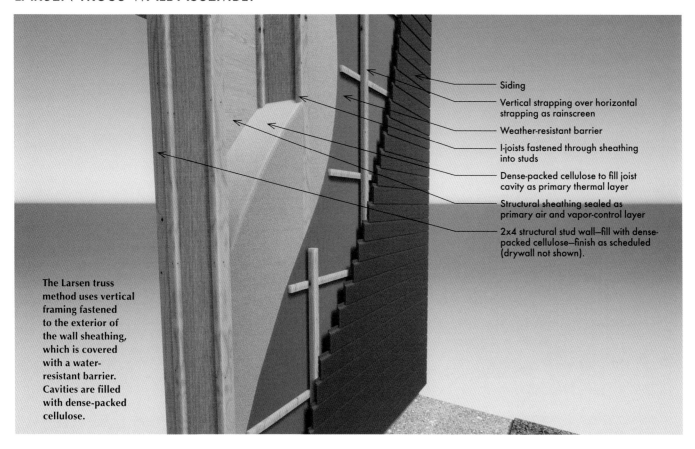

Siding

Vertical strapping over horizontal strapping as rainscreen

Weather-resistant barrier

I-joists fastened through sheathing into studs

Dense-packed cellulose to fill joist cavity as primary thermal layer

Structural sheathing sealed as primary air and vapor-control layer

2x4 structural stud wall—fill with dense-packed cellulose—finish as scheduled (drywall not shown).

**The Larsen truss method uses vertical framing fastened to the exterior of the wall sheathing, which is covered with a water-resistant barrier. Cavities are filled with dense-packed cellulose.**

This particular construction method is popular among Passive House builders, mostly because it doesn't trap moisture and its air and vapor control layers are located on the warm side of the assembly. This minimizes the risk of condensation (and mold and mildew). When the assembly consists of mostly bio-based materials with high vapor permeability, its carbon footprint can be extremely low (or even sequester carbon) and the drying potential is very high. (We'll revisit this in the next chapter.)

**Double stud** This is a tried-and-true method that has been around for decades. It usually consists of a structural 2x4 (or 2x6) stud wall with an additional

**A Larsen truss wall under construction.**

## DOUBLE-STUD WALL ASSEMBLY

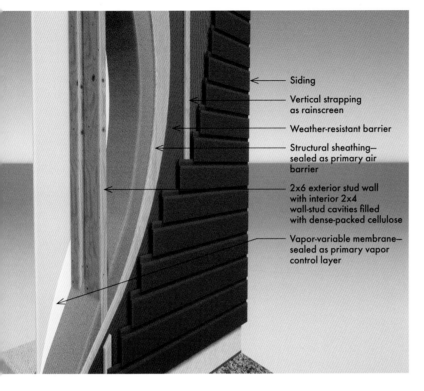

Siding

Vertical strapping
as rainscreen

Weather-resistant barrier

Structural sheathing—
sealed as primary air
barrier

2x6 exterior stud wall
with interior 2x4
wall-stud cavities filled
with dense-packed cellulose

Vapor-variable membrane—
sealed as primary vapor
control layer

2x4 (or 2x3) interior stud wall. Rather than wrapping the exterior in a blanket of insulation, the double-stud wall creates a thick, well-insulated assembly where cavity insulation is able to fill all the space between the stud layers.

A double-stud wall is easy to detail and very easy for traditional builders and designers to adopt. Most of the details are very similar to a typical stud wall. And like the Larsen truss, it can be made largely of bio-based materials with a low (even sequestering) carbon footprint. Relatively affordable and simple to construct, the double-stud wall is a hero of the PGH crowd. For more on double-stud walls, see the "Efficient Framing" section in Chapter 7.

**This double-stud wall shows a 2x6 structural exterior stud wall with an interior 2x4 nonstructural stud wall. Dense-packed cellulose insulation fills the cavity. On the exterior, sheathing is applied followed by a water-resistant barrier, vertical strapping, and siding.**

**Framing for the double-stud wall at the Maquoit Bay House shown in progress (see the Case Study on p. 42).**

Cathedral ceilings, which follow the roof slope, present some unique challenges when it comes to insulating and thermal bridging.

# ROOFS

The laws of physics are universal for walls and roofs, so it's no wonder that the same techniques for insulating and mitigating thermal bridging are used with roofs. The big difference is that the roof is at the top of the thermal envelope where the stack effect increases the difference between outdoor and indoor temperatures and increases the potential for greater heat loss. (This is why roofs should be even more insulated than any other assembly.) The other big difference, of course, is that the roof is going to see rain (and snow in colder climates), which means that the roofing material must be both waterproof and water-vapor proof.

**Attics vs. cathedral ceilings** Attics are easy. Sort of. There's a large flat floor at the bottom where we can pile on fluffy cellulose or fiberglass. We can just keep piling it on until the desired R-value is met. Sounds easy, but we also need to think about venting this attic space and keeping interior moisture from leaking into it. More on this in the next chapter about moisture migration.

Cathedral ceilings are more difficult. In case the term *cathedral ceiling* is new to you, picture a finished attic with sloped ceilings. This assembly must do the exact same things as the wall assembly described earlier, except that heat transfer is a much bigger deal here. The prescription is greater R-values and minimizing thermal bridging.

**Strapping** If you're in the business of design or construction, you're probably familiar with strapping. But in case you aren't, strapping is simply strips of wood that run perpendicular to the framing. In New England, it's common to have strapping between the framing and drywall for ceilings.

The original reason for adding strapping to the ceiling was to distribute the deflection (or bending) of the floor or roof joists. Strapping helps distribute deflection across more framing members, so it is far less pronounced. If there were no strapping, a rogue joist or rafter would telegraph through the drywall and appear as a permanent bump, or worse, a crack. Strapping actually helps us thermally as well by acting as a thermal break for most of the ceiling surface.

If the rafters are deep enough to give you insulation with the R-value you need, then strapping will be the easiest way to take a big swing at thermal bridging. If you are in a cold climate and the framing depth is not enough, adding strapping is an opportunity to

kill two birds with one stone—adding depth for more insulation and increased R-value, and creating a thermal break.

**Truss or I-joist rafters** A cheaper way to get more depth and thermal separation in a roof system is to go with deeper framing members even if they aren't needed structurally. There is greater material cost, but the labor costs would be exactly the same. Believe it or not, wood I-joists do a fair job of reducing thermal transfer. The web of an engineered wood I-joist is usually only $3/8$ in. (sometimes $1/2$ in. or even $5/8$ in.), which is significantly less than dimensional lumber at $1\frac{1}{2}$ in. Combined with strapping on the interior, this is enough to create a significant thermal break. Even better than I-joists are truss joists, which allow insulation to be packed between the webs.

**Offset framing** Similar to a Larsen truss or a double-stud wall, this methodology is a simple way to increase depth and create a substantial thermal break by adding additional framing members, held off from the structural rafters. Typically, this is done by using 2x4s, 2x3s, or even 2x6s ripped in half and fastening them to the structural framing with plywood, OSB, or whatever the sheathing material for the project may be.

In this cathedral ceiling, 2x strapping creates a service cavity deep enough to accommodate small LED ceiling lights without compromising the air control membrane above.

To increase the depth of a roof framing system and add a thermal break, 2x4s are attached to the bottom of the structural rafters.

Insulation is being installed over an existing roof as part of a renovation. A 2-in. layer of polyiso insulation is installed over the roofing membrane, followed by nailbase, sheathing-faced polyiso insulation board for the roofing.

Remember, the only structural role that offset framing has is to support the ceiling and possibly some of the weight of the insulation. The choice of materials can be based on what is most economical.

**Roof outsulation** Just as with exterior walls, layers of rigid insulation can be applied to the exterior of the roof sheathing to create a continuous thermal barrier and break. This sometimes results in two layers of sheathing to create a suitable surface for roofing—one right over the rafters and a second layer over the insulation. In some cases, strapping can be used in combination with a standing-seam metal roof. This saves the cost of a second layer of sheathing, but you'll find that roofing contractors prefer to have a solid surface to work on.

## FOUNDATION WALLS

It's alarming but true that foundations across the country are still left uninsulated. Perhaps not-so-good designers and builders don't understand the risks of mold and mildew or are just cutting corners and saving money. Insulating foundation walls may not be as important as insulating above-grade walls, but that's no reason to ignore them completely. Retrofitting a foundation is usually a costly endeavor, so this is not the place to trim costs. You have one good shot at getting your foundation right and that's when it's being installed the first time. Below are some examples of Pretty Good foundation wall assemblies.

**ICFs** Insulated concrete forms (ICFs) have been growing in popularity. Typically, they are hollow polystyrene blocks that are both the formwork for concrete and the insulation. They are relatively easy to install.

A concrete ICF foundation wall after the concrete has been poured. The wood straps reinforce the wall during the pour.

ICFs go together like LEGO® blocks, braced and reinforced with steel rebar and filled with concrete. Special care needs to be taken during the pour so that the walls remain level and plumb.

An R-20 wall is easy to achieve with ICFs, and some brands even offer different combinations of thickness of polystyrene to achieve greater values. If a finished basement is planned, then ICFs tend to be a very cost-effective approach. Most types come with plastic webs on the inside that can be used to attach drywall.

**Exterior insulation** Just like the outsulation approach for walls and roofs, insulation can be added to the exterior of the foundation walls using EPS, XPS, mineral wool, or another insulation approved for ground contact. Below grade, it's easy to add insulation until you reach your target R-value. It's when the foundation wall pops above grade that this strategy gets tricky. If above-grade walls are being finished with exterior insulation, they will be in the same plane as the foundation walls. The insulation on the foundation wall can be protected with a metal or fiber-cement panel or stucco.

**Interior insulation** There are situations where interior insulation makes more sense. Above-grade walls may not be hanging significantly over the concrete foundation, for example, or dealing with exterior insulation above grade seems too fussy. Maybe you plan to add an interior basement finish anyway. (Pro tip—go ahead and add some exterior insulation below grade anyway if you're in a cold climate. This is likely one of the most affordable ways to add insulation to a home, and it's very easy to do when building the foundation and very difficult to do at a later date.)

We're just going to go ahead and say it. Basements are not great spaces. Sure, sometimes you're given a site on a slope with a great daylight basement opportunity, or maybe a basement is viewed as "discounted space." Since you have to excavate for a frost wall anyway, why not dig a little more and get some space

Exterior EPS insulation being installed on a foundation wall. Note the black water-resistant barrier that has been tape-sealed to the concrete ahead of the insulation installation. These pieces will be tape-sealed to the exterior wall sheathing.

you can really use? This is a fine strategy as long as there's a real function for that space (like a workshop, game room, or home theater), but otherwise, it tends to be space that you never use. However, in the event you do plan to finish the basement, insulating to the interior is all but essential in a cold climate.

You can insulate with rigid insulation of some kind and fasten it to the concrete, then add strapping (usually vertical) and finish the wall with a moisture-resistant drywall. One disadvantage of this approach is that most types of rigid insulation used in this scenario are not necessarily good additions to the indoor environment (common additives in XPS include flame retardants and insecticides; mineral wool may have

formaldehyde and unknown other heavy metals; see Chapter 7). Another disadvantage is that strapping may not provide enough room to run wiring and install outlets.

Another approach is to build a stud wall in front of the foundation wall. This may take more square footage away from the basement, but it avoids all the issues mentioned above. However, a stud wall brings its own set of issues, primarily having to do with moisture and the potential for mold and mildew. This will be covered in more detail in the next chapter, but the drawing on the next page shows an example of how to deal with this.

## BASEMENT WALL

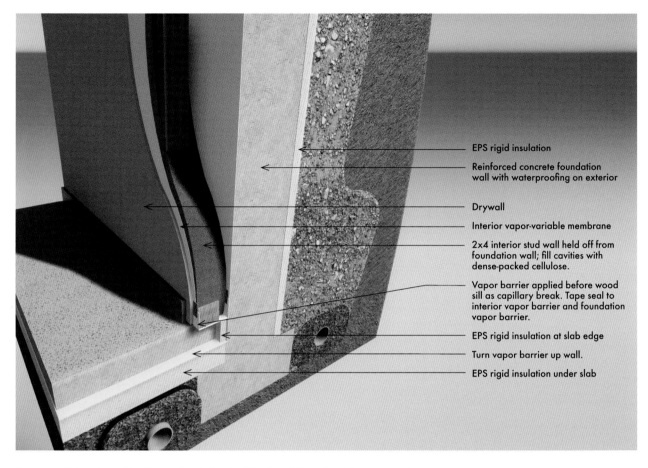

EPS rigid insulation

Reinforced concrete foundation wall with waterproofing on exterior

Drywall

Interior vapor-variable membrane

2x4 interior stud wall held off from foundation wall; fill cavities with dense-packed cellulose.

Vapor barrier applied before wood sill as capillary break. Tape seal to interior vapor barrier and foundation vapor barrier.

EPS rigid insulation at slab edge

Turn vapor barrier up wall.

EPS rigid insulation under slab

**Because cellulose is used in this interior stud wall at the foundation, the slab vapor barrier (yellow) continues up the concrete wall, isolating it from moisture in the concrete.**

Holding the stud wall away from the foundation wall provides a thermal break and the opportunity to fill the space with insulation. The vapor barrier from the slab can be installed so that it continues up the foundation wall and is sealed to the sill plate above. An additional piece of vapor barrier can be taped to the piece covering the foundation wall and lapped onto the basement slab floor. The stud wall can rest on this (or on another sill-sealing gasket). This way, all organic material is isolated from the concrete.

**Frost-protected shallow foundations** Also called frost-protected slabs, these foundations take a different approach to protecting the house from frost heaves. Water expands as it freezes, even when it's underground. If there is enough water below your foundation and it is cold enough to freeze, the force of that expansion can split the foundation as easily as a kid with a gingersnap cookie. These forces are not to be trifled with. That is why the footing of a frost wall should be well below the frost line. With a frost-protected shallow foundation, the idea is to insulate at the perimeter of the slab and let the heat of the earth prevent frost from forming below the house. A good general rule of thumb is that for every foot of depth a regular frost wall needs, a foot of horizontal insulation should extend outward from the house just below grade.

ABOVE This mockup shows the frost-protected slab at Sugar Bush House (see the Case Study on p. 108). The insulation on the right is what's below the slab. Not shown is the critical extension of insulation that extends outward from the thickened slab edge.

RIGHT The frost-protected slab ready for concrete to be poured.

## CONNECTIONS

Here's where preventing thermal bridging can get tricky. There's always a lot going on at the intersections of different assemblies, and creating a thermal break at these locations often takes a back seat to issues of waterproofing and structural support. But a PGH manages its thermal bridging even in these tough locations.

Of course, there's no *one* way of detailing any of these tricky spots. There are so many different materials, assembly types, conditions, and techniques that it would be impossible to cover them all here, but we thought it would be good to show some classic conditions and how some PGH builders and designers are able to address thermal bridging.

# WALL-TO-FOUNDATION CONNECTIONS

## OUTSULATION WALL ON FROST WALL

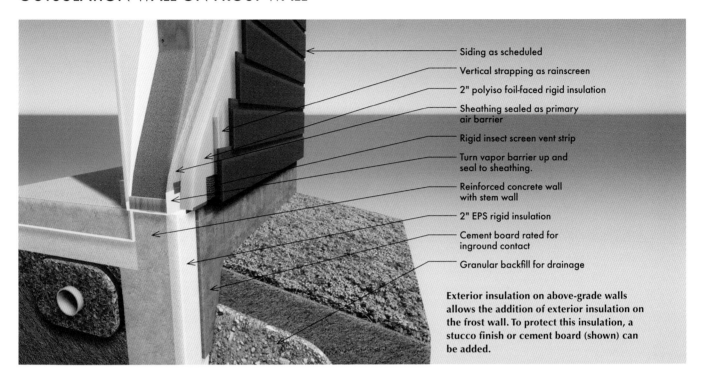

Siding as scheduled

Vertical strapping as rainscreen

2" polyiso foil-faced rigid insulation

Sheathing sealed as primary air barrier

Rigid insect screen vent strip

Turn vapor barrier up and seal to sheathing.

Reinforced concrete wall with stem wall

2" EPS rigid insulation

Cement board rated for inground contact

Granular backfill for drainage

Exterior insulation on above-grade walls allows the addition of exterior insulation on the frost wall. To protect this insulation, a stucco finish or cement board (shown) can be added.

## DOUBLE-STUD WALL ON FROST WALL

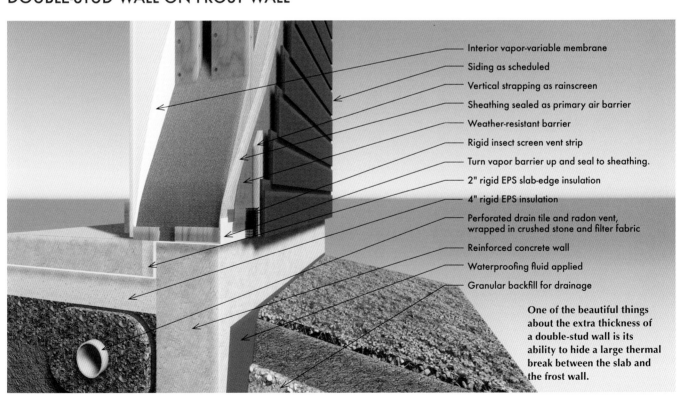

Interior vapor-variable membrane

Siding as scheduled

Vertical strapping as rainscreen

Sheathing sealed as primary air barrier

Weather-resistant barrier

Rigid insect screen vent strip

Turn vapor barrier up and seal to sheathing.

2" rigid EPS slab-edge insulation

4" rigid EPS insulation

Perforated drain tile and radon vent, wrapped in crushed stone and filter fabric

Reinforced concrete wall

Waterproofing fluid applied

Granular backfill for drainage

One of the beautiful things about the extra thickness of a double-stud wall is its ability to hide a large thermal break between the slab and the frost wall.

100    BUILDING ENVELOPE BASICS

## LARSEN TRUSS ON FROST-PROTECTED SLAB

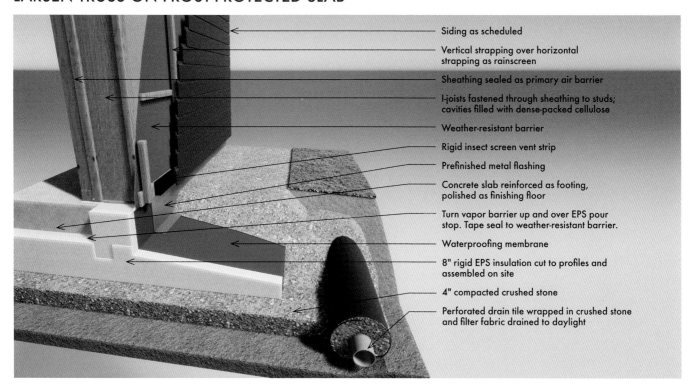

- Siding as scheduled
- Vertical strapping over horizontal strapping as rainscreen
- Sheathing sealed as primary air barrier
- I-joists fastened through sheathing to studs; cavities filled with dense-packed cellulose
- Weather-resistant barrier
- Rigid insect screen vent strip
- Prefinished metal flashing
- Concrete slab reinforced as footing, polished as finishing floor
- Turn vapor barrier up and over EPS pour stop. Tape seal to weather-resistant barrier.
- Waterproofing membrane
- 8" rigid EPS insulation cut to profiles and assembled on site
- 4" compacted crushed stone
- Perforated drain tile wrapped in crushed stone and filter fabric drained to daylight

Similar to the outsulation wall, the thick exterior insulation of the wall allows for exterior insulation of the frost wall or, as shown here, for a frost-protected slab.

# FLOOR-TO-WALL CONNECTIONS

## OUTSULATION AT FLOOR

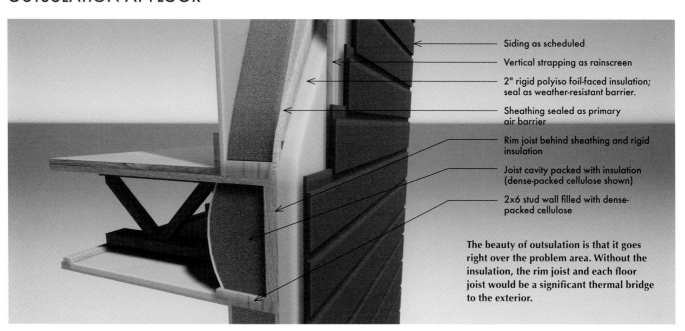

- Siding as scheduled
- Vertical strapping as rainscreen
- 2" rigid polyiso foil-faced insulation; seal as weather-resistant barrier.
- Sheathing sealed as primary air barrier
- Rim joist behind sheathing and rigid insulation
- Joist cavity packed with insulation (dense-packed cellulose shown)
- 2x6 stud wall filled with dense-packed cellulose

The beauty of outsulation is that it goes right over the problem area. Without the insulation, the rim joist and each floor joist would be a significant thermal bridge to the exterior.

## DOUBLE-STUD WALL ON BASEMENT WALL

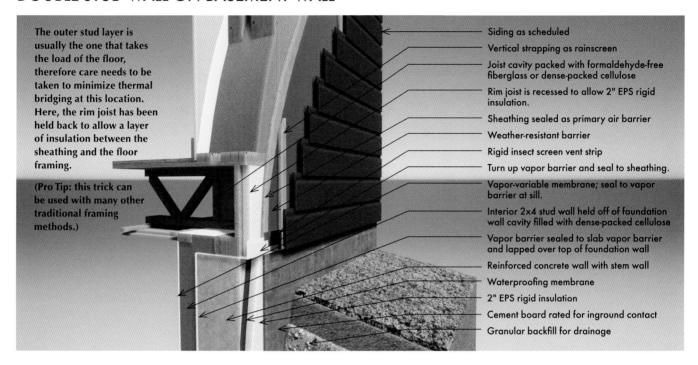

The outer stud layer is usually the one that takes the load of the floor, therefore care needs to be taken to minimize thermal bridging at this location. Here, the rim joist has been held back to allow a layer of insulation between the sheathing and the floor framing.

(Pro Tip: this trick can be used with many other traditional framing methods.)

Siding as scheduled

Vertical strapping as rainscreen

Joist cavity packed with formaldehyde-free fiberglass or dense-packed cellulose

Rim joist is recessed to allow 2" EPS rigid insulation.

Sheathing sealed as primary air barrier

Weather-resistant barrier

Rigid insect screen vent strip

Turn up vapor barrier and seal to sheathing.

Vapor-variable membrane; seal to vapor barrier at sill.

Interior 2x4 stud wall held off of foundation wall cavity filled with dense-packed cellulose

Vapor barrier sealed to slab vapor barrier and lapped over top of foundation wall

Reinforced concrete wall with stem wall

Waterproofing membrane

2" EPS rigid insulation

Cement board rated for inground contact

Granular backfill for drainage

# WALL-TO-ROOF CONNECTIONS

## RAISED-HEEL TRUSS ON A DOUBLE-STUD WALL

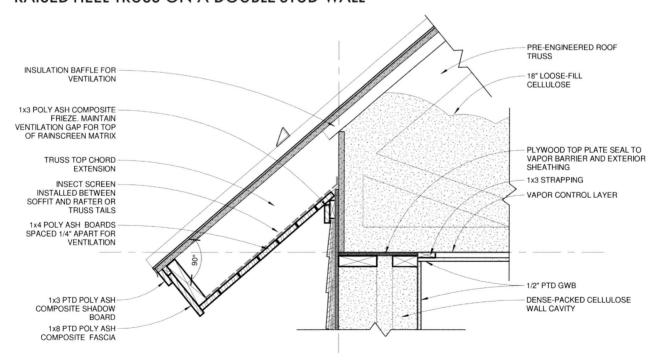

INSULATION BAFFLE FOR VENTILATION

1x3 POLY ASH COMPOSITE FRIEZE. MAINTAIN VENTILATION GAP FOR TOP OF RAINSCREEN MATRIX

TRUSS TOP CHORD EXTENSION

INSECT SCREEN INSTALLED BETWEEN SOFFIT AND RAFTER OR TRUSS TAILS

1x4 POLY ASH BOARDS SPACED 1/4" APART FOR VENTILATION

1x3 PTD POLY ASH COMPOSITE SHADOW BOARD

1x8 PTD POLY ASH COMPOSITE FASCIA

PRE-ENGINEERED ROOF TRUSS

18" LOOSE-FILL CELLULOSE

PLYWOOD TOP PLATE SEAL TO VAPOR BARRIER AND EXTERIOR SHEATHING

1x3 STRAPPING

VAPOR CONTROL LAYER

1/2" PTD GWB

DENSE-PACKED CELLULOSE WALL CAVITY

90°

The easiest way to insulate a roof is to insulate the bottom of the truss framing. Give it some depth by having a raised heel (a.k.a. energy heel) on the truss. This allows the insulation to be installed completely over the top of the wall while leaving room for ventilation via the eaves and roof ridge.

## OFFSET RAFTERS ON A DOUBLE-STUD WALL

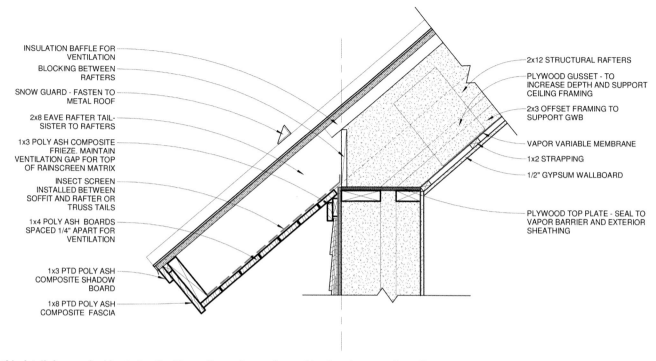

INSULATION BAFFLE FOR VENTILATION

BLOCKING BETWEEN RAFTERS

SNOW GUARD - FASTEN TO METAL ROOF

2x8 EAVE RAFTER TAIL-SISTER TO RAFTERS

1x3 POLY ASH COMPOSITE FRIEZE. MAINTAIN VENTILATION GAP FOR TOP OF RAINSCREEN MATRIX

INSECT SCREEN INSTALLED BETWEEN SOFFIT AND RAFTER OR TRUSS TAILS

1x4 POLY ASH BOARDS SPACED 1/4" APART FOR VENTILATION

1x3 PTD POLY ASH COMPOSITE SHADOW BOARD

1x8 PTD POLY ASH COMPOSITE FASCIA

2x12 STRUCTURAL RAFTERS

PLYWOOD GUSSET - TO INCREASE DEPTH AND SUPPORT CEILING FRAMING

2x3 OFFSET FRAMING TO SUPPORT GWB

VAPOR VARIABLE MEMBRANE

1x2 STRAPPING

1/2" GYPSUM WALLBOARD

PLYWOOD TOP PLATE - SEAL TO VAPOR BARRIER AND EXTERIOR SHEATHING

This detail shows a double-stud wall with an offset-rafter roof assembly. Gaps between the soffit boards allow air to flow into the ventilation baffles installed just under the roof sheathing and exit at the ridge. This ensures that the sheathing will dry in case of condensation or leaks.

**Cathedral ceilings** There is no shortage of details for cathedral ceilings, but finding one that solves all potential problems is rare. As you'll read in the next section, creating a continuous air-sealing layer for the building envelope is critical and when you are using a vapor-permeable, bio-based insulation material (the preferred insulation among the PGH crowd) then venting the cathedral ceiling cavity is a necessity. You might not agree with that last sentence but it doesn't matter because most building codes do. Shown above is a detail that ventilates the cathedral ceiling cavity.

# Air Sealing

Between 20% and 25% of a typical home's heat loss is via convection as air flows freely through the many cracks and seams of the building envelope. That's hard-earned heat or air conditioning hitching a ride on the air as it leaks to the outdoors. Preventing these leaks is the cheapest and most cost-effective

way of reducing heat transfer through the building envelope. All it takes is some care, some decent air-sealing products, and a little bit of know-how. While building a Passive House, one of the authors of this book adopted the mantra: "We're building a boat. If it leaks, we sink and we die!" because meeting the air-sealing standard of a Passive House was one of the more difficult challenges of the project. The build team embraced this idea. Any seam, penetration, or transition in the building envelope was scrutinized and tenaciously sealed with tape. Put simply, a Pretty Good House is an energy-efficient home, and an energy-efficient home is a tight home.

Let's address the "houses need to breathe" thing. It's simply not true. Humans need to breathe; buildings need to dry. When we seal our homes, we are talking about *air* sealing them, we are not *vapor* sealing them. This is a big distinction. We now have a suite of products and techniques that block the movement of air but allow the passage of water vapor (water in gas form). This allows the building envelope to dry easily while preventing air leaks that are so detrimental to the integrity of the building. (More on this in the next chapter on moisture migration through building assemblies.)

But what about oxygen and fresh air for the building occupants, you might ask? With a tight house, you need to supply balanced ventilation through an energy-recovery ventilator (ERV). We will cover that in more detail in Chapter 8 on mechanical systems and ventilation. But for the time being, it might be best to accept the premise that a healthy house leaks, but an energy-efficient house *controls* how it leaks. Rather than a home getting its fresh air through the cracks and failures of the building envelope, we can deliver fresh air to the areas that need it most (bedrooms and living spaces), exhaust stale air from spaces that need it most (kitchens, baths, and laundry), and retain 80% to 90% of the heat energy of the exhaust air in the process. It's a far superior approach to letting the house "breathe." That's something a PGH builder should never say.

## WHERE'S THE AIR BARRIER?

It helps to visualize exactly where in the building envelope the air barrier should be located. This is relatively easy to do. Just draw a line on all your details that shows where you are drawing the line, so to speak, against air leakage (see the drawing on the facing page). If you're able to keep the line continuous, congratulations. You have a complete air control layer. If you find your lines have trouble connecting at the junction of assemblies, then you have some work to do.

In a typical house, the air control layer is usually at the sheathing because this is already a continuous layer of plywood (or OSB with a pre-applied weather-resistant barrier), a reasonably airtight material. All one needs to do is tape the seams and connect the different assemblies. This sounds simple, but in practice it can get tricky where assemblies meet each other.

Building professionals often combine air control and vapor control layers. That's totally acceptable, but keep in mind that these actually are two separate things. Unlike a vapor control layer, an air control layer can go anywhere in the building assembly. You can use a vapor control layer as an air-sealing layer, or you can use the weather control layer as the air control layer, or *both*. The more air sealing, the better.

# Regular OSB: Not a Reliable Air Barrier

There's plenty of evidence to suggest that off-the-shelf oriented strand board (OSB) is a pretty lousy air barrier by itself.

Richard Pedranti, a Passive House architect in Milford, Pennsylvania, explained how he discovered this in a presentation in 2015. He was working on a Passive House in Climate Zone 6 that specified regular OSB sheathing as the air barrier. Because it was a Passive House, it was vital that air leakage not exceed 0.6 ACH50, so their team planned to do a shell test even before the windows were installed. All the openings were sheathed over, with all seams taped and sealed. This should have been their best test. Yet they were way off. The house was too leaky. After an exhaustive and frustrating search for leaks they reversed the blower door and taped poly to the outside of the OSB. Air forced through the OSB by the blower door inflated the poly immediately, showing that the OSB was the culprit. A vapor-permeable air barrier was applied to the exterior of the OSB, and the next blower-door test resulted in 0.35 ACH50.

# THE AIR-BARRIER PENCIL TEST

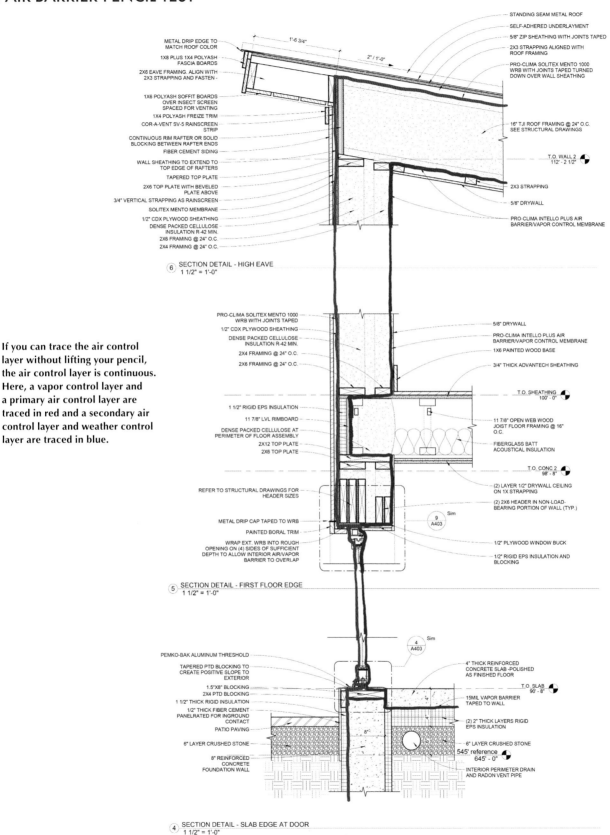

If you can trace the air control layer without lifting your pencil, the air control layer is continuous. Here, a vapor control layer and a primary air control layer are traced in red and a secondary air control layer and weather control layer are traced in blue.

STANDING SEAM METAL ROOF

SELF-ADHERED UNDERLAYMENT

5/8" ZIP SHEATHING WITH JOINTS TAPED

2X3 STRAPPING ALIGNED WITH ROOF FRAMING

PRO-CLIMA SOLITEX MENTO 1000 WRB WITH JOINTS TAPED TURNED DOWN OVER WALL SHEATHING

16" TJI ROOF FRAMING @ 24" O.C. SEE STRUCTURAL DRAWINGS

T.O. WALL 2
112' - 2 1/2"

2X3 STRAPPING

5/8" DRYWALL

PRO-CLIMA INTELLO PLUS AIR BARRIER/VAPOR CONTROL MEMBRANE

METAL DRIP EDGE TO MATCH ROOF COLOR

1X8 PLUS 1X4 POLYASH FASCIA BOARDS

2X6 EAVE FRAMING. ALIGN WITH 2X3 STRAPPING AND FASTEN -

1X6 POLYASH SOFFIT BOARDS OVER INSECT SCREEN SPACED FOR VENTING

1X4 POLYASH FREIZE TRIM

COR-A-VENT SV-5 RAINSCREEN STRIP

CONTINUOUS RIM RAFTER OR SOLID BLOCKING BETWEEN RAFTER ENDS

FIBER CEMENT SIDING

WALL SHEATHING TO EXTEND TO TOP EDGE OF RAFTERS

TAPERED TOP PLATE

2X6 TOP PLATE WITH BEVELED PLATE ABOVE

3/4" VERTICAL STRAPPING AS RAINSCREEN

SOLITEX MENTO MEMBRANE

1/2" CDX PLYWOOD SHEATHING

DENSE PACKED CELLULOSE INSULATION R-42 MIN.

2X6 FRAMING @ 24" O.C.

2X4 FRAMING @ 24" O.C.

6 SECTION DETAIL - HIGH EAVE
1 1/2" = 1'-0"

1'-6 3/4"

2" / 1'-0"

PRO-CLIMA SOLITEX MENTO 1000 WRB WITH JOINTS TAPED

1/2" CDX PLYWOOD SHEATHING

DENSE PACKED CELLULOSE INSULATION R-42 MIN.

2X4 FRAMING @ 24" O.C.

2X6 FRAMING @ 24" O.C.

5/8" DRYWALL

PRO-CLIMA INTELLO PLUS AIR BARRIER/VAPOR CONTROL MEMBRANE

1X6 PAINTED WOOD BASE

3/4" THICK ADVANTECH SHEATHING

T.O. SHEATHING
100' - 0"

1 1/2" RIGID EPS INSULATION

11 7/8" LVL RIMBOARD

DENSE PACKED CELLULOSE AT PERIMETER OF FLOOR ASSEMBLY

2X12 TOP PLATE

2X6 TOP PLATE

11 7/8" OPEN WEB WOOD JOIST FLOOR FRAMING @ 16" O.C.

FIBERGLASS BATT ACOUSTICAL INSULATION

T.O. CONC 2
98' - 8"

(2) LAYER 1/2" DRYWALL CEILING ON 1X STRAPPING

(2) 2X6 HEADER IN NON-LOAD-BEARING PORTION OF WALL (TYP.)

REFER TO STRUCTURAL DRAWINGS FOR HEADER SIZES

9
A403
Sim

METAL DRIP CAP TAPED TO WRB

PAINTED BORAL TRIM

WRAP EXT. WRB INTO ROUGH OPENING ON (4) SIDES OF SUFFICIENT DEPTH TO ALLOW INTERIOR AIR/VAPOR BARRIER TO OVERLAP

1/2" PLYWOOD WINDOW BUCK

1/2" RIGID EPS INSULATION AND BLOCKING

5 SECTION DETAIL - FIRST FLOOR EDGE
1 1/2" = 1'-0"

4
A403
Sim

PEMKO-BAK ALUMINUM THRESHOLD

TAPERED PTD BLOCKING TO CREATE POSITIVE SLOPE TO EXTERIOR

1.5"X8" BLOCKING

2X4 PTD BLOCKING

1 1/2" THICK RIGID INSULATION

1/2" THICK FIBER CEMENT PANEL RATED FOR INGROUND CONTACT

PATIO PAVING

6" LAYER CRUSHED STONE

8" REINFORCED CONCRETE FOUNDATION WALL

4" THICK REINFORCED CONCRETE SLAB - POLISHED AS FINISHED FLOOR

T.O. SLAB
90' - 8"

15MIL VAPOR BARRIER TAPED TO WALL

(2) 2" THICK LAYERS RIGID EPS INSULATION

6" LAYER CRUSHED STONE

545' reference
645' - 0"

INTERIOR PERIMETER DRAIN AND RADON VENT PIPE

4 SECTION DETAIL - SLAB EDGE AT DOOR
1 1/2" = 1'-0"

## VENTED SUSPENDED SOFFIT

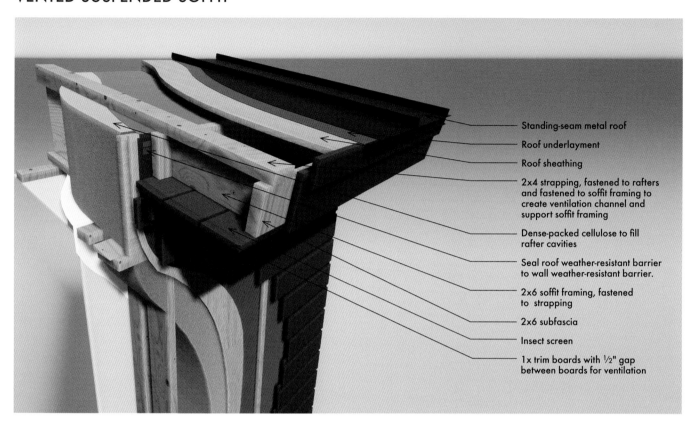

Standing-seam metal roof

Roof underlayment

Roof sheathing

2x4 strapping, fastened to rafters and fastened to soffit framing to create ventilation channel and support soffit framing

Dense-packed cellulose to fill rafter cavities

Seal roof weather-resistant barrier to wall weather-resistant barrier.

2x6 soffit framing, fastened to strapping

2x6 subfascia

Insect screen

1x trim boards with ½" gap between boards for ventilation

Adding rafter tails after the roof sheathing and wall sheathing have been connected and sealed creates a continuous air control layer. Note that this method depends on the structural capacity of the roof sheathing and the 2x4. Consult a structural engineer before using this approach.

**Roof-to-wall connections** One of the trickiest places to maintain a continuous air barrier is at the junction of the roof assembly and the wall assembly, especially if the roof is a cathedral roof. The drawing above and the photo on the facing page show a couple of options for solving this.

## MEASURING AIR TIGHTNESS

It's becoming commonplace now to measure the air tightness of a building with a blower-door test. This is covered in Chapter 10 on verification, but it should be stated in this chapter that a PGH is going to perform at least two blower-door tests. One takes place when the home is complete and airtightness can be verified and documented. The other, which is far more important, is done during construction and is often referred to as a "shell test." It's performed prior to the installation of insulation and finishes. This test is less about documenting airtightness as it is about finding leaks and sealing them up. When the blower door is installed, and the house is depressurized (or pressurized), it's the perfect opportunity to track down these trouble spots. By using smoke pens, infrared cameras, theatrical smoke machines, or even just feeling around with your hand, you can track down leaks and seal them.

With the information presented in this chapter, we hope you're ready to create a Pretty Good House with a building envelope that is appropriately insulated, continuous, and tightly sealed against the wind and weather.

Shown here is the vented suspended soffit in the field. The roof water-resistant barrier has been sealed to the wall WRB and a vent channel has been created between the roof WRB and the roof sheathing.

## ACH50: Why 50 Pascals

Air leakage is often measured as *air changes per hour at 50 pascals of pressure* (or ACH50). To do this, a house is depressurized by using a blower door to help identify air leaks. But why 50 pascals?

This pressure differential simulates a 20-mph wind gust on the outside of the house. That's a fun factoid and should help describe the force that a pressure differential can create. If you've ever been present for a blower-door test, you probably know that at that pressure, a small leak feels like a little jet of air. If water were present on the other side of that leak, it would ride the small jet and be sucked into the building envelope. The importance of a tight house is more than keeping the cold air out but keeping small failures in the building envelope from creating big moisture problems. In short, leaks suck.

## THINGS TO CONSIDER

• Have you met code requirements for insulation values? Are they up to snuff compared to the PGH R-values in this chapter?

• Are you going to perform an energy model to verify the effectiveness of the insulation values you are choosing?

• How are you handling thermal bridging?

• Have you looked closely at each location where different assemblies come together (like floor to foundation wall, or roof to wall)? Have you examined each for thermal bridging? Have you traced your air control layer through each of these details and made sure that it is continuous?

• What is your method of air sealing for your house? For each assembly?

• Do you have a long-term plan to improve the performance of your existing home? Have you had an energy audit performed?

# Sugar Bush House

TO NEW ENGLANDERS, a sugarbush is a stand of maples tapped in early spring for sap that ultimately becomes maple syrup. Naming this house after a prized forest resource seems apt, not only because it's located in a rural corner of Vermont, the country's most prolific syrup-producing state, but also because it so carefully reflects the visual qualities of the site.

Architect Robert Swinburne explains the original concept for the house this way: dark and shaggy on the outside, bright and clean on the inside. The simple design boils down to four walls and a roof, in Swinburne's mind "a light-filled chapel in the woods."

Many of the construction details were worked out on site by Swinburne and Gero Dolfus of Mindel and Morse Builders. Exterior walls are built with Larsen trusses over 2x6 structural walls, and the roof consists of 2-ft.-deep floor trusses. Both assemblies provide ample room for cellulose insulation. Beneath the floating slab-on-grade foundation is a perimeter of WarmFörm EPS forms combined with recycled EPS roughly 12 in. deep.

The two-bedroom design puts almost all of the living space on a single level. The exception is a loft that seems more like a treehouse than it does interior space. In addition to the nearly 1,700 sq. ft. of living space is an outdoor deck and a connected breezeway and garage. Outdoor surfaces are intentionally unpolished. The locally milled hemlock siding, installed over a rainscreen, is hard and heavy and should perform better in Vermont's weather than pine. It will gray naturally over time, and should any boards need replacement it will be easy to do. Shallow roof overhangs will help exterior walls dry quickly during Vermont's long stretches of humid weather.

There's no fine carpentry on the exterior of the building, Swinburne says. Pine-board walls for the garage are slatted—installed with a space between them—to allow light and air to filter through, not unlike old barns in the region. The idea is simplicity, ease of maintenance, and ample use of local resources. The outdoor stoop is constructed of locally harvested black locust, a weather-resistant wood often used for fence posts. Cherry treads for the indoor staircase

came from trees on the site, as did some of the pine for the board sheathing.

One reason for using locally harvested wood is to reduce the carbon footprint of the house, and the practice also helped reduce waste. Offcuts from the sheathing, for example, went to the end of the drive-way where neighbors picked them up for kindling. Scraps from the Advantech subflooring were used as gussets in the Larsen truss walls. No dumpster ever appeared on the site during construction.

To Swinburne, the house hit many Pretty Good House buttons: a superinsulated building enclosure, an integrated design process in which construction and design ideas were accepted from everyone working on the project, even community engagement in the form of an open house for neighbors.

**TOP** With its clean, unadorned spaces on the interior and the rough texture of native hemlock on the outside, the Sugar Bush House is a "light-filled chapel in the woods" to architect Robert Swinburne.

**ABOVE** The slatted pine siding on the garage allows air and light to filter into the space, reminiscent of many old barns in the region.

The staircase leading to a loft over the main floor of the house includes treads made from cherry trees that were felled on site.

"What stands out for me the most," said Dolfus, "is the way the house interacts with the site. The design is very simple and what makes it particularly interesting are features that were relatively inexpensive from a building perspective. That doesn't always happen when architects get involved."

## WHAT MAKES THIS A PRETTY GOOD HOUSE?

- Superinsulated building enclosure with low air leakage.
- Simple building shape.
- Local materials with minimal processing.
- Design process that involved all trades.

## The Case for Board Sheathing

The use of plywood and OSB sheathing for exterior walls and roofs is now nearly universal, and it's not hard to see why. The 4-by-8 panels go up quickly, and specialized products like Huber's ZIP sheathing can become part of the building enclosure's air barrier without the need for separate housewrap.

Board sheathing is no longer the norm, but along with hemlock siding milled from trees on site it is a low-carbon alternative to panel products that now dominate residential construction.

Gero Dolfus, the owner of Mindel and Morse Builders, gets all that, but he still prefers rough board sheathing over panel products. Why? In Vermont where Dolfus's company builds houses, softwood lumber can be harvested locally and installed rough. That means less processing, less transportation, and, as a result, a lower carbon impact. Board sheathing also is vapor open when compared to either OSB or plywood, meaning a lower risk of trapped moisture in building assemblies.

One added bonus: the chemical-free offcuts are burnable. During construction of the Sugar Bush House, the offcuts were carted to the end of the driveway where neighbors could pick them up and take them home for kindling.

LOCATION: Putney, Vermont;
Climate Zone 6A

ARCHITECT: Robert Swinburne

BUILDER: Mindel and Morse Builders

CONDITIONED SPACE: 1,679 sq. ft.

NUMBER OF BEDROOMS/
BATHROOMS: 2/2

FOUNDATION: Frost-protected slab

FOUNDATION INSULATION: EPS, R-46

WALL CONSTRUCTION:
2x6 structural wall, Larsen truss

ABOVE-GRADE WALL INSULATION:
Dense-pack cellulose, R-52

ATTIC FLOOR INSULATION:
Dense-pack cellulose, R-103.6

AIR LEAKAGE: 0.8 ach50

SPACE HEATING AND COOLING:
Wood stove, heat pump

DOMESTIC HOT WATER:
Heat-pump water heater

MECHANICAL VENTILATION: ERV

PV SYSTEM CAPACITY:
Community solar

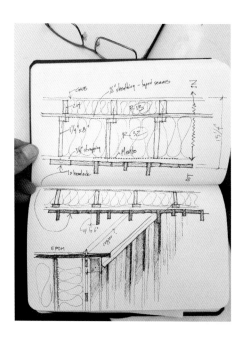

**ABOVE** Many of the construction details for the house, including trusses for the roof and walls, were worked out between architect Robert Swinburne and builder Gero Dolfus as they went.

**LEFT** White walls, generously sized windows, and light-colored cabinets and flooring enhance the simplicity of design.

CHAPTER FIVE

# WATER/MOISTURE MANAGEMENT

## CONTROL LAYERS
## CLASSIC DOUBLE-STUD WALL

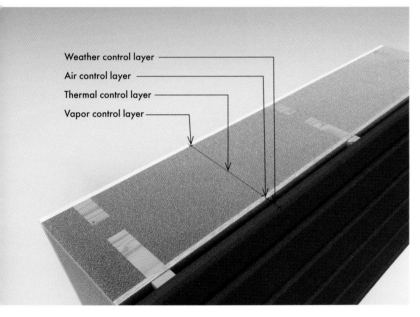

Weather control layer
Air control layer
Thermal control layer
Vapor control layer

**This cold-climate wall illustrates the basic control layers that should be continuous around the entire building envelope. The vapor control layer is a vapor-variable membrane behind the drywall. The thermal control layer is the dense-packed cellulose. The air control layer is the water-resistant barrier and sheathing; and the weather control layer is the siding backed by a rainscreen (with strapping and air gap for ventilation and drying).**

A house is always under pressure, from gravity, wind, and air, but also from water either as a liquid trying to get in or as vapor trying to get out. A Pretty Good House is designed to manage moisture migration through the building assemblies. Failure to do so could mean condensation. And where there's water, air, and organic material (such as the wood that comprises most of your building materials), conditions are ripe for mold, mildew, and decay.

When designing a PGH, keep in mind the four control layers of a building envelope (as listed by the Building Science Corporation), know exactly where those layers are in the building assembly, and ensure their continuity. We've already discussed the first two control layers in Chapter 4. The thermal control layer mainly refers to insulation and the insulative values of windows and doors. A continuous air control layer seals the building envelope as tightly as possible, and it should be readily visible on construction drawings. In this chapter, we'll focus on the other two critical control layers: the rain (or weather) control layer and the vapor control layer.

## Rain Control Layer

If you can't keep the rain outside the building envelope, none of the other layers really matter. Therefore, making sure your house will shed water (whether as rain, snow, sleet, or hail) is more important than worrying about other control layers. This seems obvious, and any builder or architect worth a damn is going to be familiar with the traditional methods of shedding rain: pitched roofs, ice and water shield in the trouble areas, good flashing details, roof overhangs, proper lapping of membranes at window connections, and so on. A PGH takes this a little further.

*If you can't keep the rain outside the building envelope, none of the other layers really matter.*

## WINDOWSILL DETAIL IN DOUBLE-STUD WALL

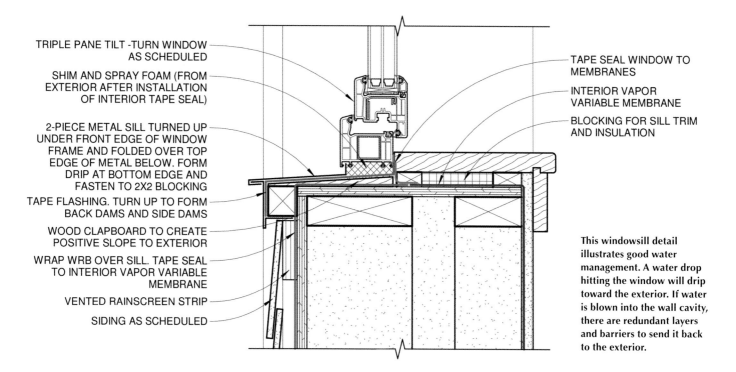

TRIPLE PANE TILT -TURN WINDOW AS SCHEDULED

SHIM AND SPRAY FOAM (FROM EXTERIOR AFTER INSTALLATION OF INTERIOR TAPE SEAL)

2-PIECE METAL SILL TURNED UP UNDER FRONT EDGE OF WINDOW FRAME AND FOLDED OVER TOP EDGE OF METAL BELOW. FORM DRIP AT BOTTOM EDGE AND FASTEN TO 2X2 BLOCKING

TAPE FLASHING. TURN UP TO FORM BACK DAMS AND SIDE DAMS

WOOD CLAPBOARD TO CREATE POSITIVE SLOPE TO EXTERIOR

WRAP WRB OVER SILL. TAPE SEAL TO INTERIOR VAPOR VARIABLE MEMBRANE

VENTED RAINSCREEN STRIP

SIDING AS SCHEDULED

TAPE SEAL WINDOW TO MEMBRANES

INTERIOR VAPOR VARIABLE MEMBRANE

BLOCKING FOR SILL TRIM AND INSULATION

**This windowsill detail illustrates good water management. A water drop hitting the window will drip toward the exterior. If water is blown into the wall cavity, there are redundant layers and barriers to send it back to the exterior.**

Our mantra when drawing up construction details is this: "Be the water drop." Water doesn't just fall straight down from the sky. Here in Maine, it exists in all three different states of matter and blows from every direction. And water has its own behavior when moving on surfaces: it clings, it spreads, it can be absorbed. A PGH detail will always shed the water away, will always work with gravity, and will always minimize or eliminate points of entry.

A leak needs both water and a driving force. Usually, this force is gravity. Sometimes it's wind. But what not-so-good detailers often fail to realize is that the pressure differential between inside and outside can be a substantial driving force. As a water drop passes a small air leak, let's say at a window connection, wind can cause the house to suck that water drop into the wall assembly. We need to either stop that entry point or give the drop a way to escape (such as a rainscreen cavity behind the siding or trim).

A PGH controls water below ground as well as above. Gone are the days when you would just pour a concrete foundation, backfill, and call it good. It's a recipe for disaster. Concrete is porous and absorbs moisture even when fully cured. While concrete is, by and large, unaffected by the presence of water, it will allow water to permeate through it, leading to the wetting of critical building elements such as sill plates, flooring, and posts. We've all been in basements that have a musty smell. This odor is an indicator of higher relative humidity, and even though it may be the norm in basements, high humidity is a major contributor to both poor air quality and mold and rot.

The first line of defense is the application of a good waterproofing membrane on the exterior of the foundation (this isn't necessary if it is just a frost wall for a slab on grade because there's no occupied space inside the walls). Available products include membranes and fluid-applied waterproofing. This is the equivalent of a weather control barrier, only below grade.

Just as air pressure can drive water into a house, hydrostatic pressure (the pressure that ground water exerts on the foundation) can push water through any flaws in the foundation or waterproofing membrane. Creating a drainage plane on the exterior of the foundation wall is a fantastic second line of defense. This can mean backfilling with a fast-draining material (like crushed stone or gravel) or installing a dimpled membrane against the foundation wall. Water drops to the footing where it can be collected and drained to daylight. If this is impossible, then of course an old-fashioned sump pump can be used in the basement. But if you're installing a sump pump, you're already assuming some failures and ruling out the use of the basement for living space.

Because concrete is thick, porous, and usually below grade, it almost always contains some moisture. Therefore, untreated wood (or any other organic material) should never come in direct contact with concrete. Through capillary action, concrete can lift water against the pull of gravity, sometimes many feet up a foundation wall. A PGH will prevent damage

from this natural phenomenon by protecting vulnerable house parts with a capillary break.

There are two common locations for a capillary break: across the top of the footing before the concrete wall gets poured, and at the top of the concrete wall where the wood framing begins.

The footing is a wide band of concrete that is poured before the foundation walls. It is wider than the walls (typically 16 in. to 24 in. wide), and it helps distribute the weight of the foundation (and thus the house that sits on top of it). Sealing the top of the footing helps prevent water from wicking up into the wall from the ground below.

ABOVE The Delta MS foundation damp-proofing system includes both a waterproof membrane and a dimpled plastic exterior that creates a drainage plane against the foundation wall surface, allowing water to sink to the storm drain located at the footing.

RIGHT Brushing a synthetic cementitious capillary break on top of the footing reduces absorption of water by the foundation wall.

# Legend of the Termite Shield

Back in the '20s and '30s door-to-door salesmen sold lumberyards things like lightning rods for barns and termite shields for houses. A termite shield is a thin strip of sheet metal with a bend along one edge. It was placed between the concrete foundation and the wood mud sill. The idea was that termites would have a difficult time crawling around this bend and would be prevented from reaching the wood.

Termite shields became popular and seemed to work. Entomologists, however, argued that this was ridiculous and akin to selling snake oil. Termites and ants negotiated angles like this in nature all the time, and an angled piece of metal was not a deterrent whatsoever. As a result, sales of termite shields declined, but houses without the termite shields began to suffer termite infestations more often than those with a termite shield. This, of course, was a

great "I told you so" moment for termite-shield salesmen, and their products became popular once again.

So what was really happening? It was not so much that the shield was keeping the bugs away from the wood, but that the shield was keeping the moisture in the concrete away from the wood. It was acting as a capillary break. Termites love wood that is soft and starting to decay. It's easier for them to nest in and consume. Without the termite shield as a capillary break, the wood was wetter and softer and more appetizing.

(Here in Maine, the authors are not experienced with termite control, but what we hear is that the termite shield is still important in termite country, not only for a capillary break but as a great location to see the tube-like structures the termites construct, giving away their presence.)

## RAINSCREENS

One of the easiest and most important things you can do for a wall assembly is to include a rainscreen. A rainscreen is essentially an air gap behind the siding, vented at the top and bottom to allow airflow behind the siding. Rainscreens are usually made by installing strapping (vertical wood strips) between the water-resistant barrier (WRB) and the siding. Wood siding, if allowed to dry properly, will be far more dimensionally stable, hang onto its finish coatings much longer, and be far more durable. This goes for other painted products that can also absorb water, such as fiber cement siding, as well.

*One of the easiest and most important things you can do for a wall assembly is to include a rainscreen.*

Vertical strapping (strips of wood typically aligned with the framing in the wall) creates a rainscreen for the white cedar siding. Air can flow behind the siding, increasing its drying potential. The yellow 3D mesh acts as the rainscreen for the shingles that will be installed below the bay window.

When dealing with siding that needs more frequent nailing, such as shingles, a rainscreen matrix can be used. This material is a plastic mesh that creates an even surface for the installation of shingles while still maintaining an air gap behind them.

# Vapor Control Layer

We need to get a little technical to discuss water vapor in building assemblies. You can rely on physics to be the same at any given time in any climate zone in the country. If you want to make tea in Florida or in Alaska, you can put water in a tea kettle, put it on a heat source, wait for the water to heat up, and pour it in a cup. The tea kettle whistles because the water is changing state, from a liquid to a vapor. Why are we talking about tea in a building-science chapter? It's because these simple principles of temperature, pressure, and the phases of water, will be discussed quite a bit and this little tea kettle will be a good reference point.

## BASIC PHYSICS OF PRESSURE AND THERMODYNAMICS

Heat flows from hot to cold, or more accurately from high energy to low energy. If you set that hot tea kettle on a trivet in a room that is 70°F, eventually the high energy heat of the kettle will radiate out into the room. Eventually the tea kettle and the water inside will become the same temperature as the room.

What is a little less intuitive is that vapor density acts in much the same way. While the water was piping hot in the kettle, you would expect the steam to escape as it moved from high pressure to low pressure. But what about when the kettle is at the same temperature as the air in the room? The whistling stopped, the steam stopped. Everything is equal, right? Well, no. There's water in that kettle in a slightly contained environment. The vapor pressure in the kettle is slightly higher. That vapor seeks equilibrium with its surroundings, just like the heat.

## Sorption and Solar Drive

Now we're getting nerdy. Everyone knows the term *absorb,* which is when a material takes in water. *Adsorption* is when water vapor adheres to a material's surface. Together they are called *sorption.* A more general term is *moisture accumulation.* Solar drive, or solar vapor drive, occurs when a moisture-loaded material such as wet siding is exposed to direct sunlight. The sun has enough radiant energy to push the moisture through the material and into whatever is behind the cladding. Rainscreen gaps are an effective barrier to solar vapor drive, especially when they are fully vented, but a WRB is also necessary.

Water vapor is often the cause of moisture-related problems in buildings. Think of a PGH as a giant tea kettle. Imagine a cold winter day. Inside, there's a family gathering. It's warm. They're making pasta downstairs, while Grandpa takes a long, hot shower upstairs. The humidity level is on the rise. It's not uncomfortable for the occupants, but there is now substantial outward vapor pressure on the building envelope (like the pressure building in the tea kettle) and that pressure is from the warm higher humidity inside toward the colder lower humidity outside. When warm moist air finds a cold surface, it will condense, causing water to accumulate in some of the worst places for your building. A Pretty Good House will have a very well-defined vapor control layer that is continuous around the entire building envelope. It can be comprised of many different materials and membranes.

Prior to the 1950s no one really worried about vapor control, because houses were built from vapor-open materials and were so leaky and draughty that they had excellent drying potential. With the invention of plywood and drywall, houses started to get tighter and less permeable, and problems with moisture became more common.

---

*A Pretty Good House will have a very well-defined vapor control layer that is continuous around the entire building envelope.*

---

## CONDENSATION: MOLD AND MILDEW'S IRRIGATION SYSTEM

For mold or mildew to grow it needs two things: organic materials (food) and high relative humidity (water). It is nearly impossible to eliminate the food source, since we build our buildings mostly from organic materials (wood and cellulose) and the dust in the air is comprised mostly of organic material. So, we must manage the relative humidity or moisture content of our building and the building assemblies to minimize the risk of mold or mildew.

The building envelopes of our homes are far less perfect, and more permeable, than the walls of the tea kettle. Each little leak is a place where vapor is allowed to escape and force its way into our building assemblies. This is why air sealing is far more important than vapor sealing. The amount of water and water vapor that can travel through a leak in the building envelope is far greater than the water vapor that can permeate through different materials. Once all the air leaks are sealed, however, we still have the problem of water vapor passing through permeable materials such as wood, insulation, or drywall. Therefore, it is important to understand exactly where the vapor control layer is located.

For example, if there is no vapor barrier on the interior of a 2x6 stud wall, then the most vapor-impermeable material in the assembly is most likely

the exterior sheathing. On a cold winter day this sheathing also will be cold, and if water vapor makes its way to this surface it will condense, form water droplets, be absorbed, and ultimately promote the growth of mold and mildew.

In the 1970s, '80s, and '90s, installing polyethylene ("poly") vapor barriers on the interior (just behind the drywall) was common practice to mitigate this problem. It had little success in all but the coldest climates and varying degrees of failures in all climates. Theoretically it was a good idea, but in practice the continuous membrane was usually flawed with uncountable staple and nail holes, tears, and other failures that allowed the moisture from the interior of the house to pass into the wall assemblies. Adding insult to injury, the poly greatly reduced the drying capacity of the wall and roof assemblies to the interior, trapping the moisture in what's called a "vapor sandwich."

A PGH needs a better vapor control layer than that. Before we dig into methodology, let's get some terminology out of the way. We're going to be talking about vapor retarders, which are classified by how open they are to water vapor movement (as classified by the International Code Council and ASHRAE):

- Class I vapor retarder, 0.1 perm or less (may also be called vapor barrier); vapor impermeable.

## Understanding Perm Ratings

Permeability is a measure of how much water vapor can pass through a material. It is typically measured in "perms," where 1 perm is defined as the passage of 1 grain (64.8 milligrams) of water vapor per hour per square foot at 1 inch of mercury (3,386.38 pascals). (That's a U.S perm, not metric.)

The lower the perm rating of a material, the less water vapor it allows through.

- Class II vapor retarder, more than 0.1 perms and up to 1.0 perm; vapor semi-impermeable.

- Class III vapor retarder, more than 1.0 perm and up to 10 perms; vapor semi-permeable.

- Vapor permeable (or vapor open) is a material greater than 10 perms.

# Wall Assemblies

There are four basic methods that a PGH designer can take to establish a vapor control layer within a wall assembly.

- **Vapor-variable membranes.** These specialized plastics have pores that open and close based on relative humidity and are capable of regulating the transmission of water vapor.

- **Insulation as a control layer.** Relying on the vapor-closed properties of certain insulation types (usually spray foam) to keep water vapor from reaching and condensing on the sheathing or other layers in the wall assembly.

- **Vapor-open assemblies.** Ordering the layers of the wall assembly so that the most impermeable is in a warm part of a wall and safe from condensation.

- **Warm sheathing as vapor control layer.** This is an "outsulation" approach, where the sheathing is used as the vapor control layer with the majority of the wall assembly's insulation on the exterior of the sheathing. This approach keeps the sheathing (vapor control layer) warm, thereby greatly reducing the risk of condensation.

## VAPOR-VARIABLE MEMBRANES

When you finished reading the previous chapter on building envelope basics, you may have come away thinking that double-stud construction is probably one of the best ways to create a high-performance wall assembly. But where is the vapor control? Every-

thing you've read in this chapter would lead you to think that this is a dangerous assembly with the Class II sheathing on the extreme cold side of the assembly. If water vapor were to migrate through from the interior to that sheathing, it could condense and become active water within the wall. To reduce the mold risk of a wall assembly like this, we need a way to stop that vapor from entering the wall—a vapor control layer on the warm side of the wall.

In the earlier days of PGH construction, some builders and architects addressed this by following the airtight drywall approach as prescribed by the Building Science Corporation at the time. Essentially, this means using the painted drywall in combination with air-sealing gaskets at penetrations as the vapor control layer. However, with the advent of more modern materials, that method is rarely used today. Instead, builders opt for vapor-variable membranes. These membranes are applied to the interior of the

## VAPOR-VARIABLE MEMBRANE

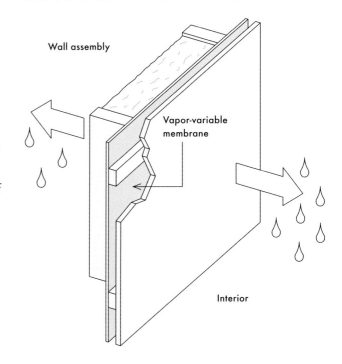

Wall assembly

Vapor-variable membrane

Interior

**Vapor-variable membranes are designed to resist the passage of water vapor from the interior into wall and roof cavities in winter but allow any accumulated moisture to dry to the interior when the season changes.**

# WRBs: Water-Resistant Barriers

Throughout this chapter (and others) you'll see reference to WRBs being used in wall and roof assemblies, usually just behind the primary weather barrier (siding or roofing) as added protection in case the siding or roofing inevitably leaks. When asphalt roofing felt was invented (originally made of cotton rag and asphalt, or a paper and wood pulp blend and asphalt), that was its sole purpose—extra leak protection. But it did have an added characteristic. Even though it repelled water it did have some permeability and could allow materials behind it to dry out.

When Dupont released the spun polyolefin membrane called Tyvek, the market was forever changed. This membrane, and others that soon followed, were designed to stop liquid water but allow significant amounts of water vapor to pass through, greatly increasing the drying potential of wall and roof assemblies.

Now the market is absolutely flooded with many different brands and types of WRBs. Some have integrated "bumps" or "wrinkles" significant enough to create a rainscreen. Others are integrated onto the sheathing. Of note is Huber's system sheathing, OSB sheathing with the WRB already adhered to it. That made air sealing even easier and "weathering in" during construction faster.

Other wraps on the market (such as Siga Majvest and Pro Clima Mento) are tightly woven polypropylene for similar permeability and increased durability. Each has its own proprietary tape for air sealing. WRBs such as these are also strong enough to retain dense-packed cellulose.

assembly (just behind the finish material). But unlike poly used in previous decades, these membranes are composed of materials that become less permeable as the humidity increases on its interior side and more permeable as the air dries. This creates a membrane that slowly opens up to allow assemblies to dry to the interior when that option is possible while still inhibiting vapor entry from the interior.

There are a number of membranes like this on the market today, including offerings from Pro Clima, CertainTeed, Siga, Delta, and Rothoblaas. Hopefully there will be even more in the future. They're all a little different, but in general they are designed to have low permeability when the relative humidity is low and higher permeability when the humidity increases. The idea is that the membrane will block vapor from migrating into wall and roof cavities in the winter, when indoor humidity is low, and open up in the summer to allow any accumulated moisture

to dry to the interior. Siga's Majrex is a little different. Rather than changing permeability to any significant extent, it is designed so that it's always harder for water vapor to get into the wall cavity than it is for trapped moisture to get out.

All of the membranes have their merits, and arguments abound as to which is better. Regardless of which you go with, make sure that a vapor-variable membrane is installed correctly and in accordance with the manufacturer's instructions. One benefit to the newer membranes on the market is that unlike polyethylene they are made from more rugged materials. But they still need to be installed in combination with tapes and other sealants to maintain the integrity and continuity of the membrane.

In a hot and humid climate, remember that the vapor drive is reversed from that of a typical cold-climate building. In these climates, we are more worried

Two different types of vapor-variable membranes are installed over the dense-pack cellulose: Pro Clima DB+, a paper-based membrane, on the walls, and the slightly more expensive Pro Clima Intello on the ceiling. Both vary their vapor permeability in response to the relative humidity, but the latter has greater variability. This wider range is more critical for the roof assembly, so it was worth the extra cost.

Closed-cell spray foam should be applied in "lifts," multiple passes 2 in. to 3 in. thick at a time. If too much is applied all at once, there can be problems with the foam curing.

about water vapor from the exterior of the building condensing on the cold innermost layer (usually drywall). Therefore, installing a membrane on the interior is unnecessary.

## INSULATION AS A VAPOR CONTROL LAYER

This approach uses the insulation itself as a vapor control layer, which means it is comprised of a vapor-impermeable material such as closed-cell spray foam. (You could also use polystyrene on the interior in this manner, but the cost, level of detailing, and level of performance of rigid EPS or XPS make them poor choices for this method.)

For a variety of reasons, most PGH builders avoid the use of spray foams whenever possible. First, spray

foams are made of toxic materials that can outgas into a home if not installed correctly, and they are unhealthy for the installers. Second, many spray foams use blowing agents with a high global-warming potential (GWP), making their ecological payback multiple decades away (and from a climate standpoint, we don't have that kind of time). But spray foams are getting much better as time progresses, with different chemicals and blowing agents. Some even have blowing agents with a GWP of 1, which helps their overall climate impact, making them similar to EPS insulation in this regard. If the spray foam is a closed-cell spray foam (and qualifies as a Class I or II vapor retarder) and can be continuous across the surface of the interior of the assembly, it is an effective vapor retarder. But be warned that spray foams have been known to shrink and pull away from the surfaces upon which they have been sprayed. This has the potential to open small fractures and cracks for both air and moisture infiltration. Therefore, the classic technique of only doing spray foam in between framing members and not completely encasing them can add up to an enormous number of tiny failures in the vapor control layer (as well as the air control layer).

## VAPOR-OPEN ASSEMBLIES

Another approach is to forgo the use of a membrane and reorder the components of an assembly based on their permeability so that the assembly is vapor open.

The Larsen truss wall method is a good example (see the drawing at left on p. 122). In this assembly, the sheathing, usually a Class II vapor retarder and the most vapor-impermeable material in the assembly, is on the warm side of the wall. From there moving out, there are vertical trusses (I-joists) filled with dense-packed cellulose, and a water-resistant barrier adjacent to a vented rainscreen cavity. From the sheathing outward, the wall is composed of highly permeable (vapor-open) materials, so that the wall can always dry to the exterior, minimizing the risk of mold or mildew.

This vapor-open construction can also be paired with an "outsulation" approach as described in the previous chapter: that is, installing layers of rigid insulation outside of the sheathing, essentially wrapping the outside of the building in a continuous layer of insulation (see the drawing at right on p. 122). If that outsulation is a material such as mineral wool or rigid wood-fiber insulation, then it, too, is a vapor-open assembly and has a very low risk of mold or mildew.

## WARM SHEATHING AS VAPOR CONTROL LAYER

You might be thinking to yourself, "if the sheathing is a Class II vapor retarder and on the warm side of the assembly, isn't that enough to have an effective vapor control layer?" The answer is yes. If you construct an assembly with outsulation as described above, then that insulation doesn't necessarily need to be vapor

In this vapor-open wall assembly under construction, the custom Larsen truss framing is fastened to the sheathing with a vapor-variable membrane between them. The membrane is designed to be installed facing out as a temporary weather barrier during construction. All the materials in the assembly beyond this layer (cellulose insulation, water-resistant barrier, rainscreen, siding) will be far more permeable, making this a vapor-open assembly.

open. It can be vapor closed (a Class I vapor-retarding material such as foil-faced rigid polyisocyanurate or XPS insulation). The strategy is to place enough of a building's R-value on the cold side of your vapor control layer, so that vapor control layer is safe from condensation.

So why, you may ask, do we even care about the vapor-open assembly if this warm sheathing method works? A PGH will always opt for drying mechanisms over wetting prevention. In other words, having an impermeable vapor control layer that keeps interior moisture out is pretty good, but having the ability to dry any moisture that does make it through is even better.

## VAPOR-OPEN WALL ASSEMBLY

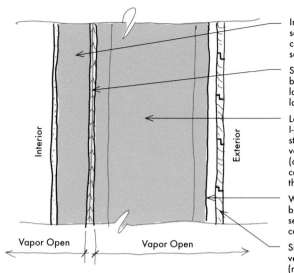

Interior

Exterior

Interior stud wall—
secondary thermal
control layer and
service cavity

Sheathing sealed as
both vapor control
layer and air control
layer

Larsen trusses (vertical
I-joist aligned with
studs) filled with
vapor-open insulation
(dense-packed
cellulose)—primary
thermal control layer

Weather-resistant
barrier membrane—
secondary weather
control membrane

Siding over
vertical strapping
(rainscreen)—primary
weather barrier

Vapor Open

Vapor Open

## OUTSULATION WALL ASSEMBLY

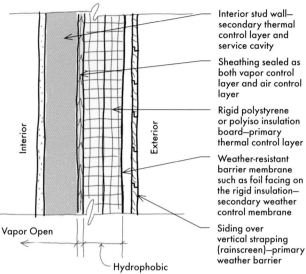

Interior

Exterior

Interior stud wall—
secondary thermal
control layer and
service cavity

Sheathing sealed as
both vapor control
layer and air control
layer

Rigid polystyrene
or polyiso insulation
board—primary
thermal control layer

Weather-resistant
barrier membrane
such as foil facing on
the rigid insulation—
secondary weather
control membrane

Siding over
vertical strapping
(rainscreen)—primary
weather barrier

Vapor Open

Hydrophobic

Both assembly strategies use sheathing as a primary air and vapor control layer. With the sheathing on the warm side of the wall, the risk of condensation is very low. In the vapor-open wall, the assembly can easily dry from the sheathing outward. In the outsulation wall, it doesn't have to because the insulation material is hydrophobic and water vapor can't condense within it. If the outsulation wall used a vapor-open rigid insulation, then its vapor profile would be similar to the vapor-open wall assembly.

# Roof Assemblies

Just like walls, roof assemblies need a vapor control layer. All the general strategies mentioned previously for walls are very similar for roofs. The major differences are that they exist at the top of the building envelope where the vapor pressure from the interior is greatest, and that to stand up to the elements their outer layer is almost always completely impermeable (asphalt shingles, standing-seam metal, EPDM roof membranes, etc.). Thus, it is even more important to get your detailing right.

• **Vapor-variable membranes with vented roofs.**
Using a vapor-variable membrane as the control layer and under-sheathing venting as a rainscreen. This relieves any vapor pressure that might build up in the assembly and allows drying to the underside of the sheathing in case there are any minor leaks that develop over time.

• **Insulation as a control layer with unvented (or "hot") roofs.** Similar to the same approach for walls, this approach relies on the vapor-impermeable properties of certain insulation types to keep water vapor from reaching and condensing on the roof sheathing.

• **Outsulation roof assemblies.** As with walls, this method puts vapor-closed insulation on the exterior of the sheathing, which is used as the vapor control layer.

• **Vapor-open roof assemblies**. Similar to the same approach for walls, layers of the roof assembly are ordered so that the most impermeable layer is in a warm part of the roof and so the assembly can dry to the exterior freely.

## VAPOR-VARIABLE MEMBRANES WITH VENTED ROOFS

As with a rainscreen for a wall assembly, roofs also can be vented. It is very common to install soffit vents at the eaves and ridge vents at the ridge to promote constant airflow at the exterior of the roof assembly just under the sheathing. This is often done to help keep the roof cool in the summertime, and it is sometimes required by asphalt shingle manufacturers to maintain the warranty on the shingles. But it has the added benefit of giving the roof assembly a way to dry itself to the exterior without compromising the weathertightness of the roof itself. It is also required by the IRC code if one's roof insulation is vapor open, such as cellulose or fiberglass batt insulation.

As stated in the previous chapter, attics are easy… sort of. There's plenty of space above the flat floor of the attic to allow for ventilation. The vapor control layer is almost always located at the floor of the attic (which usually is also the ceiling of the level below). If there are any can lights in this ceiling, they will need to be carefully sealed. This is a good spot for a vapor-variable membrane.

In the case of cathedral ceilings however, things can get a little tricky.

**Vented cathedral roof with vapor-variable membrane.** Just like a double-stud wall, a highly insulated roof composed of vapor-open insulation needs a vapor control layer on the interior side of the assembly. In a PGH, this is usually a vapor-variable membrane. And because of code requirements, the roof needs to be vented; this can be done by holding back the insulation with a baffle to create a ventilation channel.

In cold climates, sometimes we need all the insulation we can get so it may seem counterproductive to reduce the amount of insulation in the roof and introduce a cold draft directly into roof cavities using vent baffles. An alternative is to add strapping on top

of the sheathing to create ventilation channels, then install another layer of sheathing on top of the strapping to support the roofing. This has the added benefit of being easy to install from a labor standpoint, but a downside is that you need twice the amount of sheathing. This seems somewhat wasteful and makes a PGH builder/designer wince a little.

## INSULATION AS A CONTROL LAYER WITH UNVENTED ROOFS

As with a wall assembly, sheathing can be isolated from interior vapor by using a vapor-closed insulation such as closed-cell spray foam. But be mindful of spray foam's global warming impact and the chemical make-up (toxicity) of the spray foam itself. Spray foam should not be relied upon as an air control method. In this scenario, the sheathing should probably be the air

## VENTING DOESN'T COOL CEILINGS

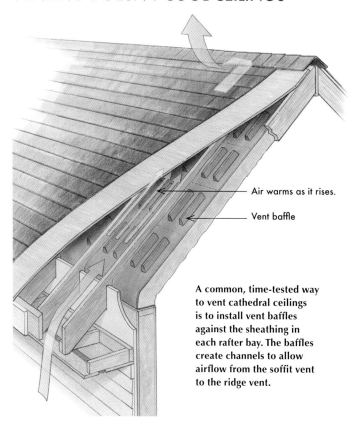

Air warms as it rises.

Vent baffle

A common, time-tested way to vent cathedral ceilings is to install vent baffles against the sheathing in each rafter bay. The baffles create channels to allow airflow from the soffit vent to the ridge vent.

## VENTED, WITH VAPOR-VARIABLE MEMBRANE

## INSULATION AS VAPOR CONTROL LAYER

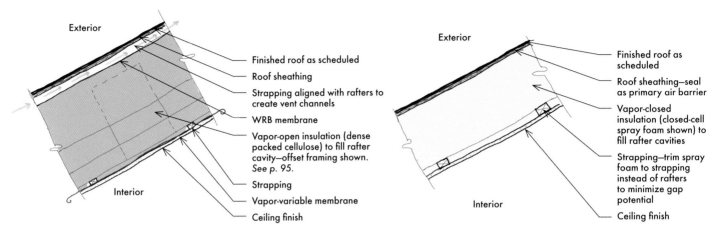

**VENTED, WITH VAPOR-VARIABLE MEMBRANE labels:**
- Finished roof as scheduled
- Roof sheathing
- Strapping aligned with rafters to create vent channels
- WRB membrane
- Vapor-open insulation (dense packed cellulose) to fill rafter cavity—offset framing shown. See p. 95.
- Strapping
- Vapor-variable membrane
- Ceiling finish

Exterior / Interior

**INSULATION AS VAPOR CONTROL LAYER labels:**
- Finished roof as scheduled
- Roof sheathing—seal as primary air barrier
- Vapor-closed insulation (closed-cell spray foam shown) to fill rafter cavities
- Strapping—trim spray foam to strapping instead of rafters to minimize gap potential
- Ceiling finish

Exterior / Interior

## OUTSULATION ROOF ASSEMBLY

## VAPOR-OPEN ROOF ASSEMBLY

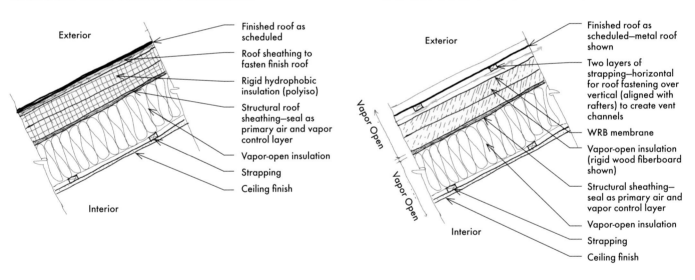

**OUTSULATION ROOF ASSEMBLY labels:**
- Finished roof as scheduled
- Roof sheathing to fasten finish roof
- Rigid hydrophobic insulation (polyiso)
- Structural roof sheathing—seal as primary air and vapor control layer
- Vapor-open insulation
- Strapping
- Ceiling finish

Exterior / Interior

**VAPOR-OPEN ROOF ASSEMBLY labels:**
- Finished roof as scheduled—metal roof shown
- Two layers of strapping—horizontal for roof fastening over vertical (aligned with rafters) to create vent channels
- WRB membrane
- Vapor-open insulation (rigid wood fiberboard shown)
- Structural sheathing—seal as primary air and vapor control layer
- Vapor-open insulation
- Strapping
- Ceiling finish

Exterior / Interior / Vapor Open / Vapor Open

Four examples of cathedral ceilings with well-managed vapor control membranes. At top left, the vapor control layer is the membrane itself. At top right, the interior surface of the vapor-closed spray foam insulation is the vapor control layer. In the other two examples, the roof sheathing is the vapor control layer.

control layer where all the seams are taped and sealed and connected to the wall assembly's air control layer.

If a roof is installed directly to the sheathing it is sometimes referred to as a "hot roof" because with the lack of ventilation behind the roof, it has the potential to reach some significantly high temperatures—high enough that some shingle and roofing manufacturers will not warranty their products with such an application.

## OUTSULATION ROOF ASSEMBLIES

By placing the majority of the roof assembly's insulation on the exterior of the sheathing, the sheathing can be used as both the vapor control layer and an air control layer. (This is a very similar approach to that used for walls mentioned earlier.) This methodology is often used with low-slope membrane roofs where the membrane can be adhered to the fiberglass facing of the rigid insulation. In higher-sloped roofs it often requires an additional layer of sheathing to support the roofing material. You might look at the detail drawing of this assembly on the facing page and think you could just use a structural insulated panel (SIP) instead of layering the sheathing, insulation, and sheathing again. You would be correct.

## VAPOR-OPEN ROOF ASSEMBLIES

A vapor-open roof is built much like a vapor-open wall. One method that is growing in popularity in the U.S. is to use a water-resistant membrane on top of the rafters to retain the insulation (usually dense-packed cellulose or fiberglass), act as a primary air control layer, and act as a secondary weather barrier (in case of any leaks). Installed above this membrane would be strapping (in line with the rafters) to create a ventilation space and help retain the insulation, followed by the roof sheathing and roof itself. Builders may appreciate this method for its elegance

in achieving an air control layer and eliminating any concern for interior membranes, but it complicates construction. They must install the strapping and the sheathing without having a solid surface to stand on. They will have to do so by using roof staging or by stepping only on the strapping. A positive aspect of this approach is that it becomes very easy to connect the roof's air control membrane to the membrane on the wall. Eave and rake details, however, can be tricky. Be sure to consult a structural engineer for help with these tricky spots if you have snow loads in your area.

**Vapor-open inverted roof.** Using a similar approach, the inverted roof places the structural sheathing on the inside of the cathedral assembly (see the drawing on p. 126). This approach uses the sheathing as a Class II vapor retarder (it also can be used as an additional air barrier). The advantage here is that the blower-door test can be performed earlier in the construction process. (Often the shell of the building is incomplete at the roof until insulation and an inner air-sealing barrier is installed.) But like the vapor-open detail mentioned above, the builder must install the membrane and additional layers while making sure not to step where the membrane is unsupported by joists.

Thinking through the various control layers on your roof is probably more critical here than anywhere else in your house. And it may also require compromises among available materials, carpenter skillsets and comfort, as well as the familiarity of all involved with the techniques that will be required.

At this point, our PGH should be well protected, from the bottom of the foundation to the ridge of the roof. The critical lesson here is that water will always find a way in. We want to make sure it finds a way out again.

## INVERTED ROOF ASSEMBLY

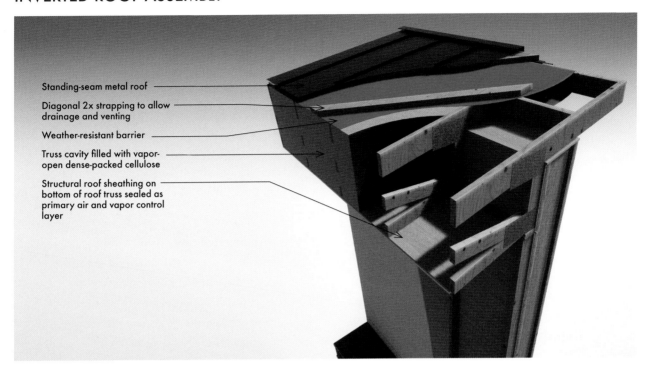

Standing-seam metal roof

Diagonal 2x strapping to allow drainage and venting

Weather-resistant barrier

Truss cavity filled with vapor-open dense-packed cellulose

Structural roof sheathing on bottom of roof truss sealed as primary air and vapor control layer

An inverted roof has its structural sheathing on the bottom, acting as both the primary air and vapor control layers. From this plane outward, the materials are vapor open to the vented air space just below the metal roof.

### THINGS TO CONSIDER

- Have you incorporated good weather control details such as roof overhangs, window and door flashing, and site water drainage?

- Are you incorporating a basement and if so, how are you waterproofing it? What methods are you using to ensure the water table stays below your floor slab? Are you insulating the walls to make sure there are no cold surfaces that could create condensation?

- Are you incorporating a rainscreen on the exterior of the wall assemblies?

- Have you defined the vapor control layer, and does it remain continuous around the whole building envelope?

- Are you using a vapor-variable membrane in the walls and/or roof? If so, are you making sure it is continuous, sealed, and placed on the warm side of the assembly?

- Are you venting your roof? If not, are you denying water vapor a way to dry to the exterior? Or are you denying water vapor a place where it can condense on a cold surface?

- Are you making sure your shell is sound before adding insulation? Are there interior moisture problems (like a wet basement) that need to be addressed first?

# Jamaica Plain Legacy

MOST OF THE PRETTY GOOD HOUSES WE'VE TALKED ABOUT so far have been new construction, but the PGH concept applies just as well to renovations. A remodel doesn't give designers and builders as much flexibility as new construction, but there is still a lot that can be accomplished in the way of energy efficiency, resource conservation, and improved comfort.

An extensive renovation of this 1930 two-story house in the Jamaica Plain section of Boston began with a request from one of the owners: Could Byggmeister Design-Build convert the garage or the basement into a home office? That got the conversation started, but Byggmeister CEO Rachel White realized that a new home office was the last thing the house needed.

Kathy and Chris, the current owners, could trace the history of their house to Chris's grandfather, its first owner. Chris's mother had grown up in the house, and he and Kathy had raised their two children there. Although it was a beloved part of the family's history, the house had not been updated in decades and was drafty, inefficient, and uncomfortable. "We told her it was going to be hard to put a home office in the garage because it was falling down," White says. "We would need to rebuild."

A new and larger deck at the rear of the house is the only obvious outward sign of a major renovation that transformed this drafty white elephant into a comfortable and energy-efficient family heirloom.

What followed was a five-month rehabilitation of the first floor of the house, including the addition of a full bath to take the place of an awkward half-bath, a down-to-the-studs overhaul of the kitchen, new mechanical systems, and a fully insulated attic—all of it carried out on a limited budget. During construction, the family moved upstairs with their two dogs, taking their refrigerator with them but giving up on their stove for the duration of the project. Other than insulation blown in from the exterior, the second floor of the house was unchanged.

"Their attachment to the house cut both ways," White says. "On the one hand it was what made it hard to touch the house, but I think it was also what made it worth it to them, to fix it rather than to move."

LOCATION: Jamaica Plain, Massachusetts; Climate Zone 5A

DESIGNER: William Harper

BUILDER: Byggmeister Design-Build

LIVING AREA: 1,536 sq. ft.

NUMBER OF BEDROOMS/BATHROOMS: 3/2

FOUNDATION: Stone

FOUNDATION INSULATION: 2-in. closed-cell polyurethane foam (R-13)

SUBSLAB INSULATION: None

WALL CONSTRUCTION: 2x4

ABOVE-GRADE WALL INSULATION: Dense-pack cellulose (R-13)

ROOF: 3-in. closed-cell polyurethane, 8-in. cellulose (R-49)

AIR LEAKAGE: 15 ach50 before, 6 ach50 after

SPACE HEAT: Ducted air-source heat pumps

DOMESTIC HOT WATER: Heat-pump water heater

MECHANICAL VENTILATION: Continuous exhaust ventilation

PV SYSTEM CAPACITY: None (shaded lot)

## JAMAICA PLAIN FLOORPLAN

**BEFORE**

**AFTER**

Byggmeister's focus is on energy efficiency and minimizing carbon emissions. In the past, the company relied heavily on spray polyurethane foam as the most reliable and efficient way to insulate renovated attics. While not giving it up entirely, Byggmeister has found ways to reduce the amount of foam it used. In this attic, originally framed with 2x6 rafters, the company put one of its low-carbon strategies to work. After building down the rafters to make the bays deeper, Byggmeister started with a 3-in. layer of spray polyurethane foam (made with a low global warming potential blowing agent) and followed with dense-pack cellulose to bring the attic to a code-compliant

LEFT The existing kitchen, which had not been updated in decades, included a cramped half-bath in one corner and a narrow doorway into an adjacent dining room. Rearranging the first floor allowed the addition of a full bath as well as a larger kitchen.

BELOW Byggmeister gutted the kitchen and rebuilt the area with new flooring, cabinets, and appliances. The new bathroom is visible at the far corner of the room and in the floor plans on the facing page.

R-49. Originally without any insulation, exterior walls got dense-pack cellulose installed from the outside. In the basement, the stone foundation was sprayed with 2 in. of polyurethane foam that both sealed and insulated.

Replacing mechanical systems eliminated all but one combustion appliance (the only holdout is a gas dryer). Those changes included boarding up a fireplace in the living room, replacing an ancient boiler with heat pumps, and adding a heat-pump water

The full bathroom on the first floor, which replaced a tiny half-bath, includes a glass-walled shower and modern fixtures. Other than insulating exterior walls, the renovation did not include any work on the second floor of the house.

## WHAT MAKES THIS A PRETTY GOOD HOUSE?

- New mechanical systems eliminate most combustion appliances.

- Air sealing significantly increases comfort.

- New insulation and air sealing reduced site energy use by 80%.

- Insulation strategies designed to minimize carbon emissions.

- Worked within existing footprint.

## Preserving a Family Treasure

Major renovations often include an enlarged footprint to provide a little more room, possibly a tear-down, particularly when the starting point is a 90-year-old house of less than 1,600 sq. ft. But in this case, Byggmeister worked with a tight construction budget to make major changes to the first floor while leaving the second floor alone. With the exception of an enlarged backyard deck, the footprint of the house remained the same. The backdrop to the work was the family's deep attachment to the house; the grandfather of one of the owners had been the original owner. "We had to be very respectful of the history," says Byggmeister CEO Rachel White. "We felt keenly the responsibility that we had because of their long history. What I really like is that we solved their problems without an addition. This is a relatively small house, and we made it work without adding on."

heater to take the place of a water heater so old that the plumber took photos of it. The changes dramatically reduced air infiltration and made the house noticeably more comfortable.

"They did not realize how much more comfortable their house was going to be," White says. "They've become these great advocates for spending money to improve comfort and efficiency, and that's not what they went into this for."

In the attic, Byggmeister used its low-foam approach, first deepening the rafter bays and then combining a 3-in. layer of spray polyurethane foam and dense-pack cellulose to bring the attic to a code-compliant R-49. A vapor-variable membrane provides air sealing and a vapor retarder.

In what was once a nightmare kitchen, even the dog now has a comfortable place to hang out. Revised floor plans widened the passage between the kitchen and the adjacent dining room.

## CHAPTER SIX

# WINDOWS AND EXTERIOR DOORS

**Windows and doors contribute greatly to a home's character and personality, as well as playing other important roles.**

A house without windows or doors would be easy to air-seal but wouldn't be very useful—most of us prefer to be able to get in and to see outside. And just as a person's eyes give us a sense of their soul, windows reveal a home's personality and give a hint of what's going on inside. Doors add character and, of course, provide actual ingress and egress.

Windows and doors have changed enormously over time, from oilskin cloth or draped animal hides to the high-tech, heavy-duty products available today. Their function, though, has remained the same—let light and solar energy in, keep wind and unwanted guests out, and allow passage of people and air as desired when open. Everybody knows what windows and doors are, so what's there to discuss? A lot of important points, actually.

This old-time single-glazed window with small panes has been repaired many times over the last 150 years or so. It's better than a hole in the wall, but not a lot better when it comes to comfort and energy use.

# The Language of Windows and Doors

The architectural term for windows and exterior doors is *fenestration,* from the Latin word *fenestrae* meaning a small opening. Fenestration also applies to other openings, and for the overall pattern of how windows and doors are arranged. It's also a term used in the fields of medicine and biology, and "defenestrate" means to throw a person out a window. "Fenestration" is a bit highfalutin and not very precise, so we'll just use the terms *windows, doors,* and *glazing.* Glazing technically means glass surfaces, but it can also mean windows and doors that have glass panels.

Windows and doors have a lot of parts, each with a specific name or names, and not all window and doors use the same parts (or names). While in general we try to avoid using trade lingo, when discussing windows and doors it makes things easier for everyone if you use the correct terms.

# Window Options

Windows and doors play an important role in your home's aesthetic appeal. From the exterior, they provide character and personality, and they may indicate what activities happen on the interior. From the interior, glazing provides views to the exterior, natural light, solar energy, and fresh air. The amount of glazing needed varies on each project, and also by location and orientation—a north-facing wall in Maine or Manitoba should have minimal glazing to minimize heat loss, while a north-facing wall in Miami or Mexicali might have a lot of glazing, with minimal glazing on the south side to minimize heat gain.

There are building code requirements for how much glazing you need, for airflow and life safety rea-

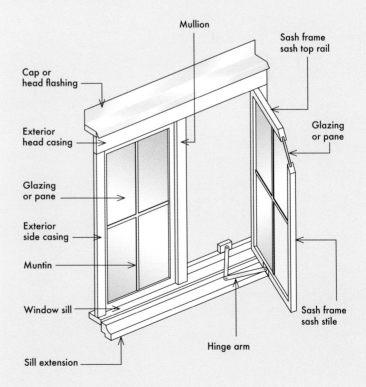

ABOVE LEFT Artfully arranged, practically sized windows: Large panes offer a broad view, cost less, and perform better than multiple operable windows of the same overall size, but keeping one smaller window that's operable provides for airflow and emergency egress. Repeating the same size and shape window ties different façades together.

ABOVE RIGHT This façade combines traditional forms with natural materials and modern details. Windows are carefully arranged and deeply inset for performance and to create shadow lines that animate the semi-smooth painted siding. The back side of most homes is designed as an afterthought, but it's worth making all sides beautiful so you can enjoy how the house looks from your back yard.

LEFT GO Logic's 1,000-sq.-ft. cottage has a simple, modest form but a strong presence thanks to its oversized, repeating window pattern. Muntins are not functional but help break larger expanses into more relatable pieces; they also help prevent birds from crashing into the reflective glass.

sons, but in many cases windows can be replaced by mechanical systems. There are rules of thumb, though: a façade with at least 15% of its area in glass will usually look better than one with less glass. Talented designers can cheat that rule, but it's a good starting point for primary façades. In most climate zones, the more glass you add, the worse the house performs from an energy standpoint. Fortunately, window and door technology has come a long way in recent decades, so you can have your views and comfort, too. But even today's best windows are no match for the performance of a well-insulated wall, so choose wisely, and invest in good quality.

## ORIENTATION

The sun rises in the east and sets in the west, but unless you're directly on the equator, the sun's position at a given date and time varies throughout the year. In the winter months, as most of us know, the sun rises later and sets earlier than in summer. What not everyone realizes is that in winter the sun rises

and sets farther south along the horizon than in summer and never gets as high in the sky in the winter as it does in summer. Those details have implications for window design and specifications, and they vary with climate zone and latitude. In a conventional house, little effort is paid to window specification or designing for performance. In 1970s-style passive

Designed by architect Steven Baczek, this modest house has a symmetrical, logical-looking arrangement of windows and doors. Note how the upper windows are fully shaded by the overhanging roof, in what appears to be midsummer. In winter, in a northern climate, those windows will get full sun and the associated solar warmth.

## WHY A HOUSE'S ORIENTATION MATTERS

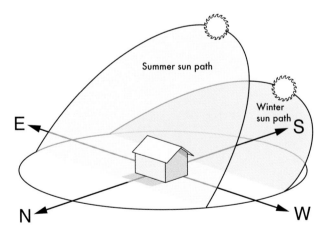

Windows and glazed doors should be selected and oriented after considering seasonal variations in the sun's path. In the northern hemisphere, the summer sun rises and sets closer to north on the horizon than it does in winter, and it is higher in the sky at midday. Window arrangements, glazing coatings, roof overhangs, and shading devices should work with the sun, gaining free solar heat in winter (but not too much) and shading the hot summer sun when possible.

This window layout takes advantage of desirable sun and views while letting in just the right amount of free solar heat and screening a less-desirable view.

solar design for cold climates, south-facing glass was maximized to get huge solar gains, which can be desirable on the coldest sunny days but counterproductive the rest of the year. In German-style Passive House design, glazing is carefully calculated, with the thermal implications of each piece analyzed for efficiency. In a Pretty Good House, we fall somewhere in the middle—we certainly care about the performance but recognize that ultra-efficient windows may not be worth the cost premium. Fortunately, there are very efficient windows that are also relatively affordable.

## MATERIALS

Most window frames are made either of wood or polyvinyl chloride (PVC, or simply vinyl), although fiberglass, aluminum, and occasionally steel or other metals also are available. Wood is traditional and naturally strong, lightweight, and somewhat insulating, so it's a common frame material for good-quality windows. Most people find it attractive, and it paints well so it's often left exposed on the interior. On the exterior, painted or stained wood windows require more maintenance than most people care to do, so wrapping the exterior with a more durable material is common—fiberglass, vinyl, and aluminum are the typical options. Because vinyl windows are usually the least-expensive option and require little maintenance, they've become a very common choice. Some manufacturers draw a distinction between PVC and uPVC, which is an unplasticized version of PVC made without phthalates or BPA endocrine disrupters. However, although quality and purity of PVC may vary among manufacturers, our research indicates that no vinyl-framed windows are made with plasticizers, so worrying about PVC vs. uPVC should not be part of the decision-making process.

A North American-style casement window with solid-wood frame and aluminum exterior cladding (Sierra Pacific brand shown). Aluminum has high embodied carbon but improves the longevity of windows, which take a beating from sun and rain. North American frames are less massive than European-style and typically have two gaskets instead of three. Installation flanges are familiar to North American builders, whereas European-style windows are usually installed without flanges.

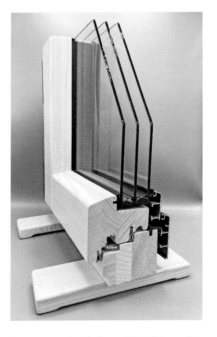

European-style window with solid-wood frame and aluminum exterior cladding (Makrowin brand shown). Wood frames slow heat flow less than insulated PVC frames but are a renewable resource and provide strength and a premium look.

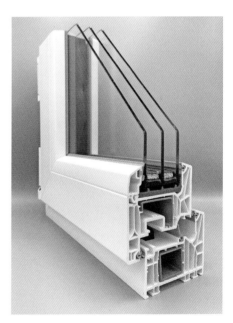

European-style uPVC window with triple glazing and steel-reinforced frames (Schüco brand shown).

Frames made from PVC are not as inherently strong as wood frames, so they are often reinforced internally with steel or aluminum. uPVC window frames are not solid, but have voids that reduce weight and warping, while slowing heat flow. Some manufacturers insulate the voids with foam to further reduce the rate of heat flow.

Fiberglass is another material that can be used for frames or for cladding a wood-framed window. Composed of glass fibers and plastic resin, it's more rigid, higher-strength, and expands and contracts less than PVC but is similarly rot-proof.

Metal windows often have a minimalist look that appeals to designers, but metal is an excellent conductor of heat (i.e., a terrible insulator) so only products that are thermally broken—usually with a hard rubber gasket separating the interior and exterior portions of the frame—should be considered for a PGH.

Other considerations are the glass coating, gas fill, and spacers that separate panes of glass. Various metals can be atomized and sprayed onto glass surfaces to change what happens with heat flow. The spaces between panes can be filled with gas, typically argon or sometimes krypton, to further slow heat flow. Over time, air will eventually displace the gas, so although krypton fill provides the highest performance, its premium price is not usually worth paying for. Argon fill comes with a low-enough upcharge that it usually makes sense in a PGH, at least a cold-climate one. The spacers are the last piece to consider; in some older dual-pane glazing the edges are continuous glass, but modern windows have stainless-steel or rubber spacers to hold the panes apart, capped with a butyl (rubber) sealant on the exterior. There are slight differences in heat conduction that matter for Passive House certification but are not enough to make a difference on a PGH.

European-style uPVC window with triple glazing and triple gasketing (Logic brand shown). Metal reinforcing isn't always necessary. The multiple chambers formed into the frames slow heat flow.

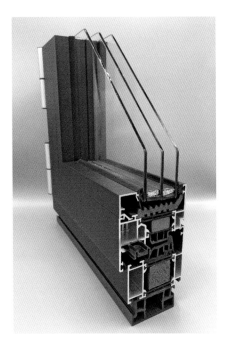

European-style aluminum-framed window with triple glazing, thermal breaks, and insulated frames (Schüco brand shown).

Fiberglass (a blend of resin and glass fibers) and related composites make durable window frames, such as this example from Alpen. This window also shows Alpen's unique triple glazing system, including a center "pane" of ultra-clear Mylar.

In most cases you don't have to worry about what the various coatings are; just look or ask for the performance values appropriate for your project (for more, see "Glazing ABC" on p. 141). An accurate energy model can help you optimize the window specifications, or you can follow prescriptive recommendations. As we discuss in more detail in Chapter 4, the original PGH model borrowed from a Building Science Corp. publication authored by John Straube called *Building America Special Research Project: High R-Value Enclosures for High Performance Residential Buildings in All Climate Zones;* Building America Report - 1005, 29 October 2010 (Rev. 1 February 2011). Window technology has advanced since this document was published, and windows with lower U-factors than listed are now relatively easy to find, but these are still good starting points.

# OPERATION

How do your windows open? Here in the Northeast, when you say "window," most people think of a double-hung, the traditional arrangement of a lower sash that can slide up and an upper sash that can slide down. A similar arrangement is a single-hung, where only the lower sash slides. There also are horizontally sliding windows. The advantages of sliding windows are that when they are open, they don't take up any space inside or outside the house, window-mounted air conditioners and box fans fit nicely, and at least in the Northeast, they are what people are used to. Their biggest downside is air leakage—the sash opens in the same direction as the air seal, so it can't be too tight or the window won't operate smoothly. They have evolved over the centuries and state-of-the-art models are reasonably good at keeping air out, at least when new, but for highest performance we are usually looking at other types of windows—ones that swing.

## WINDOW PERFORMANCE VALUES

| Climate Zone | Window U-factor (maximum recommended by BSC) | Window U-factor (maximum required by 2021 IRC) | Window SHGC (maximum recommended by BSC) | Window SHGC (maximum required by 2021 IRC) |
|---|---|---|---|---|
| 1 | — | 0.50 | — | 0.25 |
| 2 | 0.35 | 0.50 | 0.25 | 0.25 |
| 3 | 0.30 | 0.40 | 0.30 | 0.25 |
| 4 | 0.30 | 0.30 | 0.35 | 0.25 |
| 5 | 0.24 | 0.30 | 0.50 | 0.40 |
| 6 | 0.18 | 0.30 | Not required | Not required |
| 7 | 0.15 | 0.30 | Not required | Not required |
| 8 | 0.15 | 0.30 | Not required | Not required |

Note: The IRC uses the term *fenestration,* not *window.* Skylights are considered separately.

The IRC prescriptive code is getting more stringent every year, but when it comes to windows and glazed doors, PGH practitioners should consider Building Science Corporation's recommendations the maximum. The higher the proportion of windows to solid walls, the more important their U-factor, as even the best windows allow a lot more heat flow than solid walls. A U-0.30 window loses (or gains) twice as much heat per hour as a U-0.15 window. A U-0.40 window loses (or gains) 33% more heat than a U-0.30 unit.

# WINDOW TYPES

Tilt/turn

Hopper

EXTERIOR

INTERIOR

Awning

Casement

Picture

Slider

Double-hung

Single-hung

Swinging windows include casements, awnings, hoppers, and tilt/turns. Casements and awnings swing outward—casements from the side, like a door, and awnings from the top. Sometimes called crankouts, in most cases they are operated with a rotating handle and a gear, or sometimes they are "pushouts" with stays that hold the windows in place with friction. Over time, gear mechanisms can wear out but they are easily replaced. Hoppers are hinged at the bottom and swing in and are rarely seen in new homes except in basements. Tilt/turns, popular in Europe and just starting to become known in the U.S., can swing in like a door or tilt in like a hopper, using a unique mechanism that allows both operations. They do not have crank handles or stays so they can swing freely, which can be seen as a positive or negative trait. Swinging windows are generally better for high-performance homes; the sash compresses the air seal as it closes, limiting airflow.

**Double-hung windows have been the standard in traditional North American homes for centuries. They open without projecting into or out of the building, saving space, and today's models are significantly more energy efficient than older units. But the seals allow for air leakage over time, so it's best to go with fixed or swinging windows when possible.**

**RIGHT** Awning windows are hinged at the top and crank out, similar to casement windows, except that they can be left open in a light rain. They are not suitable for egress, however.

**BELOW** Tilt/turn windows, shown here in "turn" mode, are popular in Europe and gaining ground in North America. Close the window, turn the handle in the opposite direction, and they hinge at the bottom, tilting inward at the top like a hopper window—good for ventilation while providing security.

# U-Factor vs. R-Value

We say more about this topic in Chapter 4, but because we use U-factors for windows we'll also mention it here. While most people are somewhat familiar with R-value as a measure of insulating ability, for windows and doors we use the less-familiar U-factor rather than the R-value. The two are inverses of each other; U-factor describes the rate of heat flow, so the lower the value, the slower the heat flow. Slower heat flow is a good thing in every climate zone, but more important the greater the difference between average indoor and outdoor temperatures—that is, in colder climates.

**WINDOW U-FACTORS**

| Climate Zone | 2021 IRC maximum allowable U-factor | Equivalent R-value | RGH recommended maximum U-factor |
|---|---|---|---|
| 0 | no limit | N/A | 0.40 |
| 1 | no limit | N/A | 0.30 |
| 2 | 0.40 | 2.50 | 0.30 |
| 3 | 0.30 | 3.33 | 0.28 |
| 4 | 0.30 | 3.33 | 0.25 |
| 5 | 0.30 | 3.33 | 0.22 |
| 6 | 0.30 | 3.33 | 0.20 |
| 7 | 0.30 | 3.33 | 0.18 |
| 8 | 0.30 | 3.33 | 0.16 |

# Glazing ABC

Several performance values are important to understand when considering which windows to use. In the U.S., the National Fenestration Rating Council (NFRC) is the primary organization gathering this information, accessible at the NFRC website (www.nfrc.org).

**U-factor** describes the rate of heat flow. The lower the number, the slower the window gains or loses heat. A code-minimum window in northern climates is U-0.30. A PGH window should be lower; no more than U-0.20 in Climate Zone 6. Windows are available with U-factors down to U-0.09. U-factor is the inverse of R-value; U-0.20 is the same as R-5; U-0.09 is the same as R-11.

The **SHGC** (solar heat gain coefficient) describes how much of the sun's solar energy can get through the glass. Sometimes a high SHGC is desirable, such as on south-facing walls in northern climates because the windows will capture that free heat on cold winter days. But in a cooling climate, low SHGC is better because these windows block the sun's heat. Before we figured out that insulation and air sealing were the most effective ways to make a high-performance house, there were a lot of experiments using high-SHGC glass to capture heat and various contraptions to distribute the heat throughout the house, but very few of them worked well. We now know that a reliable approach includes "just right" amounts of glazing, with fine-tuned specifications.

**VT** stands for visible transmittance, sometimes called VLT for visible light transmittance. Using a scale of 0-1, with 0 being opaque and 1.0 being perfectly clear, a good range is 0.4 to 0.8. Glazing with VT values less than 0.4 will appear to be tinted. While in many cases a high VT leads to a high SHGC (i.e., untinted glass lets in lots of solar energy) and low VT usually reduces solar gain, with the variety of coatings now available those rules of thumb are not necessarily true. Also consider insect screens—they block about 40% of visible light and reduce the SHGC. Since VT includes the window and sash frames, no window can reach a VT of 1.

**CR** (condensation resistance) is a 1 to 100 measure of how likely a window will have condensation on the interior. In colder climates, heat loss, air leaks, and thermal bridging create cold spots on the window where warm, moist interior air can condense. Once you have condensation, you have the possibility of mold growth. Look for CR values of 50 or higher.

**Air Leakage** and **Design Pressure** (DP) ratings are two related but different values. Air leakage is defined by the U.S. Department of Energy (DOE) as "the rate of air movement around a window, door, or skylight in the presence of a specific pressure difference across it. It's expressed in units of cubic feet per minute per square foot of frame area (cfm/ft²)." A low rating means a tighter window, but remember that air leakage depends on how the window is installed.

Reporting the air-leakage values is not required but it can be helpful. To be reported, the windows must pass no more than 0.3 cfm per square foot at 75 pascals pressure, roughly equivalent to a 25 mph wind. For larger window areas, that amount of leakage can add up and can result in comfort problems. The best possible value is 0.1 cfm/ft², as the testing agency will not round down to zero. Air-leakage reporting is a voluntary aspect of a voluntary program, so don't be surprised if you can't find values listed, but if you can find them, be sure they are no more than 0.3 cfm/ft² and preferably less than 0.2 cfm/ft².

## HOW MANY PANES?

The number of panes can refer to how many "lites" the window has. Traditionally in the U.S., glass was shipped from Europe in limited sizes and strength, so to make a full-size window, wooden or metal muntins created a framework within the larger sash to house individual panes, called divided lites.

In high-performance design, however, the number of panes usually refers to how many sheets of glass are layered from interior to exterior to create a window. Traditional windows were a single pane thick, or single-glazed. That was effective at blocking airflow (except around the loose-fitting sash) but did little to stop heat flow or solar gain—single-glazed windows typically perform at about U-1.0 (or R-1.0) In all parts of the U.S., a PGH should have at least two panes of glass, creating a sealed pocket of air or gas between panes. All insulation is based on trapping air or another gas, so a well-made dual-glazed window is exponentially more effective at slowing heat flow than a single-glazed window. But there is a limit; the best dual-glazed windows perform about U-0.2, the same as a wall with R-5 insulation and most are closer to U-0.33 (R-3.0).

In addition to allowing more heat flow (resulting in increased energy bills and drafty houses), under-performing windows in cold climates have cold interior surfaces, resulting in increased chances of condensation. That results in mold growth and in discomfort—the cold surface draws heat from your skin via radiant heat flow, the opposite of what happens when a wood stove or the sun makes you feel warm.

In Passive House design, triple-glazed windows are required; in PGH-land we only recommend them, but they are often a sensible choice if you aren't in a mild climate. The additional layer of glass (or, in some cases, ultra-clear plastic) can reduce heat loss significantly over dual-pane windows, and comfort is increased because the innermost pane stays close to room temperature regardless of the outdoor temperature. Quad-pane windows are now available for super high performance. But glass coatings make a difference; there are dual-pane windows that outperform triple-pane windows. Also beware of claims that "triple glazing is too expensive." There are some very affordable high-performance windows and some outrageously priced, poorly performing windows, so look at the options before making a decision. An energy model can be very useful for comparing the impact of different choices.

# Exterior Doors

Doors may be solid, glazed, or a mix; when glazed, they are basically windows you can walk through. Traditionally, exterior doors were made of wood. Wood is good—it's strong for its weight, attractive, easy to work with, durable, has some insulating value, and takes paint or stains nicely. Unfortunately, it changes dimension depending on moisture content, which is dependent on humidity. Kept wet, wood will eventually rot; and if not protected with a pigmented finish, it's susceptible to sunburn (a.k.a. UV damage), which blows any finish off the surface. Frame-and-panel designs minimize wood movement but can trap water if not maintained. Laminated wood doors—slabs glued together to create a wide plank—move too much and will eventually leak air.

Contemporary doors are often made from fiberglass, steel, or aluminum, or sometimes PVC, with an insulating foam core. All are rot-resistant or rot-proof;

FACING PAGE, TOP LEFT  A solid-wood door with wood threshold should be protected by a generous overhang if possible. Wood is attractive but not ideal from an energy standpoint.

FACING PAGE, TOP RIGHT  An insulated fiberglass door that looks like wood, with an adjustable aluminum threshold, is arguably a better choice for a PGH.

FACING PAGE, BOTTOM LEFT  This triple-glazed, half-lite, European-style door has interior hinges that are different from typical North American-style hinges. The door closes against heavy-duty triple gaskets.

FACING PAGE, BOTTOM RIGHT  This European-style door has a door leaf that overlaps onto the frame, allowing for multiple gaskets.

the difference is whether they have wooden internal members and how exposed those members are to stormwater. Steel doors are usually the least expensive. They can last a long time if maintained but will rust if not, and they dent easily. The details meant to mimic traditional wood doors are often not very crisp.

Fiberglass doors typically have sharper details and won't rust. Fiberglass expands and contracts with temperature similarly to glass, so a fiberglass frame can be a good match for a glass-paneled exterior door. PVC doors are restricted to high-performance European-style doors, or inexpensive sliding doors where the relatively weak material is not stressed.

## THE PARTS OF A DOOR

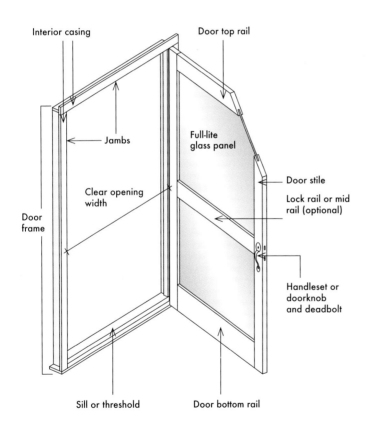

Interior casing

Door top rail

Jambs

Full-lite glass panel

Clear opening width

Door stile

Lock rail or mid rail (optional)

Door frame

Handleset or doorknob and deadbolt

Sill or threshold

Door bottom rail

**While details change from door to door, it's helpful to understand the terms we use when discussing doors.**

Doors are installed in a frame called a jamb, made up of side and head jambs and a sill or threshold. While solid-wood door thresholds are traditional, and gaskets are available that keep air and water infiltration to a minimum, they are finicky and expensive. The vast majority of new, North American-style entry doors use adjustable aluminum thresholds, with a raised section that can be set to provide good contact with a fixed gasket on the door bottom. At the head and side jambs, the door closes against a compressible nylon gasket to keep air and water out.

*European-style entry doors, like windows, have beefier, better-insulating frames and close against multiple rubber gaskets for a vault-like effect.*

Most North American-style doors have a single latch point, a doorknob or handset with or without a separate deadbolt. Also available are three-point latches, which additionally engage at the top and bottom of the door. Over time a single-latch door will leak more, while a three-point latch will ensure the door closes tightly. The three-point latch is recommended for cold-climate PGH doors but it's an expensive upgrade with a long payback period, so it's often left on the chopping block when the budget gets tight.

European-style entry doors, like windows, have beefier, better-insulating frames and close against multiple rubber gaskets for a vault-like effect.

Double doors are common for doors that lead to patios and decks and are sometimes used to create a grand main entry. They are usually hard to keep airtight and watertight over time, as any movement has double the effect. The same issue is compounded for accordion doors—the ones that open glamorously wide with multiple panels that stack to one side.

Like windows with sliding sash, sliding doors tend to leak more air and lose more energy than swinging doors, which close tightly against gaskets. But sliding doors save floor space, and need smaller frames than swinging doors because the frames aren't supporting the leveraged door weight. The best-performing units are called lift-and-slide doors; they lift up to operate and seal tightly to the sill when not in use.

Sliding doors can be appealing, especially in smaller spaces. Unlike swinging doors they don't take up floor area and with the door fully supported on the bottom, the door leaf's stiles and rails don't have the structural demands of a swinging door and can be smaller, allowing more glass for a given door size. But as with sliding windows, the mechanisms that allow the doors to slide also allow air and water to pass through, especially at the threshold. An upgrade that works better and is worth considering is a lift-and-slide door, a European approach. The gasketed door bottom sits tightly on the threshold until it needs to move. Then, wheels push down to lift the door off the track. These doors are not inexpensive but operate beautifully and perform well.

One related note: doors should always have a protective overhang. We all break that rule occasionally, but unprotected doors take a beating from sun and rain, so a bit of cover goes a long way. People entering during a rainstorm will appreciate it, too.

So, what doors should you use on a PGH? For cost-oriented projects, if the envelope and windows are all high quality, the least-expensive entry doors that will perform acceptably are North American-style fiberglass, with or without glazing. Triple glazing can be hard to find in this type of door, but the total door surface area is typically a very small percentage of the whole house. If you will be sitting near an exterior door in cold weather, however, consider going with higher-performance units—the difference in comfort will be noticeable. If you only have one or two exterior doors and they are protected from sun and rain by deep overhangs, you can even use wood doors without risking a visit from the PGH police. But don't say we didn't warn you about reduced comfort.

# Flash Your Windows and Doors Properly

Installing windows and doors is not as simple as it used to be. We are primarily interested in keeping rain and wind out, as we always have been, so we use tapes and flashing to direct stormwater away from the building. We also know that enough windows and doors will eventually fail at the sill, often resulting in significant moisture-related damage, which means that it's good insurance to install sill pans.

Sill pans can be made of various materials, but we prefer flexible membranes because they don't conduct heat like metal pans and they aren't as bulky as plastic pans (though those

also work). The idea is to plan for the day when a window or door leaks, usually through joints in the frame, and allow any water to drain away safely. Framing in a slope, or using a shim to create one, or including a vertical back dam, are important if the pan is to do its job. (You might be surprised how many get installed flat without a slope or back dam.)

# Skylights

Roof windows and skylights are very similar; the only difference is in how they are installed, with an integral curb vs. a site-built curb. We'll use the term *skylight* to cover both options. They provide daylight to the spaces under the roof, they may vent to provide airflow, and some types can even fold out to create a code-compliant emergency escape. They provide views of the sky and allow light to flood in, brightening any space during the day. Author Michael's childhood bed was under a venting skylight; sleeping looking up through maple leaves to the stars was a pleasant experience, as long as he remembered to close it during rainstorms. (Skylights are now available with rain sensors that will automatically close the window.)

Sounds dreamy, right? Unfortunately, if a window makes a lousy wall, a skylight makes a horrendous roof. The 2018 IRC for Climate Zones 3-8 only requires skylights to perform at U-0.55, equivalent to R-1.8, while the rest of the roof must be at least R-49 in zones 4-8. If you only have one skylight, this may not have a big impact on performance, but skylights are often used in multiples. They aren't quite as bad as a hole in the roof, because if properly installed they do shed water and resist air infiltration. But compared to the rest of the roof, thermally they are not a lot better. They also allow unwanted solar gain in hot months. Interior blinds are available, but once solar energy has passed through the glass, most of it stays inside the house. Blinds are mainly to block light and solar glare.

Skylights provide daylight and sky views, but they come with an energy penalty.

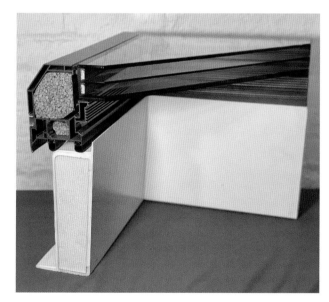

While it's best to keep holes out of your roof as much as possible, if you want a skylight, go for a high-performance version such as this Lamilux unit from foursevenfive.com, which has triple glazing, double gasketing, thermal breaks, and a system to reduce the chances of condensation.

While contemporary name-brand skylights rarely leak when installed properly, a welcome change from older, site-built units, they do tend to be condensation machines. It's very rare to see one that doesn't have water damage around the lower portions (the culprit is thermal bridging that leads to condensation). Warm, moist air tends to rise, so when it finds cold surfaces at a skylight, the moisture in the air turns to liquid water. Water damage leads to mold, rot, and other microbial growth—not what we want in a PGH.

Higher-performing, triple-glazed skylights are available that have better seals and are designed to resist condensation. If you have to use a skylight, seek out one of that type. Available down to around U-0.14 for the unit (about R-7), they still perform poorly compared to the rest of the roof, but they are better than typical skylights, which have about half the insulating value.

While tubular skylights provide daylight in rooms where sunlight may not otherwise reach, LED ceiling fixtures provide similar quality of lighting without having an energy-sucking hole in the roof.

Another product that fits into this category are solar tubes. Made from metal tubes with reflective mylar coatings, they have a clear plastic dome on the exterior and a glass ring on the interior that direct sunlight into interior spaces. The effect, during daytime hours, is like a medium-wattage ceiling fixture, and at night they have optional LED lights on the interior. To reduce energy costs and operating carbon loads, a PGH should provide for daylighting (see Chapter 9), so these are good, right? Unfortunately, not really—in most cases they are a net energy loser. With the low cost and easy installation of LED fixtures, it's usually better to burn a few watts of energy with artificial lighting than to install what amounts to a chimney through your roof. The quality of light through the translucent glass ring is pretty similar to a recessed light, anyway.

## THINGS TO CONSIDER

- Use the best units you can afford.

- Use enough glazing, but not too much.

- Energy modeling will help you fine-tune glazing specifications so your home will be comfortable without using excessive amounts of energy to heat and cool.

- Be sure your window and door layouts take advantage of desirable views and solar gain and contribute to an attractive, inviting home.

- When remodeling, think carefully about replacing windows and doors. They are rarely the most important thing to address, and the replacements may only last a fraction as long as the originals.

# Timeless Barn

It looks very much like a barn and workshop from the outside, and that's exactly what it used to be. But a deep energy retrofit transformed the building into a high-performance home without diminishing its vernacular charm.

FROM THE OUTSIDE, this 50-year-old structure still looks very much like the barn and workshop that it once was. Some interior features—especially the exposed rafters and board sheathing—also appear to be unchanged. But appearances are deceptive. Below the surface, this is a state-of-the-art house that is fully insulated, airtight, and equipped with modern mechanicals.

Its transformation began when interior designer Stephen Peck and his husband John Messer went looking for a property in southern Maine that they could use as a base during the winter when life in rural Downeast Maine seemed too isolating. The lot they found came with both a house and a barn-workshop,

but it was the outbuilding that really caught Peck's eye. He began shaping a plan for its rehabilitation, and sought out Chris Briley for help with architectural and engineering questions.

The barn had some charming features—exposed rough-sawn frame and sheathing, the unique wood-panel flooring—but there was no mistaking the fact that it was a barn that smelled like the mice who lived there. "It used to be some dude's workshop," Briley says.

The deep energy retrofit that Briley mapped out with Emerald Builders started with replacing the existing foundation, which Briley calls "a complicated mess." Ultimately, the building was lifted up and moved out

## WHAT MAKES THIS A PRETTY GOOD HOUSE?

- Renovation preserves much of the original structure.

- Air-sealed to 0.25 ach50.

- Insulated mostly with dense-pack cellulose, a recycled material with a low carbon impact.

- Heating and cooling with ductless mini-splits.

- Whole-house ventilation with an ERV.

- High-quality triple-pane windows.

- Exterior siding is western hemlock.

of the way so new frost walls and foundation could be installed. The owner had no need for a full basement so there was no reason to spend the money on one, but an enclosed crawlspace that was insulated and integrated into the building envelope provided room for mechanical systems.

Emerald stripped exterior walls of the siding down to the board sheathing, then added a layer of ZIP sheathing for shear strength and as an air barrier. That was followed by 2 in. of kraft-faced polyiso, 2 in. of foil-faced polyiso, and vertical strapping for a rainscreen. The siding is western hemlock.

Although Peck had considered leaving some interior studs and boards exposed, in the end the stud bays were filled with dense-pack cellulose and used as a service cavity for plumbing and electrical.

## Floor with a History

Slabs of Douglas fir, banded at each end in metal, make up the floor, and at first it wasn't clear exactly where they had come from. But owner Stephen Peck remembered seeing a coffee table with the same kind of top and realized the flooring had originally been hatch covers on World War II Liberty Ships. When the ships were decommissioned in nearby Portland, the hatch covers were set aside, then rounded up by the barn's original owner to become flooring.

Rough, and splattered with oil and paint, the panels were a challenge to clean up to the point where they could actually be used as finished flooring. The Emerald crew carefully sanded the floor to reduce roughness while preserving its historic patina. Floors were then coated with epoxy to lock wood fibers in place and finished with polyurethane. "They are the true showpiece of this project," Peck says of the fir panels. "There isn't another floor like it in the world."

Many of the interior finishes are unchanged, but there was still room to add some contemporary detailing like this stair rail.

**ABOVE** The single bedroom is on the upper level, at the end of a catwalk that spans the length of the building.

**LEFT** The modern kitchen faces the living area in an open floor plan. A separate dining area is located across the room.

# FLOOR PLANS

**FIRST FLOOR**

**SECOND FLOOR**

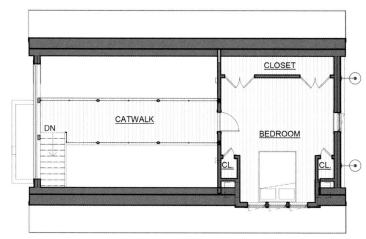

LOCATION: Falmouth, Maine; Climate Zone 6A

DESIGNER: Stephen Peck

ARCHITECT: Briburn

BUILDER: Emerald Builders

LIVING AREA: 1,423 sq. ft.

NUMBER OF BEDROOMS/BATHROOMS: 1/1

FOUNDATION: Concrete frost wall

FOUNDATION INSULATION: 4-in. EPS (R-20); crawl-space fully in the envelope

SUBSLAB INSULATION: 4-in. EPS (R-20)

WALL CONSTRUCTION: Existing studs and board sheathing, plus exterior layer of ZIP sheathing

ABOVE-GRADE WALL INSULATION: 4-in. polyiso, plus 4-in. dense-pack cellulose (total R-39)

ROOF INSULATION: 16-in. I-joists with dense-pack cellulose (R-61)

AIR LEAKAGE: 0.25 ACH50

SPACE HEAT: Ductless mini-splits

DOMESTIC HOT WATER: Electric resistance

MECHANICAL VENTILATION: ERV

PV SYSTEM CAPACITY: None installed

The roof is another sleight of hand that preserves the look and feel of the barn. In its original condition, the roof was supported by site-built trusses. A catwalk below the trusses traveled the length of the ridge to a room at the far end of the building that would become the bedroom. The team managed to keep those features while building in room for insulation. The bottom chords of the trusses were removed, and two steel beams were worked in to support a strengthened catwalk, and then two new beams were added to support the roof. Above the original board sheathing is a vapor-variable membrane that serves as the air barrier, new I-joists, and new sheathing. The 16-in.-deep rafter bays are insulated with dense-pack cellulose, protected by a vapor-open membrane. A 1-in. vent channel allows outward drying.

None of this is apparent from the outside of the building. Emerald Builders designed an eave overhang system that makes it look as if the roof is conventionally framed. "Actually," Briley says, "that was one of the hard things about it, to do all these modern things and keep it looking like a vernacular barn structure."

**ABOVE LEFT** One arresting detail of the house is its unusual flooring, made from Douglas-fir hatch covers salvaged from World War II Liberty Ships when they were decommissioned in nearby Portland, Maine.

**ABOVE** The timber rafters and plank sheathing in the roof conceal a high-performance assembly consisting of a vapor-variable membrane, new I-joists, and dense-pack cellulose.

# CHAPTER SEVEN
# MATERIALS

A Pretty Good House in progress. What seems like a lot of progress is only the beginning. Many layers, pieces, finishes, coatings, and fasteners are yet to be installed.

A staggering number of materials, products, and compounds go into the construction of a typical house. Two hundred years ago, products were simple and local. A century ago, only luxury goods were imported. Now, the palette of available materials is vast and planetary, and what you choose as a Pretty Good designer or builder will influence the environ-ment, the local economy, and the health of the build-ing occupants. And as the owner of a Pretty Good House, you have the ultimate say on what does and does not go into your home.

Of course, with all the complexity of these prod-ucts comes a complex set of decisions and criteria for evaluating them. Choosing can be difficult. One product may have recycled content, be very durable, and require little maintenance, but be extremely high in embodied energy and embodied carbon (like aluminum). Another might have high insulative qualities, saving energy, but be composed of potentially toxic materials (like some spray foams). So how do you choose? Unfortunately, there are no pat answers. The metrics vary by climate, region, aesthetics, application, priorities, and even one's own value set. It's up to you to balance the different attributes and make that determination yourself. The good news, however, is that we can discuss each of these major attributes and help you focus your efforts on deciding which materials to use, which to use sparingly, and which to avoid altogether.

# Embodied Carbon

In the past five years, the urgency of this particular metric has come to the forefront, and it is arguably one of the most important. Embodied carbon is the amount of carbon that is released into the atmosphere to harvest, manufacture, and deliver that material to the jobsite. "Carbon" is an abbreviated term for carbon dioxide ($CO_2$), whose excessive production is at the root of global warming. This is very similar to *embodied energy*, a term that has been around a lot longer, with one small difference. Embodied energy refers to the energy used without regard to how it is produced. Embodied carbon explicitly measures the production of greenhouse gases in the atmosphere at all points in the process.

Often you will see embodied carbon measured in tons of $eCO_2$ (which stands for embodied carbon dioxide). Sometimes you might find it expressed as tons of $eCO_2e$, which stands for embodied carbon equivalence. This is because not all products release $CO_2$ directly but gases they do emit have a destructive effect that can be compared to $CO_2$'s.

The science of counting carbon in our building materials is relatively new. It was long assumed that opera-

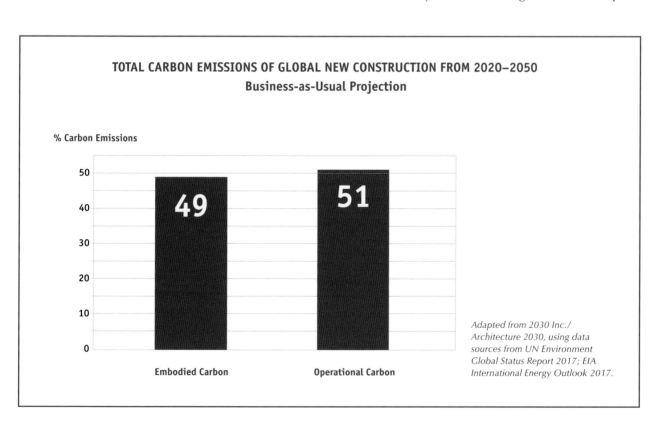

**TOTAL CARBON EMISSIONS OF GLOBAL NEW CONSTRUCTION FROM 2020–2050**
**Business-as-Usual Projection**

% Carbon Emissions

Embodied Carbon: 49
Operational Carbon: 51

*Adapted from 2030 Inc./ Architecture 2030, using data sources from UN Environment Global Status Report 2017; EIA International Energy Outlook 2017.*

tional energy (the energy a building uses throughout its life to heat, cool, and operate) would be of far greater environmental impact than the amount of energy (and emitted carbon) that went into creating the building in the first place.

This line of thinking is flawed because it fails to take into account the urgency of addressing climate change. If we had 100 years to get our carbon emissions under control, this reasoning might be sound. The carbon problem, however, is far more urgent. The IPCC (Intergovernmental Panel on Climate Change) performed an in-depth study on the building sector for its 2018 report. It found that buildings accounted for approximately 40% of the carbon released into our atmosphere. This puts the burden of doing something about it at our feet as builders, architects, and homebuyers. According to the report, there is an 85% chance of keeping the global temperature rise below 2° Celsius (the point at which climate change might not be reversible) if the building sector can be completely carbon neutral by 2050. That means that we have less than 30 years to tackle this problem.

---

*This may be the worst moment in human history to be adding $CO_2$ to the atmosphere.*

---

Building a net-zero home would reduce carbon emissions by 50% over the next 30 years, but embodied carbon would still account for the other half. This may be the worst moment in human history to be adding $CO_2$ to the atmosphere. The short term may outweigh the long-term goals in some of our decisions. When the magnitude of this problem sinks in and we realize that across the entire globe all of our buildings must be carbon neutral by 2050, it may seem overwhelming. But there is a strategy to deal with this issue and that is as follows:

1. Greatly reduce the amount of embodied carbon in the materials we use.
2. Specify carbon-sequestering materials.

## CARBON SEQUESTRATION

"Buildings are the problem, but buildings are the solution."
—Erin McDade, Architecture 2030's Senior Program Director

A tree in the forest thrives on the nutrients in the ground, the energy in sunlight, and the $CO_2$ in the atmosphere. Every tree, plant, and blade of grass, takes in carbon dioxide and expels oxygen. Plants store this carbon within their cell structure and literally build themselves with the carbon they've extracted from the atmosphere (or ocean). When the tree falls over and decays, that carbon is slowly released back into the atmosphere (adding to the atmospheric $CO_2$). When wood is burned, that release is immediate. But

A Pretty Good House avoids high-embodied-carbon materials (concrete, steel, most spray foam, and brick) when low-embodied-carbon materials will do. Better choices include wood, cellulose insulation, and bio-based materials such as straw bale, shown here.

what if you cut that tree down and stored the carbon in your building as lumber, or flooring, or insulation? That carbon would be sequestered and wouldn't be released until it decayed or is burned. Here we start to see the genesis of a solution. But for this strategy to be truly helpful, those plants must be replaced immediately.

---

*Pretty Good builders and designers are always brutally honest with themselves about the sustainability of their products.*

---

Certification by the Forest Stewardship Council (FSC) is currently the best national standard available to verify that the lumber or forest products you use are sustainably harvested. Certified products (along with straw bales, hempcrete, and other rapidly replenished bio-based materials) can actually have a negative embodied carbon number and can help offset the total embodied carbon of other products used in construction. Here in Maine, we have plenty of small, local sawmills whose operators know exactly where their saw logs are coming from. Many small woodlots are sustainably managed. Not every part of the country is as lucky, but if you know the source of the lumber you intend to use and that it's sustainably harvested, the wood should count as if it were FSC certified. Pretty Good builders and designers are always brutally honest with themselves about the sustainability of their products; make sure you're not convincing yourself that a non-FSC piece of wood is just as good as FSC lumber. It must be sustainably harvested and the forest sustainably managed or else it's doing more harm than good.

For help in deciding which materials have the lowest embodied carbon, visit the websites of Building Transparency (https://www.buildingtransparency.org/), Carbon Smart Materials Palette (https://materialspal-ette.org/), or Builders for Climate Action (https://www.buildersforclimateaction.org/resources.html).

So is a PGH house carbon neutral? We've always said that the PGH approach is a common-sense approach to designing and building a quality home. It would be common sense to say that by 2050 every new house absolutely should be carbon neutral, and that until then every house should be as carbon neutral as possible.

# Resource Efficiency

Steve Konstantino, one of the PGH founders and the host of the Building Science Discussion Group in Portland, Maine, is fond of saying, "The most sustainable building is the one that is never built." He may not have coined this phrase, but it is a reminder that building things is not inherently good for the planet. It's worth asking, "Do we need to use this much material? Is there a more efficient way to use what we have?" Be smart: Use as little as possible, choose materials with the least impact, consider salvaged and recycled materials, look for local materials, and practice efficient framing.

## EFFICIENT FRAMING

In a house, the framing lumber is often the single greatest material in quantity, volume, and cost. In a standard wall, 10-15% of the wall will be lumber. That's a lot! If a two-story house has 1,800 sq. ft. of floor surface area, that's more than nine tons of framing lumber in the walls, floors, and roof.

Wood, we know, is a mediocre insulator. Framing lumber has an R-value of about 1.25 per inch. That's at best a third of most insulation materials. The more framing in your wall, the less room for effective insulation.

Builders used to throw lumber into a wall with abandon. If we had a beam to support, it wasn't uncommon to see six or more studs lined up next to each other. We would add studs just to make sure we had

Wood framing displaces insulation in the wall. Sometimes multi-stud posts are unavoidable, but when that's the case, have a strategy to insulate the post so it does not become a significant thermal bridge.

nailing for interior trim later. Skimping on lumber was a sign of either a mediocre or a penny-wise, pound-foolish builder.

As we learned more about building science and how to improve performance, we began to wonder about the downside of all that framing. Overbuilding didn't help structurally and it hurt thermally. This realization led to what is often called Advanced Framing, or Optimal Value Engineering (OVE) framing. The goal is to use enough framing to meet structural needs, but no more than that.

The first, and perhaps most consequential, step is to consider whether standard 16-in. on-center framing is needed. Spacing is dictated first by structural concerns. Wall strength is a function of both the dimensions of the studs and how close they are to each other; the closer together the studs, the stronger the wall. Then, we need to make sure the spacing works with the sheet goods we use—plywood and drywall, for example. Typically, those sheets are 8 ft. long, so 16-in. o.c. spacing works well. However, 24-in. on center spacing is often fine structurally, and it, too, is compatible with standard sheet goods. This holds true for walls, floors, and roofs. Engineers often call for stacking, where a roof rafter is directly above a second-floor wall stud, which is directly over a floor joist, which is directly over a first-floor stud, and so

## EFFICIENT FRAMING

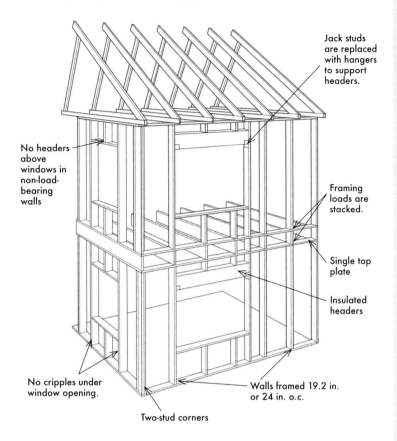

Jack studs are replaced with hangers to support headers.

No headers above windows in non-load-bearing walls

Framing loads are stacked.

Single top plate

Insulated headers

No cripples under window opening.

Walls framed 19.2 in. or 24 in. o.c.

Two-stud corners

**This drawing, from the Building Science Corp., illustrates efficient framing and how a continuous load path can be maintained from the roof to the foundation.**

on down to the foundation. This direct load path helps ensure that less framing can do more work.

The next step is to look at all the other places we put framing where we don't need it.

- Where a wall intersects another wall, putting a stud on each side of the intersection just to catch drywall is unnecessary. Nailing a few scraps horizontally between the closest studs is plenty.
- Walls will often have double top plates—the horizontal pieces at the top of the wall that the studs are all nailed to. You don't need the second plate, especially if you are stacking the framing.

## Efficient Framing for a Pretty Good Renovation

When renovating a house, it's obviously preferable from an environmental perspective to maintain as much of the existing material as possible, but many old homes, especially here in New England, are underbuilt by current standards and may require structural remediation to even meet code. Doing so with the fewest materials and the least disruption is usually preferable.

- If your floor joists are bouncy, it takes much less material to add a single beam below the existing joists than to sister each joist individually.

- If you are stripping the siding, you can add fiberboard sheathing over the existing sheathing rather than replacing it.

- Changing nonbearing walls involves much less work and material than changing bearing walls.

- Engineered lumber may allow structural repairs or support in less height than solid-sawn lumber.

As with new construction, an engineer may need to sign off on the work. And it is important to be aware of any dangerous materials, like lead paint or asbestos insulation, that are often found in older houses.

- Above any opening (like a door or window) that has a load above, you need a structural header. Use only the size specified by the engineer or code in each opening. Get rid of them entirely in openings without any load above.
- In a cathedral ceiling, try to use the rafter required for strength, and then gusset down to a nonstructural piece to provide room for insu-

lation. This both saves lumber and provides a thermal break.

- Similarly, a double-stud wall typically uses 2x4s for both walls, with a significant space in between, rather than a single wide stud. This eliminates a thermal bridge.

Wall sheathing provides resistance to racking, but we rarely need to cover the entire wall in plywood, and sheathing is not the only way to achieve structural integrity. Some builders are substituting some or all of that low R-value plywood (R-1.25 per in.) with a product like fiberboard insulation, which has less shear strength but an R-value of 3.6 per in.

Of course, none of this can happen without the agreement of an engineer or code enforcement officer. In our double-stud framing, we are often told that the structural exterior wall requires either 2x4s 16 in. o.c. or 2x6s 24 in. o.c. We usually choose the 2x4 option because the walls are easier to lift, 2x4s are a lot cheaper and can come from smaller trees, and the volume of lumber is less than the 2x6 option.

Reducing waste doesn't necessarily improve performance, but it doesn't harm it either and it certainly cuts down on the carbon footprint of the house. Some of the strategies come in the design phase. Sheathing typically comes in 8-ft.-long sheets. Designing a house around 2-ft. modules ensures an efficient use of wall and roof sheathing, which can run into the hundreds of sheets. Framing comes in increments of 2 ft.; most yards stock from 8 ft. to 16 ft. long, with 10 ft., 12 ft., and 14 ft. in between. Designing with those dimensions in mind, and making sure you don't end up with 60 floor joists that are 14 ft. 1 in. long, will make a big difference as well.

TOP A double-stud wall can be built with smaller dimensional lumber, and the space between inner and outer walls eliminates a thermal bridge.

RIGHT Here, wood-fiber insulation is used as a carbon-sequestering material that also provides structural stability as roof sheathing.

Most of the opportunities, though, come on site.

- The first step is to order the right-length lumber so you're wasting as little as possible. We love working with pre-cut studs, which come slightly under 8 ft. so that the top and bottom plates end up giving you an 8-ft. ceiling. You can frame an entire house without having to cut any studs that way.
- The next is to use the right lumber once it arrives on site. If you need a 9-ft. piece, don't cut it from a 14-ft. length if there are 10-ft. lengths around.
- There are always scraps piling up. Use them instead of a fresh piece whenever possible for framing smaller openings, for blocking, and at wall intersections.

While most houses use lumber made directly from a tree (solid-sawn lumber), there is a whole world of engineered lumber as well, and this can be a much more efficient use of materials. Engineered joists (often called I-joists because of their profile) can span greater lengths than similarly sized 2x material, and because the strength is in the top and bottom flanges, you can cut large holes in the web for ductwork, drain lines, and so forth without weakening the joist. They work well for rafters as well.

For areas where we need even more strength, laminated veneer lumber (LVL), composed of multiple plies of wood veneer glued together with a very strong resin, is often used in places where we might have previously used either a steel beam or multiple solid-sawn pieces. There also is parallel strand lumber

When dimensional lumber isn't strong enough but steel is overkill, laminated veneer lumber can be used for beams and headers, as is the case with this ridge beam. It will transfer more than 50% of the roof load to posts at each end.

Panels made of cross-laminated timber can be used in residential as well as commercial construction. Here we see CLT panels being installed for a Canadian Passive House project called Wolfe Island Passive House. The CLT panels will be exposed on the interior as the finished surface, and a thick layer of wood fiberboard insulation will cover the exterior.

# Green Building Advisor

If PGH was conceived at our discussion group in Portland, Maine, it was born in the virtual pages of the Green Building Advisor (GBA) website, and the midwife was Martin Holladay, then-editor. Michael wrote up our first session for GBA, and it was immediately clear that we'd tapped into the zeitgeist. Comments on that and follow-up pieces helped us think things through. Martin was our first, and best, cheerleader.

Beyond PGH, though, GBA has made a huge difference in the green building world. Martin was already a well-known and respected writer and researcher in our small corner of the building world. When he took over the launch of GBA, he had already spent a generation looking at what worked and what was the other kind of BS.

The website quickly became an essential part of the community and was immediately a place where current or would-be homeowners could get the opinion and advice not only from Martin (who was endlessly patient and generous, no matter how many times the same questions were asked), but also from the stable of experts who he attracted to the site.

The rapid diffusion of information was remarkable to see. Many clients came to us after already learning the basics of building science from the site. They often knew more than we did on certain subjects. It made the designer-contractor-client collaboration that much more rewarding.

GBA's cross-fertilization with *Fine Homebuilding* magazine improved both organizations. Martin has retired from running GBA but still contributes articles, and of course the book he wrote, *Musings of an Energy Nerd* after his GBA column of the same name, is now essential reading for the good kind of BS.

(PSL), which consists of smaller pieces of wood glued up with the grain oriented for maximize strength. This is good for structural beams and posts. Both use much less wood to get the strength of solid-sawn.

There is a relatively new area of construction using cross-laminated timber (CLT) to build large wooden structures. CLTs are large panels made from many smaller pieces of solid lumber. They are strong, perform better than steel in fires, and allow wood buildings of heights not previously possible, including the 18-story Mjøstårnet in Norway. At 85.4 meters (280 ft.), it is currently the world's tallest timber building.

Before we assume that these engineered products are preferable, though, we need to consider the embodied energy (or carbon) of the materials compared to what they are replacing. Wood is inherently carbon-absorbing, but even with solid-sawn lumber, there is the energy required to harvest, mill, dry, and transport it. And the more we learn about soil science, the more we realize that monoculture tree plantations absorb much less carbon than a thoughtfully managed, selectively cut forest.

With engineered lumber, you need to add in the energy required to make the glues, transport all the components to one place, and assemble the pieces. These kinds of calculations are presumably beyond all but the most dedicated Pretty Good Homeowners, but there are many resources out there (like Green Building Advisor; www.greenbuildingadvisor.com) to help.

# Recycled Content

By and large, recycled content and recyclability are good things. The ability to divert a material from a landfill and reuse it also saves the embodied energy and resources required to make a new version of that product. Topping the list of recycled materials are steel and aluminum.

The American Institute of Steel Construction, or AISC, states that "By weight, 81% of all steel products are recovered for recycling at the end of their life." And that "Steel is the most recycled material in the world, with domestic mills recycling more than 70 million tons of scrap each year. Currently, structural steel includes 93% recycled content!"

Steel's ability to be recycled is one of its greatest attributes (along with its phenomenal durability and strength-to-weight ratio), but as discussed earlier it has very high embodied carbon. Even steel with an 85% recycled content has three to six times as much embodied carbon by weight as non-FSC laminated veneer lumber, thanks mostly to the tremendous heat it takes to forge it. This makes it a difficult material

Hidden steel members will strengthen a wall where big corner windows don't leave enough room for shear walls. (For more on this house, see Case Study 2 on p. 42.)

(For more on this house, see Case Study 2 on p. 42.)

to justify if there's another bio-based, less impactful material that can do its job.

Similarly, aluminum is very high in embodied energy. The recycled content is usually around 80-85%, but because of the amount of energy it takes to produce or recycle aluminum (about four times that of steel) it should be eliminated or at least confined to very discrete areas where its corrosion resistance and malleability are highly advantageous (such as windows).

The hard-pine ceiling of this porch is made from salvaged flooring pulled from the same house.

Where recycled products really shine are in composite materials: plastics, fiberboards, composite claddings, and cellulosic materials. Some great examples are cellulose insulation, acoustic ceiling tiles, composite decking and siding, interior finish boards, even countertops. By and large, the higher the recycled content, the better it is for the environment, so you will likely see a lot of products with high recycled content in a PGH.

The ultimate in recycling is to salvage and repurpose material. This is where the do-it-yourselfer can really make an impact. By shopping at ReStores, architectural salvage stores, or online marketplaces and doing some legwork or applying a little elbow grease, you can find doors, windows, cabinets, flooring, hardware, plumbing fixtures, lumber, and even insulation.

## LOCAL IS GOOD

Just like the local-food movement, buying local building materials supports a local economy and shrinks the length of the supply chain. This usually lowers a material's overall embodied carbon by minimizing transportation distance and reducing the amount of third-party handling the product might need. It can have the added benefit of using local (and potentially cleaner) energy sources. For example, here in New England, if we can use lumber products from a local mill that uses wood from a local forest, not only has transportation been reduced (compared to lumber purchased at a big box store), but the power used to process it came from a relatively clean electrical grid when compared to the Southeast U.S. (For a map that provides average emission rates for the grid subregions in the U.S., go to www.epa.gov/egrid/power-profiler)

This same idea plays out globally. Many of our building products come from overseas. Europe's energy grid is typically cleaner than ours here in the U.S., while grids from Asia are dirtier. Of course, composition of fuel sources varies all over the globe, but this could play a role in your decision making for products.

---

*A PGH should give preference to local products over those that originate from farther away, especially from overseas.*

---

Transportation also can represent a huge percentage of a product's embodied carbon. Bamboo is often touted as a green flooring choice, for example, but choosing a product shipped from China over a locally sourced hardwood floor probably doesn't make sense environmentally

In short, a PGH should give preference to local products over those that originate from farther away, especially from overseas.

# Toxins and Indoor Air Quality

Most Americans spend a lot more time indoors than outdoors, and the indoor air quality of most homes is worse than the air outside. Volatile organic compounds (VOCs) are not always health hazards, but some are—notably, formaldehyde, which occurs naturally in some materials and in the past has often been used as a binder in composite materials. Many petroleum-based products release phthalates, or plasticizers, which are health hazards. Spray foam and other materials release isocyanates, which cause flu-like symptoms or worse. The solution is to use materials that do not contribute to poor indoor air quality, and to use filtered mechanical ventilation, which typically leaves the indoor air quality higher than that of the outdoor air.

The United States has no proactive governing body that regulates toxins in building products. We are at the mercy of the free market (and our litigious society) to act as the guardians of our health when it comes to our built environment. There was a time when there was no Food and Drug Administration. That was until we realized we needed safety standards and clear labeling to protect the public. We are at a similar point in time for building products. They now consist of far more complex compounds and chemicals, many of which are unregulated.

We cannot trust the building industry to prioritize our health over their profit. As PGH builders/designers, we do our best to choose materials that are safe for the homeowner. This is a daunting task, and you're probably thinking to yourself, "I'm a builder not a chemical engineer. How am I supposed to track down every chemical that goes into my building?!" Trust me, you're not going to.

Thanks to pressure from consumers, product specifiers, and rating systems like the Living Building Challenge, a growing number of companies are releasing Environmental Product Declarations (EPDs). These are standardized forms listing the health and environmental impacts of a product, and the more that are issued, the more informed decisions we can make. Don't be afraid to ask manufacturers or distributors for them. At best, they will have one to share. At worst you will be bringing the public's desire for EPDs to their attention.

Some of us have worked extensively with clients suffering from MCS (Multiple Chemical Sensitivities), such as the owner of the Low-Chem House featured in Case Study 7 (p. 178), and have learned to watch for a few things.

There are some trigger words that should immediately make you suspicious. If you hear a material is "mold or mildew resistant," "waterproof" or "water repellent," "nonstick," or "flame resistant," your next question should be, "What's in it?" Chances are you're going to have some homework to find a less-toxic replacement. One resource is the Green Science Policy Institute, which has developed an approach to avoiding toxic chemicals called Six Classes (www.sixclasses.org). As the name suggests, it defines six categories of chemicals to avoid, including PFAS, antimicrobials, and flame retardants.

———— ▬ **A V O I D** ▬ ————

## PFAS OR HIGHLY FLUORINATED CHEMICALS

Highly fluorinated chemicals are typically found in products designed to be stain resistant, waterproof, or (most famously) nonstick. In the building sector, these will often be found in wood-floor finishes, paints and coatings, carpet and tile, and adhesives and sealants. These convenient chemicals perform wonderfully but are known to cause some harmful long-term effects. PFOA or perfluorooctanoic acid, the most studied fluorinated chemical, has been linked to kidney and testicular cancer, elevated cholesterol, decreased fertility, thyroid problems, and decreased immune response to vaccines in children.

In 2008, the phase-out of PFOA began, but most of the replacements are already showing similar detrimental effects. If a product is "PFOA free," don't celebrate without further checking. Another unfortunate feature of highly fluorinated chemicals is that they don't go away. They find their way into our water supply and our food chain and stick around. In fact, the Green Science Policy Institute states that PFAS, chemicals not found in nature, can be found in 98% of humans right now.

———— ▬ **A V O I D** ▬ ————

## ANTIMICROBIALS

If something is antimicrobial, that sounds like a good thing, but if you're sensitive to mold and mildew, chances are good that you're also sensitive to antimicrobial chemicals. These are usually found in household products but can often be found in building products like paints, wall coverings, bathroom

accessories, door hardware, grouts and mortars, ceiling tiles, equipment (like front-loading washing machines), and joint compounds.

Antimicrobials such as triclosan (which also goes by its trademarked name Microban) have been linked to hormone disruption, negative developmental and reproductive effects, and increased allergen sensitivity and asthma. And while triclosan was banned from soap and other household cleaners by the FDA in 2016, it persists in the building industry, where the FDA has no regulatory authority. Many manufacturers have phased triclosan out anyway, but as with PFOA, its replacements may have similar side effects. It is best to avoid antimicrobials whenever possible.

———— ▬ **A V O I D** ▬ ————

## FLAME RETARDANTS

Flame retardants are found in building materials as well as combustible household goods. Applied flame retardants are known to have some harmful side effects and they are incredibly pervasive bioaccumulatives (flame retardants have been detected in nearly all Americans). The effects are most harmful to children and have been linked to developmental and hyperactivity issues. They also have been linked to liver, thyroid, and reproductive cancer. The chemicals of most concern are organohalogens and organophosphates like polybrominated diphenyl ethers (PBDEs) and chlorinated tris (TDCPP).

The building industry takes fire protection very seriously, and ensuring that products and assemblies meet building code is critical to life safety. That said, XPS insulation under a slab doesn't need a fire retardant. Use untreated EPS instead. Flame retardants can also be found in carpets, carpet backings (yes, even the recycled ones), rigid insulation (especially XPS), foam insulation, floor coatings, wood coatings, textiles, and fire-retardant paints. In short, a PGH approach is not to use products treated with flame retardants. Try to use materials that are naturally flame resistant, such as dense-pack cellulose, drywall, or plaster.

--- **A V O I D** ---

## BISPHENOLS AND PHTHALATES

These chemicals are the hardest to avoid. Bisphenols are used to make plastics more rigid and durable. Phthalates are used to make plastics more flexible. There are many chemicals that fall into these two categories each with varying degrees of toxicity. Bisphenols are hormone disrupters. Bisphenol-A (BPA) in particular simulates estrogen and has been linked to asthma and neurodevelopmental problems such as hyperactivity, anxiety, depression, and aggression, especially in children. In adults, it is also associated with type 2 diabetes, heart disease, obesity, prostate cancer, and decreased fertility.

Bisphenols can be found in many household products. In the building industry they can be found where there are clear plastic parts or materials such as polycarbonate sheeting. They can also be found in epoxy resins, coatings, and adhesives.

Phthalates have been shown to cause cognitive deficiencies, behavioral problems, asthma, and allergies and are likely carcinogens. Phthalates can be found in a wide array of building products. Leading the list is PVC (polyvinyl chloride). Not all PVC plastics contain phthalates, but most do. Other products include carpets and carpet backing, vinyl flooring, wall coverings, electric wire jacketing, flexible ductwork, roof and waterproofing membranes, paints and coatings, and adhesives and caulks.

On a building project this is a difficult category to avoid altogether, but a pretty good approach is to use PET, HDPE, and LDPE plastics (recycle numbers 1, 2, and 4, respectively) and avoid PVC (3) and the catch-all code 7 (for any plastic that doesn't fall into the other six classes). For plumbing, you can substitute HDPE pipe for PVC. For electric cable jacketing, you can use MPPE instead of PVC, but you'll quickly find that this is difficult to come by other than in low-voltage wiring.

--- **A V O I D** ---

## SOLVENTS

Solvents are the leading generators of VOCs. In the building industry, they can most often be found in paints and sealants (things that are fluid when applied but will be hardened when dried). Not all solvents are health risks, but hydrocarbon solvents and halogenated organic solvents certainly are. They become dangerous when inhaled, absorbed through skin, or consumed (usually when trace amounts make their way into drinking water). They have been linked to cancer, temporary dizziness, headaches, or *brain fog*, a term used for reduced cognitive abilities.

---

*It's a Pretty Good approach to avoid harsh solvents and VOC-emitting paints and sealants whenever possible, and to opt for water-based and low-emission products.*

---

Thanks to LEED and many other programs bringing the dangers of VOCs to light, almost every paint manufacturer makes a low- or even zero-VOC version of its paint. Some of the tougher exterior coatings, however, still pack a punch of VOCs when applied, and care should be taken when using them. With all of these new cleaner offerings for paints and sealers we now just need to specify them and use them, even if they cost a little more. It's a Pretty Good approach therefore to avoid harsh solvents and VOC-emitting paints and sealants whenever possible, and to opt for water-based and low-emission products.

## AVOID

### CERTAIN METALS

On the periodic table there are many heavy metals that can be harmful to humans, but in the building industry we are really only concerned with four: arsenic, cadmium, lead, and mercury. For the most part, these have slowly been removed from common products, but like a bad penny, they keep turning up. They have been linked to increased cancer risk, neurological disorders, and adverse cardiovascular effects. The young and pregnant and nursing mothers are highly susceptible to these.

For those of us working with old buildings, lead can often be found in roofing and flashing components, pipe fittings, solder, tiles, and, of course, old paint and paint dust. The latter can be difficult to remove safely. If you encounter lead paint, seek professional assistance for abatement.

Mercury can still be found in CFL light bulbs (we're not using those anymore, right?) and was used in paints as late as 1991.

Arsenic once was found predominantly in pressure-treated wood in the form of CCA (chromated copper arsenate), phased out beginning in 2003. If you encounter older pressure-treated wood, there's a high probability that it contains arsenic.

Cadmium still sometimes shows up in paints or resilient flooring. But a builder's most likely encounter with cadmium will come from smoke or fumes from welding and cigarette smoke while on the job.

# Some of Today's Material Choices

We all want products that are affordable, durable, low-maintenance, nontoxic, and sustainably produced. These qualities can be difficult to define precisely. In this section we'll address how they relate to some typical building product categories. (Keep in mind that the authors are from New England, which may play into some of our choices.)

### CONCRETE

As mentioned earlier in this chapter, cement is very high in embodied energy, so it has a very high GWP (global warming potential). Because of this, there has been a trend among planet-conscious builders and designers toward reducing its use where possible. As a result, the popularity of using frost-protected slabs and helical piers as foundation systems has grown in the past few years. Likewise, some designers have gone so far as to eliminate slabs in basements opting instead for a wood floor over sleepers, rigid insulation, and a strong vapor barrier (sometimes called a "slabless slab").

Another way of reducing the GWP of concrete is to replace some of the cement with other ingredients such as slag, fly ash, or pozzolans. Slag is the glass-like byproduct left over after a raw metal has been smelted. Fly ash is the powdery byproduct of coal-fired power plants. The term *pozzolans* covers a wide range of other natural (and man-made) powders derived from magmatic rocks or certain clays and shales. A PGH builder/designer might just put a call into the local concrete plant where they order their concrete and see if there are recipes available that use cement replacements.

### FRAMING

Pretty Good builders/designers prefer wood over metal framing and FSC (or sustainably harvested wood) over wood of unknown origin (see p. 157). Likewise, they will prefer local framing material over materials that have traversed great distances. These choices are more sustainable and support a local economy.

# A NEW TAKE ON SLABS

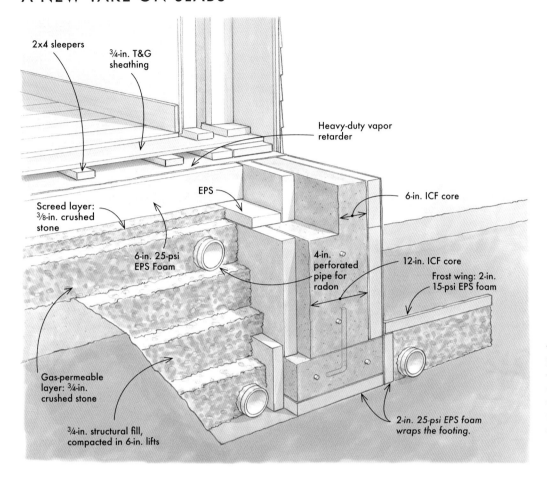

- 2x4 sleepers
- ¾-in. T&G sheathing
- Heavy-duty vapor retarder
- EPS
- 6-in. ICF core
- Screed layer: ⅜-in. crushed stone
- 6-in. 25-psi EPS Foam
- 4-in. perforated pipe for radon
- 12-in. ICF core
- Frost wing: 2-in. 15-psi EPS foam
- Gas-permeable layer: ¾-in. crushed stone
- ¾-in. structural fill, compacted in 6-in. lifts
- 2-in. 25-psi EPS foam wraps the footing.

With a properly compacted base, a concrete-free slab floor can be constructed using EPS rigid insulation, a vapor barrier, and sleepers beneath a subfloor of sheathing.

## SIDING AND TRIM

**Local wood** Lately, we've been leaning toward using local, naturally rot-resistant woods such as eastern white cedar and sometimes stained pine or hemlock. In other parts of the country, local rot-resistant wood might be red cedar, cypress, or even redwood.

**Thermally modified wood** Thermal modification (a.k.a. torrefaction) refers to a heat treatment of wood where the wood is placed in an anerobic (or oxygen-free) kiln. Without oxygen, the wood won't burn but it becomes substantially more resistant to decay and pests. The process transforms less desirable (and less expensive) wood such as poplar into a wood that looks and behaves more like a tropical hardwood.

**Acetylated wood** Acetylization is a pressure-treating process in which wood (usually radiata pine because

Eastern white cedar shingles being installed over a rainscreen matrix. Also visible are aluminum-clad windows and pre-stained spruce vertical siding.

## COMPARISON OF SIDING AND TRIM

| TYPE | Local Wood | Thermally Modified Wood | Acetylated Wood | Fiber Cement |
|------|-----------|------------------------|-----------------|--------------|
| **PROS** | Low embodied carbon, even negative if FSC certified or from a sustainably harvested forest.<br><br>Natural finish means no coatings.<br><br>Local material. | Great looking.<br><br>Highly durable and naturally rot resistant.<br><br>Local material (depending on location).<br><br>Great workability. | Pressure treated without looking like it's been pressure treated.<br><br>Highly durable and rot resistant.<br><br>Takes stains and coatings well.<br><br>Great workability. | Resource efficient—made mostly of silica.<br><br>Can have a high recycled content.<br><br>Durable.<br><br>Fire resistant.<br><br>Affordable.<br><br>Comes in an incredible array of shapes and sizes. |
| **CONS** | Good detailing is required to prevent water damage.<br><br>A natural finish will not age uniformly, a potential drawback.<br><br>If painted, it will need maintenance over time. | Pricey.<br><br>Will not age uniformly based on exposure. Like a natural wood, it grays over time (and rapidly where it is exposed to water) and darkens where exposed to sun.<br><br>If painted, it will need maintenance over time. | Not local (which raises an otherwise low GWP score).<br><br>Will not age uniformly based on exposure. Like a natural wood, it grays over time and rapidly where it is exposed to water.<br><br>If painted, it will need maintenance over time, but less than unacetylated wood. | High embodied carbon.<br><br>Difficult to work with—requires special sheers or sawblades.<br><br>Erupts a cloud of unhealthy dust when cut by power tools.<br><br>Still a painted product.<br><br>Thermal expansion needs to be considered and manufacturer instructions followed. |

The Royal River home, designed by Briburn and built by Taggart Construction, features an entrance canopy with Douglas fir posts and ceiling, FSC Philippine mahogany decking, and torrefied poplar siding. All of the lumber will weather to gray over time.

| TYPE | Engineered-Wood Composite | Fly-Ash Polymer | Vinyl Siding |
|------|---------------------------|-----------------|--------------|
| **PROS** | Affordable.<br><br>Good workability.<br><br>Relatively low embodied carbon. | Highly durable and resistant to moisture.<br><br>High recycled content.<br><br>Easier to work with than fiber cement. | Very inexpensive.<br><br>So leaky that it's naturally venting.<br><br>Easy to install. |
| **CONS** | Nonhomogenous, so end cuts and rips are left rough if exposed.<br><br>Most brands cannot be mitered.<br><br>Short track record.<br><br>Still a painted product.<br><br>Proprietary "resins" are suspect. | Can be "chippy" to work with, so finer saw blades and more care is needed.<br><br>Subject to thermal expansion. | Looks inexpensive.<br><br>Very leaky.<br><br>Ages poorly.<br><br>Toxic to make.<br><br>Extremely difficult to recycle.<br><br>Toxic to dispose of. |

today most acetylated wood comes from New Zealand) is treated with acetic anhydride, an industrial-strength vinegar. It is nontoxic and the process leaves the wood dry and resistant to rot and pests.

**Fiber cement** Fiber cement is made primarily from cement, wood pulp, and silica. We are starting to veer away from fiber-cement products (because of their incredibly high embodied carbon) in favor of other composite sidings.

**Engineered-wood composite** This is a newer and rapidly evolving sector of the siding and trim market where wood composites are shaped into trim and siding profiles. The leading brand in this category is made from wood strands, wax, and an undisclosed binding resin and coated with a zinc-borate primer

(essentially a fancy OSB shaped into siding and trim boards).

**Fly-ash polymer** This type of composite, also known as "polyash," is composed primarily of fly ash (a coal-burning byproduct) mixed with a proprietary polymer binder. It comes in a wide variety of shapes and profiles and is gaining traction in the market.

**Vinyl siding** We rarely use vinyl siding; it is not really a high-quality product and is made from PVC.

# DECKING

If our clients don't mind routine deck maintenance and are less concerned about splinters and minor cupping and twisting, we often suggest local cedar. For projects with bigger budgets, we've been recommending thermally modified (or torrefied) local hardwoods, or acetylated woods with an FSC certification. Also in the higher budget category are higher-end wood or bamboo deck composites. These dense boards usually have the look and feel of an exotic wood species, but with higher durability and stability.

Many deck composites are PVC based, a disadvantage. While some of these composite-decking options are more affordable, they are still not cheap. Manufacturers try to make it look like wood but results are mixed.

We have been avoiding tropical hardwoods altogether because of their negative climate impact. If for aesthetic/durability reasons you or your client insists on a naturally rot-resistant tropical hardwood, you should also insist on FSC certification and avoid

**Spruce decking on the Low-Chem House (see p. 178) was treated with AMF Safecoat EXT sealer.**

woods from unidentified South American plantations. Historically, this particular region has been rife with corruption and sustainability credentials are dubious. Instead, perhaps look to Indonesia or other countries with a good track record of sustainable plantation-farmed hardwoods.

Ipé is a beautiful, very hard, and super durable tropical hardwood. However, because it is an incredibly slow-growing tree and so sought after for high-end decks, it is the cause of immense deforestation. If your clients can afford ipé, they can afford just about any decking on the market. A Pretty Good builder/designer should be able to help those clients to make a better choice.

## PRESSURE-TREATED WOOD

We have been specifying an MCA (Micronized Copper Azole) treatment over the more readily found ACQ (Alkaline Copper Quaternary), Copper Nathenate, or ACC (Acid Copper Chromate). The latter should only be used in extreme exposures such as marine industrial applications when nothing else will do. Chromated Arsenicals (CCA) have been restricted by the EPA, so you're not likely to find them (but if you do, don't use them).

**MCA PROS:**
• Usually kiln-dried so it arrives dry like regular lumber.
• Usually lacks the greenish tint of others.
• Healthier to work with than others.

**MCA CONS:**
• Typically a little more expensive.
• Can be harder to find.

## INSULATION

**Cellulose** Hands down, one of our favorite types of insulation is cellulose, both dense packed and loose fill. It is typically made from recycled paper and wood pulp (and treated with borate). Since most of

the cost is in mobilization and prep work for installation, the added cost of more depth is rather small. As a bio-based product with high recycled content, it can be carbon neutral or even carbon sequestering. Its application is usually to fill cavities (between studs, joists, rafters, etc.). Loose-fill cellulose can be used as attic insulation by being blown on top of the attic floor at whatever depth is desired.

**Fiberglass** Fiberglass is one of the most popular insulation materials, mostly for its affordability and its resistance to rot, fire, and pests. It is available as loose fill and in batts. Only recently has formaldehyde-free fiberglass insulation been available. Even now, if you buy off-the-shelf fiberglass batt insulation, there is a good chance it will contain urea formaldehyde (a known carcinogen) in its binding agents. Even when formaldehyde-free fiberglass is available

It is a rare sight to see three different types of insulation in one photo. Here, cellulose (dense-packed behind polyester mesh) is used as the insulation for the double-stud wall. Closed-cell spray foam is used for the hard-to-reach area between the timber joists, and mineral wool batt insulation fills the ceiling service cavity as acoustic insulation between floor levels.

## COMPARISON OF INSULATION TYPES

| TYPE | Cellulose | Fiberglass | Rigid Extruded Polystyrene (XPS) | Rigid Expanded Polystyrene (EPS) |
|------|-----------|------------|----------------------------------|----------------------------------|
| **PROS** | Relatively affordable.<br><br>High recycled content.<br><br>Low in embodied carbon.<br><br>Good acoustic properties (when packed tightly).<br><br>Inhibits air convection within the insulation cavities. | Affordable.<br><br>Readily available.<br><br>Inert, naturally pest, rot, and fire resistant.<br><br>Comes in many shapes, sizes, and densities. | Relatively affordable.<br><br>High R-value per inch (R-5 per inch).<br><br>Can be used below grade.<br><br>Comes in many different densities.<br><br>Can bear weight.<br><br>Largely unaffected by moisture. | Relatively affordable.<br><br>High R-value per inch (slightly less than XPS).<br><br>Can be used below grade.<br><br>Comes in many different densities.<br><br>Can bear weight.<br><br>Mostly unaffected by moisture.<br><br>Much less embodied carbon than XPS (but still fairly high). |
| **CONS** | Prep work is time-consuming.<br><br>Installation can be very dusty (respirators required).<br><br>Limited to interior (low-moisture) applications.<br><br>Limited to cavity-filling installations. | Glue binders can contain added formaldehyde or outgas VOCs.<br><br>Does not stop convection within a wall.<br><br>Inhaled glass fibers can be harmful; respirators recommended for installation. | Very high embodied carbon equivalent.<br><br>Can contain pesticides or flame retardants.<br><br>Typically cannot be left exposed (due to flame-spread properties).<br><br>Limited to rigid applications. | Lower R-per inch than XPS.<br><br>Typically cannot be left exposed (due to flame spread properties).<br><br>Limited to rigid applications. |

we prefer dense-packed cellulose not only for its better environmental credentials but also because it is a much better draft-stop within the wall cavity.

**Rigid extruded polystyrene (XPS)** High R-value and versatility have made extruded polystyrene board the go-to insulation for many in our industry. However, we have been avoiding it whenever possible because the blowing agents used during the manufacturing process typically have a very high global warming potential (over 700 times that of $CO_2$). Also, XPS is often treated with a flame retardant and an insecticide. This may increase its versatility, but it's usually

Extruded polystyrene (XPS) insulation is often used below a slab, but expanded polystyrene (EPS) is a better choice even if its insulating quality is a little lower.

| TYPE | Mineral Wool | Polyisocyanurate | Wood-Fiber Insulation Board | Spray Foam Insulation |
|---|---|---|---|---|
| **PROS** | Can be used below grade.<br><br>Comes in many different densities, thicknesses, and rigidity.<br><br>Inert, naturally rot resistant.<br><br>Fire resistant.<br><br>Hydrophobic (sheds water without absorbing).<br><br>High recycled content. | High R-value per inch.<br><br>Flame resistant.<br><br>Comes in many thicknesses and facings.<br><br>Inert, naturally rot resistant. | Bio-based product.<br><br>Low embodied carbon.<br><br>Can have high recycled content.<br><br>Nontoxic materials.<br><br>Comes in many different densities, thicknesses, and rigidity. | High R-value per inch (for closed cell, lower for open cell).<br><br>Able to reach tough spots and fill small gaps.<br><br>Vapor impermeable (for closed cell).<br><br>Easy installation. |
| **CONS** | Same R-value as cellulose and fiberglass for higher cost.<br><br>Still often contains added urea formaldehyde in glue binder. | Limited to rigid applications.<br><br>Limited to above grade.<br><br>R-value drops slightly as temperature decreases. | Limited to above grade.<br><br>Very few manufacturers— so costly or increased transportation. | Potentially high global warming potential.<br><br>Potentially toxic (VOCs during install and after if not properly installed).<br><br>Difficult to remove.<br><br>Usually more expensive than other options. |

unnecessary for the common home construction application and only introduces toxins to the project.

**Rigid expanded polystyrene (EPS)** Expanded polystyrene (the stuff that Styrofoam cups are made from) is a better choice than XPS. Its R-value may be less (R-4 per inch), but the expansion gas used in its manufacture is $CO_2$. It also does not have a flame retardant, and an insecticide is added only when specified.

**Mineral wool** Mineral wool is spun basalt and steel slag (an industrial byproduct). It is pressed and shaped into a wide variety of boards and batts. Because it is made of inert materials it is suitable for below-grade applications. And as it is unaffected by water, it can even act as a drainage board on foundation walls. Mineral wool is naturally fireproof, making it an excellent choice against stove flues. Its drawbacks are that it is relatively high in embodied carbon and the binders that hold the fibers together are typically phenol and urea formaldehyde-based. Only recently has the industry begun to offer a mineral wool product with bio-based binders, but these are still hard to come by. For these reasons, we typically relegate this product to exterior use only.

**Polyisocyanurate** Polyisocyanurate is a urethane-based rigid insulation board that doesn't need flame retardants. It is therefore good for exterior roofs and walls. It is porous and therefore not suitable for below-grade installations. While having one of the highest insulative values per inch (R-6.5), it has a unique characteristic in that it loses a little thermal resistance as temperatures decrease (the opposite of what you'd want from an insulation). One reason that

This Passive House project in Connecticut uses fiberboard insulation on the walls and roof to provide a continuous thermal break.

it is often selected by PGH builders is that it comes with different facings such as foil that can act as the water-resistive barrier for an exterior envelope. It also can be found as a salvaged material from commercial re-roofing projects.

**Wood-fiber insulation board** Pretty Good builders and architects all seem to love wood-fiber insulation board. It is a good, bio-based alternative to rigid foam, is extremely low in embodied carbon, and is vapor permeable (which has its advantages at times). The insulation board is composed of fluffed wood fibers pressed together with a paraffin and polyurethane-based resin. It comes in a wide range of thicknesses and densities so it can be used in many applications both inside the home and out. Its only real drawback is cost. Presently there are

only two brands available in the U.S., and they are imported from Europe. However, at least one new manufacturer is beginning production here and is due to begin selling its product in late 2022.

**Spray foam insulation** The world of spray foam insulation is changing rapidly, and for the better. If we were writing this book only five years ago, we would have just said, "Don't use the stuff." Back in the day, all closed-cell spray foams were made with blowing agents with a massive GWP, some as high as 5,000 (5,000 times that of $CO_2$). With the advent of HFC blowing agents, that was reduced to around 700 (still not great). But now there are spray foams on the market using HFO blowing agents with a GWP as low as 1. Now we're talking.

No matter what product you use, spray foam is still toxic to apply and a full hazmat suit with respirator is needed. While that may send a prickly chill down the spine of the chemically conscious, a properly installed spray foam installation should be inert when complete. It will outgas VOCs as it cures but will cease once curing is complete. There have been cases of improperly installed spray foam that have resulted in lingering odors and continual outgassing of VOCs. These cases are rare but very difficult to solve.

Having an R-value of up to 7 per inch and the ability to expand and fill tricky spots makes this a go-to insulation for a lot of builders. Its expense and potential toxicity, however, make it less appealing to others. Some builders and architects erroneously believe that you can air-seal a project with spray foam. Over time, spray foam can shrink at different rates than the adjoining wood and tiny cracks and gaps can occur. A house insulated with spray foam may test well for air sealing on day one, but years later could test much worse.

## PAINTS AND CAULKS

As previously stated, paints can be a significant source of VOCs. Choosing a no- or low-VOC paint is relatively easy, but paint may contain other dangerous chemicals such as binders, anti-bacterials, or fungicides. There are several certification programs trying to help identify paints that aren't destructive to indoor air quality, including Green Seal, Greenguard, the Scientific Certification Systems' Indoor Advantage Gold, and the Allergy and Asthma Friendly Certification Program.

Natural paints, such as milk paint, are readily available. Another approach is not to use paint on the walls and to color a room with pigmented plaster. These are typically more expensive options but yield beautiful results.

Caulk is typically used as a gap filler between different materials (like wood trim and drywall) to seal cracks and seams. Caulking products can off-gas many of the same chemicals as paint. And as with paint, there are many low- or no-VOC caulks. Or simply avoid caulk—its function inside the house is purely aesthetic, and outside it can usually be replaced by flashing, tapes, or gaskets.

In this chapter we've really just scratched the (non-toxic) surface. We learn more every day about new products and methods to improve the performance, sustainability, and our indoor air quality. Fortunately, the level and quality of research and data keep getting better. Builders and designers are finding new, more efficient, and lower-carbon ways to build, and most are eager to share best practices to accelerate the search for lower-impact housing.

## THINGS TO CONSIDER

- Have you thought about the embodied carbon your project represents? Or material substitutions that could lessen the project's climate impact?

- Where do your materials and products come from? Are there local options available?

- Will the products you selected impact the indoor environment? Do they outgas VOCs or contain any of the six classes of chemicals?

- Have you considered the end life of the materials you've chosen? Are they destined for landfill or incinerator, or can they be recycled, downcycled, or easily reused?

- If renovating, can you reuse materials in your renovation? Are you minimizing demolition to keep as much as possible intact?

# Low-Chem House

**This simple Maine home was designed not as an architectural tour de force but as a refuge from unhealthy building materials and other environmental hazards.**

THE OWNER'S HEALTH PROBLEMS, which began while she lived near a bus station in Boston, were originally attributed to mold, environmental toxins such as petroleum, and a virus. Jill was eventually diagnosed with myalgic encephalomyelitis, and her sensitivity to chemical fumes, pollution, and other environmental hazards prompted her to look for a healthier place to live. Jill and her mother began traveling to possible locations where they counted the number of cars that went by, a barometer of how clean the air should be. In Oxford County, Maine, some 125 miles to the north, they found a wooded lot where little traffic passed.

"I think they had one or two cars in an hour," said architect Emily Mottram. "They're remote but still in a good school district for her two children."

The location was half of it. They also needed a house that offered similar advantages, and that meant cutting adhesives and plastics wherever possible. A good start was finding Jesse Stacy, a builder who already was using board sheathing and flooring rather than plywood or oriented strand board.

"That was normal practice for him," Mottram said. "It wasn't more expensive or complicated. Their whole house smelled like pine boards while they were building it. It was absolutely wonderful."

As Mottram and Stacy selected materials and components for the house, Mottram would sometimes ask for samples and scraps—a baggie of cellulose insulation, a bit of gypsum drywall, a piece of Romex electrical cable. She'd box them up and send them to the owner to see if any of the material prompted a reaction. The strategy was to eliminate all possible plastic, adhesives, and potential chemical irritants until no further cuts were practical. Flooring and trim came

**ABOVE** No-VOC paints and finishes help keep indoor air free of toxins. Kitchen cabinets were built by a local artisan who favors solid wood over sheet goods.

**LEFT** Flooring was delivered to the site unfinished, part of a strategy to limit the owner's exposure to chemical irritants.

# FLOORPLANS

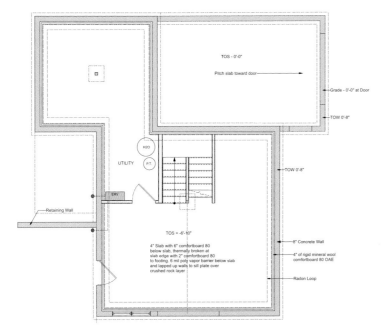

**FIRST FLOOR**

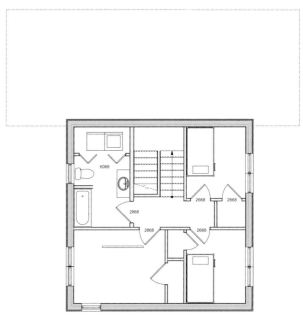

**SECOND FLOOR**

LOCATION: Oxford County, Maine; Climate Zone 6

ARCHITECT: Emily Mottram

BUILDER: Jesse Stacy, Stacy Brothers General Contractors

LIVING AREA: 1,400 sq. ft.

NUMBER OF BEDROOMS/BATHROOMS: 4/2

FOUNDATION: Full basement, poured concrete

FOUNDATION INSULATION: R-15 continuous Comfortboard 80 mineral wool

SUBSLAB INSULATION: R-20 Comfortboard 80 mineral wool

WALL CONSTRUCTION: Double-stud wall

ABOVE-GRADE WALL INSULATION: R-42 dense-pack cellulose

ATTIC FLOOR INSULATION: Vaulted ceiling, R-60 dense-pack cellulose

AIR LEAKAGE (IN ACH50): Unknown

SPACE HEAT: Ductless mini-split heat pumps

DOMESTIC HOT WATER: A.O. Smith heat-pump water heater

MECHANICAL VENTILATION: Broan ERV

PV SYSTEM CAPACITY: None

unfinished; kitchen cabinets were built by a local shop, made with solid wood, and painted with zero-VOC paints. The siding is wood, and Mottram used metal roofing instead of asphalt shingles. The owner went so far as to buy a soy-based release agent for the concrete forms. Mechanical ventilation took care of whatever irritants might have remained in the air.

Mottram makes no claims of architectural grandeur in this compact 1,400-sq.-ft. home. Originally planned as a simple 24-ft.-by-24-ft. two-story box at roughly 1,150 sq. ft., it grew slightly with the addition of a one-car garage and a 14-ft.-by-14-ft. first-floor primary bedroom that the owner's mother could use in the future. The full bath on the first floor will give the house aging-in-place potential.

The double-stud wall design, whose exterior walls and vaulted ceiling are insulated with dense-pack cellulose, is heated with ductless mini-split heat pumps and ventilated with a Broan ERV.

The meticulous attention to detail paid off. Mottram urged the owner to stay mostly away from the job site until the house could be completed and thoroughly cleaned. Since move-in, Jill has experienced no sensitivity problems. But she has enjoyed the views of the White Mountains in the distance. "It's an absolutely perfect spot," says Mottram. "They really lucked out."

A second-floor bedroom with a bunk overlooks a one-car attached garage.

## WHAT MAKES THIS A PRETTY GOOD HOUSE?

- Building products are selected with chemical sensitivities in mind, minimizing or eliminating adhesives, plastic, and petroleum-based components.

- All-electric mechanical systems keep fuel-burning appliances (including wood) out of the mix.

- A superinsulated building enclosure and a compact building design.

- Mechanical ventilation dilutes any remaining indoor air contaminants and keeps air quality high.

- Close collaboration between owner, architect, and builder.

- Carefully chosen site is far from busy roads.

Simple is good: The two-story home comes with a minimum of architectural embellishment but an attention to detail that keeps indoor air quality high.

## Keeping Indoor Air Healthy

Most kitchen cabinets are made with panel goods that contain some type of adhesive. Even when drawer fronts and face frames are solid lumber, cabinet boxes are typically made from particleboard or plywood whose fibers are bonded together with glue—and the glue can be an issue for people with extreme chemical sensitivities. The problem can be minimized if not eliminated by finding a cabinetmaker who works with solid wood throughout and uses low- or zero-VOC paints and finishes to complete the work, as local cabinet maker Henry Banks did for this home. The same logic can be applied to trim and flooring. In this case, those products came unfinished and were finished on site with products like Vermont Natural Coatings.

**TOP** Adhesives used in panel products can be a problem for people with chemical sensitivities. Local cabinetmaker Henry Banks works with solid wood instead, keeping VOC off-gassing to a minimum.

**ABOVE** Flooring and trim were finished on site with products that emit no or low VOCs, including products from Vermont Natural Coatings.

The house sits on a carefully chosen site in rural Maine where nearby vehicular traffic is limited but the views of the White Mountains are not.

# CHAPTER EIGHT

# MECHANICAL SYSTEMS

Mechanical systems include the equipment needed to heat, cool, ventilate, control humidity, deliver clean water, and drain waste water. The primary reason for mechanical systems is occupant comfort and health. For the most part, the building itself doesn't care how warm or cold it is, but humans like the indoor temperature and humidity to be within a certain range. Most people prefer the indoor temperature to be between 65°F and 75°F in winter, and 68°F to 80°F in summer, and for the relative humidity (RH) to be at least 20% and no more than 60%. High humidity exacerbates the risk of mold and fungal growth, so we try to limit indoor relative humidity to 60% or less.

More than one function can sometimes be combined into a single piece of mechanical equipment, but more typically they are separate. Either way, the "system" is as important as the "equipment"; the design is critical or the parts will not add up to a whole.

## Heating

Let's start with the oldest technology: heat. Presumably, a campfire was our first mechanical system, also serving as a stove for cooking meat and the centerpiece of a room for sharing meals. Fire as a source of warmth and comfort is deeply ingrained in our minds, which unfortunately can lead to some poor choices for heating a high-efficiency home.

A central tenet of the Pretty Good House is reducing the amount of heating and cooling required to keep a house comfortable. As our methods have improved, this has gotten easier to achieve. In many cases, the

A common sight in New England—an old, inefficient oil boiler, which has been converted to run on natural gas (methane).

challenge is finding a system that isn't too powerful for the house's needs.

The huge furnaces (which heat air) and boilers (which heat water) many of us grew up with, or still have, produce so much heat that they would only have to run for a short time in a well-built house. While this might sound like a good thing, almost all equipment is more efficient when it runs consistently over longer periods rather than starting and stopping frequently.

Thus, in a PGH, it's especially important to choose equipment carefully. This is typically beyond the ability of a homeowner (or even the builder); mechanical

## Wood Stoves

There is something very emotional about the feel, look, and smell of a wood fire, presumably going back hundreds of thousands of years. PGHs have a tense relationship with wood stoves, as well as with fireplaces, chimneys, and gas fireplaces. First, they are blunt objects functionally. It's possible to regulate the heat from a wood stove, but typically it's within a narrow range, and it's temporary. Most wood or gas stoves will produce a lot of heat quickly. In a PGH, that means the house will get very hot, and you'll either have to quench the fire quickly or open a window.

Second, wood stoves require exhaust. The combustion gases have to leave the building immediately or they will kill you. Those exhaust routes, typically a stove pipe or a chimney, are large, permanent holes in your building, allowing a lot of conditioned air to escape. They are also thermal bridges themselves, extending from outside to inside.

Third, these devices need air for combustion. In a drafty house, there's plenty of air coming in from all sides, but in a tight house, you need to plan for makeup air or you will either choke the fire or, worse, choke yourself if the stove backdrafts. This makeup air is another hole in the house, and another route for cold air to get in.

Finally, wood stoves are combustion sources inside your home. Well-sealed units performing flawlessly may not allow smoke to enter the house, but over time things deteriorate or get knocked loose. That can have deadly consequences.

Plenty of people still favor wood stoves, especially if their land has hardwood timber to harvest or if they live in an area that frequently loses power during the winter. But we do not recommend them, and in fact getting rid of chimneys in a renovation is one of our favorite activities. Save your fire lust for a winter solstice bonfire or a camping trip and enjoy your quietly humming heat pump the rest of the time.

engineers, mechanical contractors, or their suppliers usually figure this out. The essential information for sizing equipment is:

- Where the house is located (for the range of temperatures in a year).

- How big it is (volume to be heated/cooled).

- How it is built (airtightness and R-values).

- The quantity, size, and location of windows and exterior doors, along with their performance numbers.

Other issues, like passive solar, exposure to wind, or the shape of the building, also can come into play, but they are less important.

## CHOOSING HEATING EQUIPMENT FOR A PGH

**Air-source heat pumps** In the past decade or so, air-source heat pumps (ASHPs) have become increasingly popular in the U.S. and many other temperate regions for heating (and cooling) homes. Particularly in a PGH, they have many advantages over the alternatives we discuss later in this section.

---

*Reducing demand by building better is always a better solution than increasing power supply, even if it's through renewables.*

---

First and most important, ASHPs are very energy-efficient when designed and installed correctly. Second, they run on electricity. Burning fossil fuels on site has a long history, but it comes with risks to health and safety and a lot of embodied carbon as well as carbon emissions. With the drastic reduction in the cost of photovoltaic (PV) panels for on-site energy generation, the efficiency of electricity-generating plants, and the option to buy "green" power produced by wind turbines, dams, and solar farms,

most PGHs aim for all-electric energy sources. Whenever we talk about energy sources, though, we want to reiterate that reducing demand by building better is always a better solution than increasing power supply, even if it's through renewables.

Third, ASHPs come in a variety of outputs and configurations. A PGH will have a lower heating and cooling load than most other houses, and finding equipment that works well at low loads can be tricky. Experience has taught us that most systems work better with several outdoor units feeding the indoor units, rather than one large unit for the whole house. This modular approach can make it easier to hit the right balance. Also, ASHPs typically have electronically commutated motors (ECMs), which can modify the power output to match the demand.

You may hear the term *mini-split* used to describe these ASHP systems. Technically, mini-split refers to the simplest configuration: one outdoor condenser unit paired with one indoor unit. More complex configurations are sometimes called *multi-splits*. These are both ductless systems. Some people prefer a ducted system, which allows conditioned air to be delivered directly to more locations and allows for better filtration. Ducted systems also appeal to those who dislike the look of the wall cassettes, which admittedly are large, intrusive, and not terribly attractive. However, there is an efficiency drop in ducted systems, and in a small PGH there may not be a need for much distribution. Conditioned air will remain in the house much longer than in a drafty house, and rooms will tend to maintain similar temperatures. Ducts also take up valuable wall-cavity space, need to be carefully sealed to maintain effectiveness, and are difficult and expensive to clean.

Most units can run in heating and cooling mode. Even here in Maine, summers are already getting longer and hotter, and more and more clients are requesting cooling capacity. It is much cheaper and easier to install one ASHP system than one heating system and one cooling system.

The air-source heat pump unit on the right is a "mini-split" that feeds one wall cassette in the kitchen/living room. The larger unit on the left is a "multi-split" feeding several bedroom units.

**ABOVE** This ducted system has ductwork hidden in the soffit above the cabinets. The grills, from Architectural Grille, are installed with the drywall. They are easy to clean and provide a sleek, flush look.

**LEFT** Ductless mini-split systems that include wall- or floor-mounted indoor units are easier, and cheaper, to install than ducted systems.

## How Can There Be Heat to Pump When It's 10° Outside?

This is a question that skeptics sometimes ask about ASHPs. Molecules that exist as a gas at normal temperatures can be forced to turn into a liquid under high pressure. As the liquid is forced through an expansion valve, it turns back into gas that rapidly cools as it expands, absorbing heat from the surrounding air. By controlling whether the refrigerant evaporates and condenses inside or outside, we can either heat or cool the house. These refrigerants turn from liquid to gas at a very low temperature (down to boiling temperatures of about -40°F [-40°C]). Thus, even in the depths of a New England winter, the outside air is still warm enough for the refrigerant to evaporate, albeit at lower efficiency. Don't believe it when people say heat pumps don't work in cold weather!

ASHPs have become ubiquitous, especially in efficient homes. This makes the contrarians among us a little nervous. The quality of both design and installation varies widely. A single loose fitting, allowing refrigerant to escape, can easily outweigh the environmental benefits of the energy efficiency. Many older refrigerants are very dangerous greenhouse gases. Newer-generation refrigerants are much less destructive, and in fact $CO_2$ itself, first used as a refrigerant in the 19th century, is making a comeback both for its useful properties and for its benign effects on global warming in this application.

Longevity is another concern. One advantage of a traditional boiler is that it's basically a big hunk of cast iron with a flame and some pumps. They can typically last 50 years or more. Heat pumps have a much shorter life span and rely on sophisticated electronics

and fans to operate. On the other hand, since there's no combustion, they require much less maintenance than boilers or furnaces.

Even with the caveats, ASHPs make sense for a PGH. They also are relatively cheap to purchase and install, and the carbon payback, compared with other systems, is very fast, depending on what is generating the electricity that runs them.

**Ground-source heat pumps** Air-source heat pumps are so named because they use air as the medium where heat is gathered and waste heat is dumped. There also are ground-source heat pumps (GSHPs), which typically use pipes buried in the ground or in a body of water as the heat source. They take advantage of relatively stable temperatures in a water source or in the earth to warm and cool interior space. They are not the same as geothermal systems, which pull heat from hot springs or other uncommonly warm areas underground.

GSHPs have their adherents, but as the price and efficiency of ASHPs improve it gets harder to make their case. GSHPs require significant excavation to bury the lines, and the pumps that move the water often draw enough power to use up any energy saving elsewhere. On the positive side, they have been in use longer than ASHPs and are a well-understood technology. If you're doing a lot of excavation, or have a pond on your property, a GSHP may make sense.

**Radiant heat** Living spaces can be heated by water that circulates through tubing in the floor. It's easy and inexpensive to bury the tubing before concrete is placed for a slab-on-grade (see the photo on p. 8), and it provides an invitingly warm surface in the winter. Polished concrete can be beautiful as a finished floor and can be dyed or stamped as well. There are also several systems that allow you to easily install radiant tubing under wood flooring, tile, or stone.

The hot water for a radiant system is supplied either by a boiler or sometimes just by a water heater if the demand is low enough. Either of those can be gas- or

Schluter's Ditra Heat radiant-floor system is both a decoupling membrane to prevent tile and grout cracking and a grid for the electric heat (dark lines). The heating cable snaps into the space between the studs on the membrane, and tile is laid in thinset over the mat.

electric-fired. All of the authors used radiant systems in our early high-efficiency homes. But it became clear that a radiant system can produce more heat than the house needs.

This type of radiant system is also very slow to respond. An early house of Dan's had a radiant slab; the client went on a vacation and turned the thermostat down during her absence. She called a day or two after her return and complained that her house was still cold and that she had no hot water. The combined heat and hot water system was still struggling to warm up her concrete slab. These systems work best if you want the same temperature everywhere, and just leave the thermostat alone for the entire heating system.

It is often claimed that radiant heat is somehow more efficient than other systems, or that you can keep your house cooler because the floor is warm. In our experience, neither is true.

You can also create a radiant floor with an electric heat mat. This would be expensive and inefficient over a large area, but we often use this system in bathrooms to provide occasional supplemental heat. Both Schluter and Laticrete, the major suppliers of tile waterproofing and backing materials, have very user-friendly radiant floor systems and most tile installers have experience with one or both (see the photo above).

**Furnaces** Furnaces are the most common heating system in the U.S. Typically with gas (or oil) but sometimes with electricity, a furnace heats air and sends it out through supply ducts to the various areas of a house. Cooler air goes back to the furnace through return ducts so it can be reheated and redistributed. These systems are called *forced hot air (FHA)*. Filters

## A COMPARISON OF HEATING SYSTEMS

| Type | Pros | Cons | Powered by | Ability to meet low load* | Ease of install* | Cost to operate |
|------|------|------|-----------|---------------------------|------------------|-----------------|
| ASHP | Efficient, all electric | Shorter lifespan | Electricity | 5 | 4 | $ |
| GSHP | Efficient, all electric | Pumps can kill efficiency | Electricity | 5 | 1 | $$ |
| Radiant | Warm floors | Very unresponsive | Various | 3 | 3 | $$$ |
| FHA | Flexible, easy to damp up and down | Oversized for PGH, need room for ductwork | Gas typically | 2 | 1 | $$$ |
| Hydronic | Easy to zone, easy to modify | Oversized for PGH | Gas or oil | 2 | 2 | $$$ |
| Wood stove | Can harvest own fuel, no need for power | Very hot or very cold; source of particulate; requires chimney/stove pipe | Firewood, pellets | 1 | 5 | $ |

* Best (5) to Worst (1)

help remove particulates and allergens from the circulating air and must be replaced on a regular schedule.

The ductwork for the furnaces can do double duty for an air-conditioning system. Neither system, though, provides ventilation, and the ductwork is very rarely sized for the different airflow requirements of a ventilation system.

FHA systems are very responsive and can be zoned to deliver to many different rooms. The efficiency of older furnaces isn't that great, and the ducts require a lot of interior space. Because of that, either the furnace, the ducts, or both are often located outside the conditioned space, usually in the attic. They lose significant amounts of heat before it can be delivered to where it's needed. And since ducts are difficult to air-seal well, they are not only losing heat from cold ductwork, they are also pumping hot air out through the cracks (in cooling climates, of course, they are absorbing heat and blowing cool air out). The ductwork is expensive to install and zoning is very hard to get right, and while the filtration is a significant advantage, if the clients don't replace or clean the filters they can in fact worsen air quality. Finally, forced-hot air systems are usually oversized for a PGH, reducing their efficiency even more, so they are typically not a good choice.

Here in Maine, *hydronic* systems are much more common than forced hot air. Also called forced hot water, the typical hydronic system involves a sealed system pumping hot water from the boiler to radiators throughout the house, then returning the cooled water to the boiler to be reheated. There are many different types of radiators, from the cast-iron beasts we see in older houses to European-style panel radiators to radiant heat (where the floor is essentially turned into a radiator). Hydronic systems are easy to zone; some systems allow you to adjust the temperature at the radiator, allowing for more control. Hydronic systems are also relatively cheap and easy to install.

# Cooling (Air Conditioning)

The planet is heating up, faster than we thought it would. As this chapter was taking shape in 2021, the Pacific Northwest in the U.S. was not just breaking but destroying heat records. Portland, Oregon, hit 113°F. Temperatures in Portland, Maine, were well into the 90s in June, a rare occurrence. Historically in Maine, the ocean breezes, the mountains, the tree cover, and, of course, the northern latitude help keep summers mild. Even in August, average highs in Portland rarely hit 90°F, and average lows are often below 60°F. But summer heat advisories are becoming increasingly common.

This obviously points to the need for immediate action on global warming, but it also means that many of us are including or retrofitting air conditioning (AC) in our projects, often for the first time.

As with heating, the best first response for a PGH is diminishing the load (see Chapter 4 for more info). Overhangs that block summer sun but let in lower-angle winter sun, deciduous trees or vines that only block the sun when there are leaves, thoughtful use of windows, shades, and low-e coatings, and, of course, insulation and air sealing will all keep your

# Designing and Commissioning the Mechanical System

For the most part, a Pretty Good House seeks to simplify high-performance building by providing rules of thumb and guidelines. When it comes to heating and cooling systems, however, rules of thumb don't work very well. Some form of energy modeling is necessary. Building codes usually require ASHRAE Manual J calculations to determine room-by-room heat loss. The results can be accurate, but the calculations often are fudged to make things easier for the supplier or contractor. Oversizing equipment is often not desirable, as heat pumps work most efficiently near their maximum capacity and their efficiency drops off dramatically if oversized. Oversized air conditioners can't dehumidify the air effectively.

No matter which system you choose to heat, cool, or ventilate, designing the system carefully is critical. If you have enough heat capacity to meet the absolute coldest temperature you'll ever hit, which might be only 15 hours per year, your system will be oversized the other 364 days and 9 hours. Instead, we use what's called a design temperature. It is typically a temperature linked to a percentage of the year on which it will occur.

For example, the ASHRAE manual lists Portland, Maine's design temperatures for heating as -1.7°F (-18.7°C) / 99.6%, and 3.2°F (-16°C) / 99°. This means that, on average, the temperature is above -1.7°F 99.6% of the year, and above 3.2°F 99% of the year. Some

charts will also include the number for 98%. For cooling, our numbers are 86.7°F (30.4°C) / 0.4% and 83.3°F (28.5°C) / 1%, meaning, again, that temperatures are above those temperatures for those percentages of the year.

At the opposite end of design is making sure your systems are performing as designed. Are the heat pumps running at the expected rate? Is the ventilation moving the expected amount of air? It is a step often overlooked but critical, especially in a high-performing home, where efficiencies can easily be lost due to poorly functioning equipment. We cover what is involved in detail in Chapter 10 on verification and client education.

Verifying that equipment is operating as designed is called "commissioning," which can be done by the contractors who installed the equipment, the manufacturer, or a third-party auditor. But it is critical that it be done, and the results recorded. It is a good time, as well, to make sure that the homeowner understands things like maintenance schedules, filter replacement or cleaning, and who to call for servicing or repairs. Make sure you have a plan for commissioning before contracting for the work to be done. If the installer isn't planning on doing it, tell them you are planning on it and they will need to make corrections if the equipment isn't performing to specs.

cooling load down. Simple things help: opening the windows at night to flush the house with cooler air, then closing them during the day to keep the hotter air out; choosing a lighter roof color in hot climates to reflect heat; and using fans to cool off individuals rather than the whole house.

If it's really hot for days (and nights) straight, even a PGH will sooner or later heat up uncomfortably. If you're heating with air- or ground-source heat pumps, you already have a source of air conditioning. Essentially you are just reversing the operation of the system, capturing heat from inside and releasing it outside. As with heating, a cooling system needs to be designed to match the load, and the design criteria may not be the same.

All AC units are, in fact, heat pumps. The big outdoor units you are used to seeing are doing essentially the same work as the outdoor units of a mini-split. Their efficiency has improved significantly in the past decade. They pair well with forced-hot air systems, using the same ductwork. The systems that aren't heat pumps are typically called *evaporative (or swamp) coolers*, and they use the cooling effect of evaporating water instead of refrigeration. They are simpler, cheaper, and more efficient than heat pumps in dry climates (and are fairly easy to make yourself), but much less effective and can worsen humidity.

If you need to cool only one room (like a home office or bedroom), a window unit can make sense. As with other systems, make sure you air-seal well and change or clean the filters. EPA's Energy Star is a good guide to units' efficiencies.

However you cool your PGH, be aware of humidity. As we know from the classic example of summer condensation on a soda can, warm, moist air will condense on a cold surface. The magic number here is the dew point. A function of relative humidity and temperature, the dew point is the temperature at which water vapor will condense into liquid on a surface. And we know that condensation inside your

house can cause all sorts of problems, mold and rot chief among them.

To stay above the dew point, you can either keep the house hot enough (above the dew point temperature) or drop the humidity (thus lowering the dew point). In a hot, humid climate, the summer dew point can be above 70°F, and at 90°F and 72% relative humidity (which can happen in humid parts of the U.S. in summer), the dew point temperature is 80°F.

Additionally, at the warmer end of the range that humans like, humid air is much less comfortable than dry air at the same temperature. We cool our body by sweating: it is much easier for our bodies to get rid of that sweat through evaporation in drier air. "It's not the heat, it's the humidity" is, in fact, exactly right.

## DEHUMIDIFICATION

Dehumidification is an essential complement to cooling in humid climates. Most air conditioners, including heat pumps, can handle dehumidification. They simply blow the warm, humid air over the cold coils (this is what produces the drips that invariably fall on your head as you walk under a unit). Central AC systems may have add-on dehumidifier units (and, for that matter, humidification units, for arid climates or for heating season in cold climates).

As with short-cycling in a heating system, a potential problem with a PGH is that your cooling system won't run long enough to dehumidify the air. This can kick the unit into "dry" mode, which steeply drops the temperature of the coils to condense more water vapor from the conditioned air, using significant energy in the process. You can also use a standalone dehumidifier, but these need to be emptied or plumbed to a drain, and typically do a good job of dehumidifying the immediate area but not the whole house. Many older homes in Maine have damp basements, and it's not uncommon to have a dehumidifier running in them much of the year. Dehumidifiers can be significant energy users, so research carefully if

you go that route. If you will need to dehumidify the house frequently, a separate system with its own ductwork will be much more effective and efficient.

Humidity, of course, can be a problem year-round. Other than water leaking in from outside, indoor humidity is the most destructive source of moisture and must be managed. Much of it comes from simply occupying the house—cooking, bathing, cleaning, watering plants, pets, and simply breathing. Inexpensive digital hygrometers (devices that measure relative humidity) can help you monitor humidity levels. Typically, houses are best kept between 30% and 50% relative humidity. In winter, falling below 30% can lead to all the problems of dry air (cracked skin, bloody noses, etc.). In summer, rising above 60% can lead to condensation and comfort problems. An excessively dry house is not dangerous to the structure in the way an excessively humid one is.

## VENTILATION

Ventilation is the final piece of the HVAC equation. We want to get excess humidity out of our house ASAP, in any season, before it can cause problems. In a kitchen or bathroom, it is relatively simple and common to install a range hood and a bath fan. These units should be vented to the exterior—recirculating, ventless range hoods or bath fans vented into the attic are ineffective at best, destructive to your house or health at worst. Fans should have effective dampers to prevent outdoor air from blowing in when the fans aren't running.

Research into indoor air quality (IAQ) has been a huge help for builders and designers in the past decade or two. The most commonly used standard

**TOP** Ductwork for a standard range hood can exit either through the back and then go up or down the wall cavity, or through the upper cabinet into the floor cavity above. Venting to the exterior is critical, as is sealing the ductwork and making sure the backdraft damper operates freely.

**LEFT** Island ranges are always tough to ventilate. Island hoods are the best solution, but must be thought out carefully and tested to make sure they are functioning.

for ventilation is called ASHRAE 62.2. ASHRAE is the American Society of Heating, Refrigerating and Air-Conditioning Engineers, and Standard 62.2 is titled *Ventilation and Acceptable Indoor Air Quality in Residential Buildings*. It is the basis for most building code ventilation requirements.

The foreword states that "The standard describes the minimum requirements to achieve acceptable IAQ via dwelling-unit ventilation….Dwelling-unit ventilation is intended to dilute the unavoidable contaminant emissions from people, materials, and background processes."

The kitchen is a major contributor to poor IAQ. If you have a gas stove, the combustion exhaust (including carbon monoxide and formaldehyde) is an issue before you even begin cooking. We often recommend induction stoves, since they are all electric, very safe, and energy efficient.

Even without combustion, cooking produces fine particulate (objects small enough to pass through your lungs into your bloodstream), airborne hydrocarbons (some of which are carcinogenic), and other pollutants. There are three effective strategies we've found: ducted range hoods, salads, and take-out.

*No matter how careful you are to build your house with healthy materials, there is still a need for ventilation.*

Assuming you'll tire of the latter two eventually, let's focus on range hoods. There are two parts to gauging how well they exhaust: air movement and capture area. The first is measured in cubic feet per minute (cfm). There are various rules of thumb for sizing

With a makeup air kit, a pressure switch in the range hood's exhaust duct opens a gate when the fan starts, allowing fresh air in. When the fan is turned off, the gate closes to keep cold air out. In this case, outdoor air is pulled through a duct beneath the floor.

these fans. In a PGH, we recommend a fan with a capacity of 300 cfm, strong enough to ventilate but not overpowering.

In a reasonably airtight home, there is another complication. Unless there is a hole somewhere letting in as much air as you're trying to exhaust, your range hood or bath fan isn't going to do much. In a drafty house, there are plenty of places for that makeup air to come in, but in a PGH you need to plan for it.

There are various ways to provide makeup air, but increasingly we are using a relatively simple method that does a good job sealing itself when not in use. It is a duct from the exterior with an electric damper. It is wired so that it opens when the range hood turns on and closes when turned off. Where to bring this air in is, naturally, the subject of some debate. Some argue for bringing the air in close to the range hood, so you are not cooling down the whole room. Others argue for bringing it in under the refrigerator, to cool down the coils and help it run better. ASHRAE currently recommends bringing 60% in through the kitchen, the rest from elsewhere in the house. This is another area of research; hopefully we will have more definitive information someday soon.

More and more range-hood manufacturers are now selling makeup air kits, which makes planning and installation much simpler. (Note that the building code doesn't require makeup air unless the fan moves more than 400 cfm—which rules out most bath fans).

Another consideration is how effectively a range hood captures airborne pollutants. If pollutants from cooking don't end up in the hood, the fan is just exhausting fresh conditioned air. The effective capture area is a function of fan speed, shape of the hood, distance from the range surface, and size of the stove.

The best hood would be a foot wider than the range in all directions and about 10 in. above the burners. This would make it a little tough to cook, though, so we make compromises. The smaller the hood and the farther away from the stove, the more ineffective it is.

## Checking the Capture Area of a Range Hood

An easy way to check how well your hood is venting is with a smoke stick or similar device. These are inexpensive pen-sized tubes with a wick that produces nontoxic smoke. It's easy to see if the released smoke is going into, or around, the hood. By releasing smoke in various locations around the stove, you will start to see the boundaries of your capture area.

A TEC Fog Puffer is useful for testing a range hood's capture area. It creates visible fumes like a smoke stick but is safer and doesn't leave smoky odors.

The ductwork for this bathroom fan/light vents directly to the exterior and is within the insulated shell the whole way, reducing the chance of condensation. It is also carefully sealed to make sure no humid air leaks inside the house.

This is especially true for island hoods, which have to draw air from all four sides and don't have the backsplash or flanking upper cabinets to help direct air into the hood.

Bath fans are simpler but still require some thought. In a cold climate especially, the warm, humid exhaust air from your shower can easily condense in the exhaust ductwork, and you want to make sure that cold condensate doesn't drip back on your freshly shampooed hair or pool in the ductwork and grow mold or mildew. With a unit that vents out through a wall, make sure that the ductwork pitches slightly toward the exterior, so condensate can escape. Also, assemble the ducts so that the connections funnel water out of the house.

It is trickier if your only option is vertical, either through the roof or with a significant rise before turning horizontal. Your best bet is to make sure that the ductwork stays warm (and thus above the dew point) by careful insulation and air sealing. A more powerful motor, or an additional in-line fan closer to the exterior, can help ensure that the exhaust keeps moving and has less chance of condensing.

## WHOLE-HOUSE VENTILATION

Now that we've taken care of the major sources of airborne pollutants and moisture, what about the rest of the house? We've all heard that a house needs to breathe, right? Well, wrong. A house is not a living organism and thus has no need to breathe. What it needs to do is stay dry. Occupants, on the other hand, do need to breathe. A whole-house ventilation system helps with both.

In most older homes, the ventilation system is the air moving into and out of the house via drafts. You don't really know where the intake air is coming from, or the exhaust air is going to, so you may have good or bad IAQ depending on which way the wind is blowing and how hard. Is it pulling air from the meadow next door or from the moldy crawlspace? Is it pushing to the exterior or into a wall or ceiling cavity?

Once you start doing a better job air sealing, whether in a PGH or a Pretty Good Reno, you need to be more deliberate. In bedrooms, $CO_2$ from respiration can easily build up to unhealthy levels overnight. During the many hours of the day when neither the bath fan nor the range hood is running, there are still indoor pollutants that need to be diluted and moisture that needs to be exhausted. The way to address this is through a well-designed ventilation system. The essential elements are that the system is:

- Balanced (the same amount of air that is being exhausted also is entering).

- Comprehensive (all areas of the house are getting adequate ventilation).

- Room-specific (it's better to supply some rooms and exhaust others; especially true with supplying bedrooms and exhausting bathrooms and kitchens).

- Sized right.

- Carefully ducted:

  ➤ Run as short and as straight as possible. Excessive length and bends significantly reduce airflow.

  ➤ Rigid metal or plastic. If you need flexible ductwork to make a difficult-to-access connection, like at a dryer, keep it as short as possible.

➤ Within the conditioned space. Going from warm interior to cold attic and back again (or the opposite in summer) wastes considerable energy.

➤ Airtight. All ductwork should be air-sealed at all connections with either a duct mastic or mastic tape.

There's a catch: there is an energy penalty. In pleasant weather, opening windows may provide enough ventilation. But once the weather is hot, cold, or humid enough that you close the windows, any ventilation by definition involves an exchange of conditioned air (cooled, heated, or dehumidified) with unconditioned air. Once conditioned air is exhausted, the incoming air must be heated, cooled, or dehumidified. So the goal should be sufficient ventilation but not over-ventilation. ASHRAE 62.2 or whatever your building code requires is a good place to start. A simple air-quality or $CO_2$ monitor can help adjust the system once it's in place.

**Heat- and energy-recovery ventilation** The most common systems for providing balanced ventilation are heat- and energy-recovery ventilators. Heat-recovery ventilators (HRVs) have heat-exchanging cores that capture as much as 90% of the heat in the

## HEAT-RECOVERY VENTILATOR

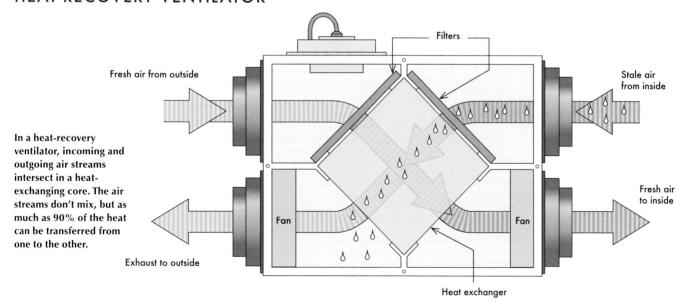

Fresh air from outside

Filters

Stale air from inside

In a heat-recovery ventilator, incoming and outgoing air streams intersect in a heat-exchanging core. The air streams don't mix, but as much as 90% of the heat can be transferred from one to the other.

Fan

Fan

Fresh air to inside

Exhaust to outside

Heat exchanger

This sophisticated Zehnder ERV brings in fresh air and exhausts indoor air via the large black ducts. The heat is exchanged inside the white unit, and the metal manifold on top distributes the supply lines and collects the return lines using Zehnder's proprietary "comfotube" ductwork.

## Can I Use My Heating or Cooling Ductwork for Ventilation?

While it would be wonderful to run only one set of ducts, the short answer is no. With rare exceptions, the requirements for duct sizing and delivery are different enough that it would reduce either the effectiveness or the efficiency of a ventilation system such that it would be ineffective, overventilate, or use ridiculous amounts of energy to operate.

Most systems are ducted from a central unit to the main spaces in the house, exhausting from areas that create moisture and odors and supplying to living and sleeping areas. Others are point-source ventilators, meaning they ventilate single rooms. Which system is best depends on many factors, including climate, occupancy, and whether bathrooms are on the same system as the rest of the house.

Some homes use exhaust-only ventilation, essentially leaving a bath fan running on low speed continuously. This usually saves money initially, but the energy saved using balanced ventilation eventually pays for itself, and because the incoming air is filtered instead of coming in through random gaps in the structure, the indoor air quality should be higher as well.

Much (virtual) ink has been spilled on whether and where to use an HRV or an ERV, but in the end the quality of the unit itself, along with the installation and the maintenance of the unit and ductwork, outweighs any advantage of one system over the other.

airstream, effective in both winter and summer. With an energy-recovery ventilator (ERV), moisture also is transferred, making dry outdoor air more humid in the winter and moist outdoor air less humid in the summer. A couple of systems are available that can switch between the two functions.

# Hot Water System

As we do a better job of reducing heating and cooling loads, we discover that the lowly hot water system often becomes the largest single energy consumer. The two basic methods for delivering hot water are storage and on-demand. The typical hot water heater with a big tank is the most common version of a storage type, either gas- or electrical-fired. On-demand systems also are called tankless. Typically, these are suitcase-sized, wall-hung units that take cold water and quickly bring it up to temperature but have no tank for storing hot water. Tankless units can also be gas- or electrical-fired, and sometimes very small units are placed directly at point of use and supply only that sink, washing machine, or shower.

Design and layout decisions can help the hot water system perform better. The first, as is often the case with a PGH, is to keep it simple. The shorter the runs from the water heater to the faucet, the faster hot water will be delivered and the less water will have to be heated. Keep bathrooms, kitchen, and laundry as close together as you can. Stack the second-floor bath over the first-floor bath. In a compact system, use a manifold delivery system, where a large (1 in. or ¾ in.) line feeds a central manifold from the water heater, and then smaller lines distribute the water to various fixtures. In a more spread-out layout, a typical trunk-and-branch (multiple ¾-in. lines feeding a smaller set of fixtures) will get hot water faster and thus waste less waiting for it.

You may want to consider a drainwater heat-recovery system. As with HRVs and air, these systems capture heat from hot water going down the drain. Typically, a heat-recovery system consists of copper pipes wrapped around the drain line. Savings of up to 20% on energy consumption are possible, but you need a fair amount of space below the drain line, and these systems must be carefully planned before plumbing is roughed in.

A carefully organized plumbing system can save water and energy. This manifold system is one method.

Insulating hot water lines can help, too, at least up to a point. It will help hot water stay hot on the way from the water heater to the fixture but will only slow, not stop, the loss of heat in lines that sit unused for a while. (On a related note, insulating cold water lines can help keep condensate from forming on them, especially if you have well water or another particularly cold water source. Inside a wall, this condensate can cause mold or rot.)

Turning down the temperature on your water heater can make a significant difference as well. It obviously takes less energy to heat water to 120°F than 140°F. If you need to temper your hot water with cold to use it safely, you can (and should) turn the temperature down.

What type of water heater to choose? Heat-pump water heaters make a lot of sense. These units are extremely energy efficient in heat-pump mode, but slow to recover. They can be run in "electric heater" mode, which means they operate like a standard electric water heater, heating via an electrical heating coil. This is faster but no more efficient than any other

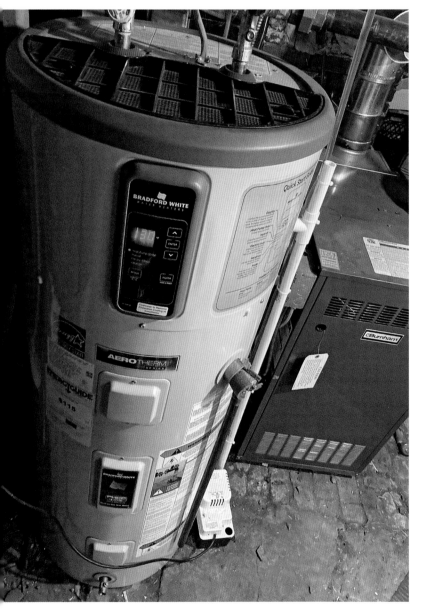

LEFT A heat-pump water heater uses a small heat pump to supply hot water to a well-insulated storage tank.

ABOVE This tankless water heater supplies hot water on demand, without storage. It's a good choice for a house with low or occasional consumption.

water heater. There also is a "hybrid" mode, which uses the heat pump unless demand picks up. These units cool and dry the air around them, so they need a lot of airflow, which doesn't work in every house.

When demand is low, a tankless on-demand system may provide enough hot water. The advantage of tankless units is cost, longevity, and relatively simple construction. They also can help when space is at a premium; since you don't have a storage tank, their footprint is insignificant in comparison. However, they are inefficient and require either having a combustion appliance or a large power supply.

*Cheaper isn't always better. Make sure you and your installer are confident that you're picking something that will last.*

If you are consistently using more hot water (usually because of household size), you are probably better off with a storage unit, which refers to any unit with a tank. You will always have a significant supply of hot water ready to go. Gas-fired water heaters are available, but we rarely use them. They are more expensive, require venting and servicing, and are another combustion source inside the house. The standard electric hot water heater with a 50-gal. tank is cheaper, easier to install, and will last at least as long.

With the great advances in photovoltaic panels, we never do solar hot water systems anymore. When we did, we combined a large, well-insulated storage tank with a small on-demand water heater. What little demand the solar hot water system didn't meet, the on-demand could.

Cheaper isn't always better. Make sure you and your installer are confident that you're picking something that will last. Water heaters can sometimes be installed by a talented homeowner, but most will

require one or more licensed professionals, and possibly also a permit from your municipality.

No matter how good the equipment gets, the essential lesson of reducing demand remains. A well-insulated and air-sealed home will be more comfortable to begin with, and by reducing demand you can both simplify and shrink the size (and cost) of your equipment, helping to pay for the better construction methods. The HVAC industry is in the midst of some huge changes. It is safe to assume that much of the technology discussed here will either be improved upon or obsolete before too long, so make sure you or your contractor stays abreast with current best practices.

## THINGS TO CONSIDER

- Know your demand! More is not better with heating and cooling—don't oversize your equipment. Running often is better than running too infrequently.

- Try to design away some of the load, with careful siting, strategic placement of windows and overhangs, and, of course, obsessive insulation and air sealing.

- A tight house requires ventilation. Make sure you have controlled air coming in to make up for the air you're exhausting.

- Cooling needs to be coupled with dehumidification. Cool, moist environments lead to condensation, mold, and rot.

- The different equipment can either work together or at cross-purposes. Together is better. Think through your mechanical system design *before* you begin construction.

- With renovations, when possible make improvements before replacing your aging HVAC system, then replace with equipment sized for smaller loads.

# Meadow View House

A metal roof and exterior cladding of Corten steel will help protect this house in the foothills of the Sierra Nevada mountains from wildfires. The simple rectangular shape and gable roof give the house a conventional flavor.

THIS HIGH-PERFORMANCE HOME in the foothills of California's Sierra Nevada mountains is a blend of modernist and conventional styles that suits both the architect who designed it for his family and his wife who grew up in an upstate New York farmhouse. It has a barnlike gable-roof design with a building enclosure and mechanical systems that are thoroughly up to date.

After working as an architect in southern California, Jeff Adams left city life behind and moved north. He joined Atmosphere Design Build in Grass Valley where he embraced the sustainable building principles and energy-efficient designs the company specialized in. The three-bedroom Meadow View House grew out of his interest in putting those ideas to work. Adams was lucky enough to find an ideal location—a

**ABOVE** The exterior may mimic the classic lines of a barn, but the interior has a more modernist feel with an open floor plan, simple trim, and broad exterior views.

**LEFT** The house has a single full bathroom, located on the second floor, that will serve the entire family. It incorporates a separate room for a claw-foot tub where a hot soak comes with great views.

lot at the top of a knoll that had once been ranched and provided both expansive views and good solar exposure.

The 1,986-sq.-ft. house is rectangular, with a wrap-around porch on three sides of the building and strategically placed cutouts to mark recessed doorways. These details make the simple shape of the house more interesting visually without making it unnecessarily complex or fussy. On the ground floor, an entry hall leads to a mudroom and half-bath on one

side and a wide-open kitchen and great room on the other. Upstairs, Adams worked in three bedrooms while finding room for a tub room and a book nook.

Material selection in this wildfire-prone region is an important part of the design. Steel roofing meets cool-roof objectives and is also highly fire-resistant. Exterior walls are made of Corten steel, which will weather naturally, require little to no maintenance, and also is fire-resistant. Although steel has high embodied carbon, it's also easy to recycle. Stucco

# FOUNDATION DETAIL

**FACE OF FRAMING**

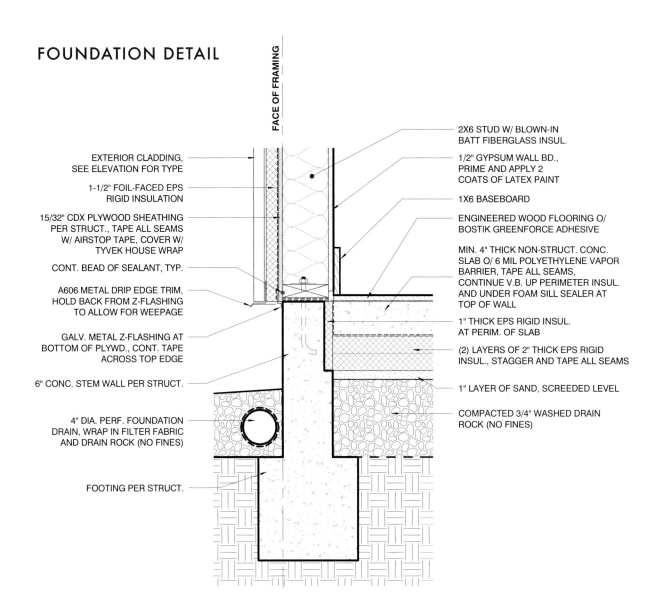

EXTERIOR CLADDING,
SEE ELEVATION FOR TYPE

1-1/2" FOIL-FACED EPS
RIGID INSULATION

15/32" CDX PLYWOOD SHEATHING
PER STRUCT., TAPE ALL SEAMS
W/ AIRSTOP TAPE, COVER W/
TYVEK HOUSE WRAP

CONT. BEAD OF SEALANT, TYP.

A606 METAL DRIP EDGE TRIM,
HOLD BACK FROM Z-FLASHING
TO ALLOW FOR WEEPAGE

GALV. METAL Z-FLASHING AT
BOTTOM OF PLYWD., CONT. TAPE
ACROSS TOP EDGE

6" CONC. STEM WALL PER STRUCT.

4" DIA. PERF. FOUNDATION
DRAIN, WRAP IN FILTER FABRIC
AND DRAIN ROCK (NO FINES)

FOOTING PER STRUCT.

2X6 STUD W/ BLOWN-IN
BATT FIBERGLASS INSUL.

1/2" GYPSUM WALL BD.,
PRIME AND APPLY 2
COATS OF LATEX PAINT

1X6 BASEBOARD

ENGINEERED WOOD FLOORING O/
BOSTIK GREENFORCE ADHESIVE

MIN. 4" THICK NON-STRUCT. CONC.
SLAB O/ 6 MIL POLYETHYLENE VAPOR
BARRIER, TAPE ALL SEAMS,
CONTINUE V.B. UP PERIMETER INSUL.
AND UNDER FOAM SILL SEALER AT
TOP OF WALL

1" THICK EPS RIGID INSUL.
AT PERIM. OF SLAB

(2) LAYERS OF 2" THICK EPS RIGID
INSUL., STAGGER AND TAPE ALL SEAMS

1" LAYER OF SAND, SCREEDED LEVEL

COMPACTED 3/4" WASHED DRAIN
ROCK (NO FINES)

LOCATION: Rough and Ready, California; boundary between Climate Zones 3 and 4.

ARCHITECT: Jeffrey Adams

BUILDER: Atmosphere Design Build

LIVING AREA: 1,986 sq. ft.

NUMBER OF BEDROOMS/BATHROOMS: 3/1.5

FOUNDATION: 6-in. concrete stemwall

FOUNDATION INSULATION: 1-in. EPS at perimeter (R-4)

SUBSLAB INSULATION: 4-in. EPS (R-16)

WALL CONSTRUCTION: 2x6 advanced framing

ABOVE-GRADE WALL INSULATION: Blown-in-batt fiberglass (R-23) with 1½-in. EPS exterior (R-6)

ATTIC FLOOR INSULATION: R-60 blown-in cellulose

AIR LEAKAGE: 0.95 ach50

SPACE HEAT: Ductless mini-splits

DOMESTIC HOT WATER: Rheem Prestige heat pump 80 gal.

MECHANICAL VENTILATION: Broan HRV

PV SYSTEM CAPACITY: 5.6-kW with Tesla Powerwall batteries

The architect's tastes trended toward more modernist themes while his wife, who grew up in New York State, liked a more traditional style. The house is a blend of both.

The house has no fossil-fuel-burning appliances. The induction range in the kitchen has been a hit, what the designer/owner calls "one of the final pieces to the all-electric puzzle."

## WHAT MAKES THIS A PRETTY GOOD HOUSE?

- Simple building shape.

- Uses a practical approach to high-performance building design with windows and building assemblies appropriate to the budget and the climate.

- Exterior details suited to a wildfire region.

- All-electric operation, including ductless mini-splits, a heat-pump water heater, and a 5.6-kW solar array.

- Rigorous air sealing.

- Advanced framing.

- Insulation includes neither polyurethane foam nor XPS.

## Rethinking the Mini-Split Approach

With very little air leakage and plenty of insulation, heating and cooling loads are relatively low. Adams chose a ductless mini-split heat-pump system consisting of two outdoor compressors and two indoor units, one upstairs and one downstairs. He was particularly influenced by the work of Carter Scott in Massachusetts, who built two-story houses that could be heated and cooled with two mini-split units. At the Adams house, the first floor has an open floor plan, so the space has relatively uniform temperatures. Upstairs, however, there are three bedrooms. The couple's teenage son likes to keep his door closed, so his room has a tendency to overheat. In hindsight Adams would have looked into a ducted mini-split for better air circulation on the second floor, even if he had to sacrifice a little efficiency to do so.

and fire-cement panels, both of them fire-resistant, complete the exterior cladding. Adams also eliminated roof overhangs, not only to make the house less prone to fire but also to save a little money.

From his work at Atmosphere, Adams knew that air tightness in the building enclosure was critical for energy performance. In his location, on the cusp between Climate Zones 3 and 4, improving airtightness from 2 ach50 to 1 ach50 reduced energy use by 30%, a major savings. In the end, Adams got leakage down to less than 1. Part of that strategy is a variable-permeance vapor retarder and air barrier at

# FLOOR PLANS

## FIRST FLOOR

1 ENTRY HALL
2 KITCHEN
3 GREAT ROOM
4 MUD ROOM
5 1/2 BATH ROOM
6 FLEX ROOM
7 STAIRWELL
8 WALK-IN PANTRY
9 COVERED PORCH
10 MECHANICAL CLOSET

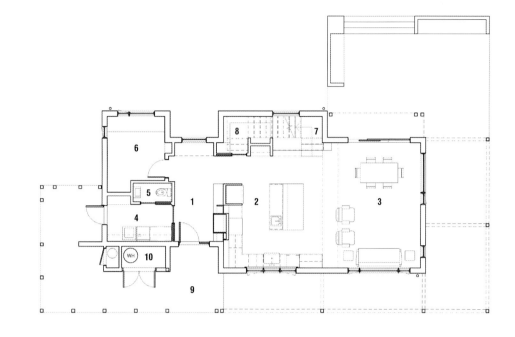

## SECOND FLOOR

1 BEDROOM 1
2 BEDROOM 2
3 MASTER BEDROOM
4 WALK IN CLOSET
5 FAMILY BATHROOM
6 TUB ROOM
7 BOOK NOOK
8 HALLWAY
9 STAIRWELL
10 LINEN CLOSET
11 MECHANICAL CHASE
12 BALCONY

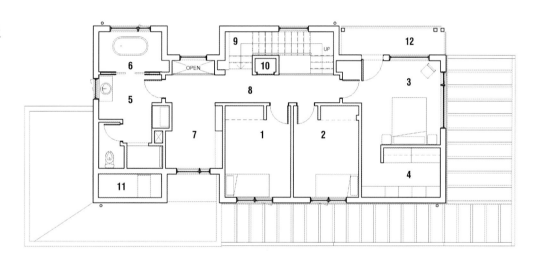

the bottom of the roof trusses that keeps all mechanical, plumbing, and electrical systems in conditioned space.

With R-60 of blown insulation in the ventilated attic, and a continuous layer of exterior insulation over blown-in-batt fiberglass insulation in the 2x6 walls, two ductless mini-split heat pumps—one on each floor—take care of heating and cooling. A 5.6 kW solar array on the detached carport gets the house

to net-zero, and two Tesla Powerwall batteries keep things running when the grid is down.

Adams, an avid cook, also put in an induction range and has been pleased with how it's worked out. "I don't feel like you're sacrificing in any way," he says, "assuming you have cookware already suited for induction. I love it, and it's one of the final pieces to the all-electric puzzle."

# CHAPTER NINE

# ELECTRICITY AND LIGHTING

## ENERGY CONSIDERATIONS

1 A photovoltaic system (or plan for one), with an unencumbered sloped roof facing within 30° of south and a conduit running from the mechanical room to the roof.

2 Air-source heat pumps for heating, cooling, and minor dehumidification.

3 LED wafer lights in ceilings, but use them sparingly. Ideally, they should illuminate something specific.

4 LED strip lights that reflect off the ceiling and provide ambient lighting.

5 LED strip lights under cabinets to illuminate areas where you are working.

6 Decorative fixtures with translucent shades that cast light in all directions while screening against the glare of a bare bulb (LED, of course).

7 Energy Star-rated appliances when available, such as for range hoods, dishwashers, and refrigerators.

8 Electric range, either resistance or induction.

9 Energy Star-rated clothes washer and dryer. To save energy and prevent depressurizing the house, consider condensing units that don't vent to the exterior.

10 Heat-pump water heater, 2-3 times more efficient than a conventional electric-resistance water heater.

11 Balanced ventilation system (ERV or HRV) to provide fresh, filtered air throughout the house.

12 Daylighting—design for natural light to flood areas where you will need daytime illumination.

When designing a Pretty Good House, a lot of thought goes into the elements that relate to energy use, from overall building design and layout to the equipment and devises we use. A PGH should use no more energy than necessary.

Electrical energy is the juice that runs most of the devices in our homes. It is usually provided by the grid—the network of transmission lines, substations, and generation plants spread across North America—but it can also be produced locally or on site. For the largest users of energy (heating systems, water heaters, clothes dryers, etc.), in the past it has often been less expensive to burn a fossil fuel on site than to use electricity, but that is changing. Developments in equipment technology and how energy is generated and distributed, combined with attention focused on the building details, lead to all-electric homes as an affordable, practical, environmentally and socially responsible PGH-approved approach.

Electrical-generation plants are located regionally and often run on fossil fuels, or sometimes nuclear reactors or hydro-dams. Increasingly, wind and solar energy are supplying the grid, but they are still a small percentage of the total. From an environmental perspective, in most locations even the most efficient fossil-fuel-burning devices on site can't match the reduced emissions of "clean" energy delivered by the grid, so it's best to aim for an all-electric household. Producing energy on site using photovoltaic panels is becoming ever more affordable and ties nicely with an all-electric home, making it even more environmentally responsible; we'll go into more detail later in this chapter. For situations where installing photovoltaic panels on site isn't viable, there is another option available in many places—choosing and investing in community solar or solar PV farms. In some places you can select "green energy" right on your energy invoice.

# Reduce First

Regardless of the energy source, to reduce operating costs and environmental impact, a PGH should reduce demand for energy with good design, an excellent building envelope, and efficient equipment, in that order. We talked about design in Chapter 3 and the building envelope in Chapter 4, so here we'll focus on the nuts and bolts of lighting and other electrical considerations.

First, a quick note on how the electricity enters your house. The traditional approach includes overhead cables leading to a structure with the main distribution panel (MDP) on the inside of the wall, backing up to the meter on the exterior. There is nothing wrong with that, but you can improve the aesthetics by bringing the electrical cables to the house underground. Where the MDP is mounted and other electrical penetrations are often a source of air leaks so be sure to seal the hole. Insulation around and behind MDPs is often spotty at best, so plan ahead for air sealing and insulation.

**Electrical supply lines usually enter a house via a weatherhead or other connection at the house, with an electric meter on the outside and the main distribution panel nearby on the interior. For improved aesthetics, consider bringing power in underground instead.**

## LIGHTING

Lighting can be one of the larger energy loads, though there is a lot of variation in the ways to light a house. One way to reduce electric lighting is called daylighting—providing natural light for ambient and even task lighting. There are some tricks for getting the most out of daylighting: keeping the house relatively narrow in one dimension, including plenty of windows, and painting the walls a light color are some obvious ones. Less obvious: place windows close to perpendicular walls and/or the ceiling to increase the amount of light that is "bounced" into the space; locate spaces to take advantage of direct sunlight early and late in the day, when it's closer to the horizon; at mid-day, consider overhangs on the south to reduce overheating in warm months; and when you have tall exterior walls, consider including a "light shelf," which bounces light deep into the house. (See Chapter 3 for more on daylighting.) But for those areas where daylighting does not reach or the hours of the day when the sun is down, how do you choose the right lighting?

**Lighting types** Lighting is usually considered as one of three types, or layers: ambient, task, and accent. A single fixture may serve more than one purpose. Ambient lighting provides general illumination, task lighting highlights areas where activities happen, and accent lighting is essentially decorative, with the design of the fixture or sometimes an unusual lighting color being at least as important as the quantity of light the fixture puts out.

Lighting is often described by the equivalent wattage of an incandescent bulb, which works for those of us who grew up with incandescent lighting. But as the world moves toward more efficient fixtures, it's better to use the metrics that professionals use: lumens is the output of light, and footcandles measures how much light reaches a specific location. Another important value is the light temperature, measured in degrees Kelvin: pure sunlight is 6000-7600°K, which is similar to traditional fluorescent bulbs, sometimes marketed as "cool white" because the light has a cool, bluish tone, though it's actually "white hot." On the other end are "warm white" bulbs, which are actually cooler temperatures—2700°K is the lowest, warmest, commonly available bulb. In between are more neutral color temperatures, and with LEDs you can get various primary colors as well.

**Choosing the right lighting** LED technology has revolutionized the field of lighting, and LED lamps are now used in all manner of fixtures. They use very little energy, are long-lasting, and often include dimmable and color-changing functions. Some people still prefer the warm glow of an incandescent bulb, which is actually a pretty efficient heater—about 99% of the energy it uses is released as heat, but that means that only 1% of the energy used is for illumination. Halogen and other noble-gas lamps (the industry term for bulbs and other luminaires) provide bright light but also a lot of heat (a.k.a. wasted energy). Compact fluorescent lamps were a bridge between incandescent and LED technology but are largely in the rear-view mirror at this point. They contain a minute amount of mercury, a problem on

# Lighting Design for the Pretty Good House

Lighting in a PGH need not be overly complicated or expensive, but it will be different. So how do we create pretty good light? Lighting designer David Warfel suggests three rules for lighting design for a PGH:

**Rule #1: Light What You Want to See** Many pros talk about lighting in layers, but few can really explain why we need task, ambient, and accent light. Forget technical terms and think about what you want to see and arrange lighting accordingly. What is the most important thing to see in your kitchen? It is probably the knife and tomato in your hands, not the floor. Now check the locations of the lights. Are they arranged to light the floor or the countertop?

What do you want to see in your living room? A book can be illuminated by a floor lamp, art by a recessed adjustable spotlight, and the stone fireplace by linear grazing lights. Our designs have few downlights pointed at the floor because there are always things in the room we think are more important. Look around you now. Is the brightest spot in the room the most important to see? It should be.

**Rule #2: Be a Glare Hunter** Think of glare as a bright spot in the wrong place—your eyes. Disc or wafer lights (a.k.a. "canless recessed lights") are super easy to install but make themselves the brightest spot in the room (a clear violation of Rule #1). A truly recessed source hides the light and reduces the glare so that you see the table instead of the fixture. Be careful when choosing decorative fixtures and lamps and look for shielded and shaded sources. Our rule of thumb is that if you can see the lightbulb then you need a different fixture to get Pretty Good lighting. Bare bulbs look great in catalogs and showrooms but become sources of glare at home. A lovely open chandelier will put more light on the ceiling than your table (another violation of rule #1) and put glare in your eyes. Look for fixtures with soft fabric shades instead.

**Rule #3: Make Change Easier** The best light is natural light; the worst is fixed white light that never changes. We need different light for different tasks, moods, times of day, and even stages of life. Why wire your home with only two choices: on and off? Think about all the activities you want to enjoy in your home. What is the right light for cooking? For a late-night snack? A dinner party with close friends? Give yourself several options in each room, like a chandelier, downlights on the table, and art lighting in a dining room. Then put them all on individual dimmers so you can get the light just right for any situation.

If you light what you want to see instead of the floor, avoid glare from disc lights and bare bulbs, and build in flexibility with options and dimmers, your lighting can be more than just enough. It can be Pretty Good.

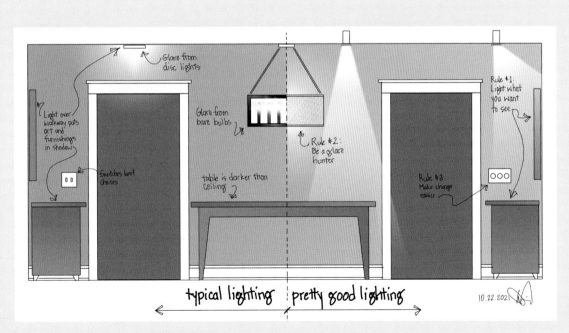

# On LEDs and Color

LED lighting is great for reducing our energy consumption and opens up possibilities for restoring some of the natural range of light we lose when we live indoors. Natural light is the best light for our bodies: Science tells us that light helps regulate virtually every function of our body and mind through a process called circadian entrainment. The research studies are pretty dense reading, but it mostly boils down to the fact that we need more natural light every day.

When was the last time you drove to the beach to watch a sunset…in black and white? Natural light outdoors comes to us in many colors from what we call cool white (pale blue) to warm white (pale amber) and all the literal shades of the rainbow. Incandescent, fluorescent, and other legacy lighting types forced us to pick one single color of light and live with it all day, every day. I even wrote articles on how to choose the right color temperature LED bulb (3000°Kelvin? 2700°Kelvin?) just a few years ago: now everything has changed.

LEDs are now available in color-changing varieties that begin to replace some of the variety available in natural light. Smartphone apps and advanced controls can keep the light inside your home in sync with the sun's light outdoors, shifting from cooler whites midday to warmer whites in the evening. The cost of such LEDs is dropping quickly to the point that a color-changing LED bulb today costs about the same as a fixed white LED cost just a few years ago. I predict that this technology will soon replace fixed white in nearly every PGH.               —David Warfel

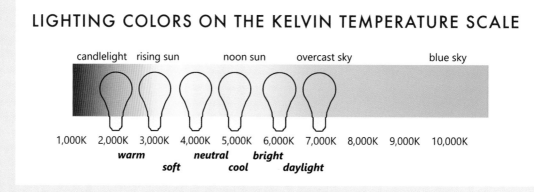

**LIGHTING COLORS ON THE KELVIN TEMPERATURE SCALE**

a large scale, but their bigger issues are a flickering appearance for some sensitive people, unattractive light quality, and a lifespan often much shorter than advertised. Most home lighting is now based on LED diodes, which are very efficient—they emit a lot of light and little heat compared to other options.

## OTHER ELECTRICAL ENERGY USERS

The rest of the energy used in the house are "plug loads," used by appliances and devices plugged into wall sockets. As always, the easiest way to reduce is to eliminate: do you really need a second fridge or a driveway de-icer? While no single device uses a huge amount of energy on a regular basis, if you have enough devices and leave them on—or even just plugged in—the cost and waste add up.

With appliances, always choose Energy Star-rated models. Energy Star is a well-known project of the U.S. Environmental Protection Agency (EPA) and Department of Energy (DOE); to be Energy Star certified, a device needs to perform significantly better than the industry average. "Significantly" varies, well, significantly among products; Energy Star refrigerators, for example, have to be at least 15% more efficient than the minimum federal efficiency standard, while televisions need to consume half the power of a typical TV when turned off. Not all appliance types are included; you won't find an Energy Star rating for kitchen ranges, for example. But for available items, start with Energy Star as a requirement and, to go further, compare the actual kilowatts per hour the device is estimated to use over the course of a year. Energy Star items often qualify for tax credits or rebates as well.

**Most appliances and energy-using equipment in the U.S. are required to have an EnergyGuide label, which shows the estimated annual energy use. Products that meet Energy Star requirements, which means they perform better than average, feature the blue Energy Star logo.**

Phantom loads are a symptom of modern life: Appliances and devices are always on standby because we don't want to wait a few seconds for them to "warm up." They are increasingly connected to the internet, which also requires a steady stream of energy. Consider putting some devices on a power strip and turning it off at the end of the day. Or get a "smart" strip, where turning off one device (say, the TV) disables the power to other outlets (such as the DVR or game system). If you aren't sure whether you have phantom

loads, turn off all of your lights at night and count how many little LED lights are still on and how fast your electrical meter is spinning.

There may be other appliances or equipment that use energy that you can't do much about, such as pumps for well water or sewer systems, water conditioning, radon fans, and other devices. But you can always look for more-efficient electrically commutated motors (ECM), you can "right-size" the equipment so it's not working too hard or wasting capacity, or you can try to design lower-energy systems and take advantage of municipal systems where available.

# Producing Your Own Energy

After reducing loads through envelope improvements, selecting efficient fixtures, appliances, and equipment, and turning things off when not in use, there is another level to the energy game—produce your own! Mostly limited to a relative handful of intrepid off-gridders 20 or more years ago, home-grown electricity via PV panels has taken off in the last decade, with dramatically lower prices, tax incentives to spur development, and net-metering to encourage decentralized production. In many situations, going with a photovoltaic system can actually have a decent return on investment—perhaps less than current stock market returns, but more secure, and much better returns than other secure investments such as bank CDs or federal treasury bonds. Usually installed on roofs, but sometimes installed as a ground-mounted array, PV panels now come in a range of sizes, types, and production capacities. Flexible panels are low-profile and can work well on curved surfaces, while more conventional panels now capture energy from low sun angles.

When annual on-site energy production equals the energy used on site, the house is considered "net zero," "net-zero energy," or "zero net energy" (NZ, NZE, or ZNE). For roof-mounted PV arrays, the roof

This house was designed and oriented to maximize PV potential. The system feeds a battery backup system before feeding back into the grid. The batteries can power essential equipment during a blackout.

surface should ideally face south at roughly the same angle above horizontal as your latitude (i.e., here at the 44th parallel, roof slopes of about 40-45° are ideal), but newer panels operate efficiently at angles far from ideal. Another option is a ground-mounted array, which may make maintenance easier and allows fine-tuning the position (see the photo on p. 217). In either case, the direct current (DC) generated by the panels goes to an inverter where it is converted to alternating current (AC) power, which is then fed to the grid. Or, for off-grid homes, the DC

power is stored in batteries, which then goes through an inverter to create AC power for home use.

## STORE YOUR OWN

Now that you've loaded your PGH with PV panels, you're good to go, right? Many people are surprised to learn that in most cases having a PV array tied to the grid doesn't help them if the grid goes down. While some systems allow for direct energy use when the sun is shining, with most systems, if you want to store solar energy for use at night or when

Built in a community of solar homes, the Slate farmhouse has enough roof real estate to hold 30 panels and be completely net zero. With a PGH budget, only 20 panels were originally installed, but room was left for future expansion of the PV system.

the electrical grid is not working, you need a battery system. For off-gridders—those who by geographic or personal choice are not connected to the energy grid—batteries are the only option other than running a generator every time they need power. Traditionally, off-gridders used banks of lead-acid batteries, not unlike car batteries. Newer technology includes lithium- or cobalt-based batteries, which run hotter than lead-acid and need a liquid or fan-based cooling system.

The best known is Tesla's Powerwall, but there are a few competitors. A Tesla Powerwall provides up to 13.5 kWh of electricity, enough to fully power a typical PGH for less than a day, but they can be installed in larger banks or used in some areas to take advantage of lower night-time energy rates. There are also controls that allow the system to prioritize essential loads, like heating, cooling, or refrigeration, to make the stored power last longer. Battery storage systems are a natural fit for photovoltaic production, but unfortunately they are still relatively expensive, especially if you need enough to power your house for more than a day. The good news is that a well-designed, well-built PGH should never freeze inside; investing in a decent building envelope has advantages beyond comfort and energy bills. If your main concern is making a pot of coffee when the grid is down, there are battery-powered coffeemakers available. But if you also want to keep your refrigerated

TOP  Two Tesla Powerwall batteries provide backup power in case the grid goes down.

RIGHT  A pair of Enphase batteries use different chemistry for a similar result.

items cold and your showers hot, at this point in time a fossil-fuel powered standby generator is usually more cost-effective than a battery system. Stay tuned, though, as battery technology is advancing rapidly as competition is driving costs down.

## ALTERNATIVE APPROACHES

Not everyone likes the look of a PV system on a roof, and some roofs are simply not conducive (though if you're building a new PGH you can—and should—design for it). If you're a fan of historical house styles or of super-clean modern lines, then a roof-mounted PV array may not be for you. (Though many of us have learned to love the look of clean, site-produced energy systems.) You might consider the flexible PV arrays mentioned above, though they cost more and produce less per square foot than conventional panels. Or you could put your array on the ground, where it can be easily cleaned; you can even get systems that track the sun's path, though they rarely

make financial sense with the current cost of PV panels. If you don't have space or desire to invest in your own PV system, you might have an option to buy power through a community solar project—a large, centralized PV "farm" that provides optimum conditions for energy production. In some ways, supporting projects like these may be better for everyone than trying to make every house into its own power generator.

On a national scale, wind power currently produces more energy than solar power—in 2021, about 8.5% of total U.S. electrical production was wind-generated, compared to about 4.1% by solar systems

In some cases, mounting an array on the ground makes more sense than on the roof. The framework can be metal, or wood, such as this one made with locust posts harvested locally. Because this array is visible from inside the house, architect and owner Robert Swinburne selected all-black panels for aesthetic reasons.

(about 30% of which is small-scale, i.e., on homes and businesses, with the remainder being utility-scale systems). Wind- and solar-powered generation are growing quickly as a percentage of total energy production. Wind turbines, sometimes incorrectly called windmills, are a common symbol of self-sufficiency. Homestead-scaled wind turbines may still make sense in some cases, where there is a reliable breeze, space, and no ordinances preventing them. Some adventurous homesteaders even make their own small-scale hydro power. But for most modern homesteaders and other PGHers, it makes sense to either plan for your own PV production or to invest in a community solar project.

## THINGS TO CONSIDER

- How will you get electricity to your house?

- Have you reduced your energy demand to the greatest practical level?

- Will you include daylighting in your design?

- Will you work with a lighting consultant who understands how to make the best of low-energy fixtures?

- Will you put devices with standby energy require-ments on a switch or power strip and turn them off when not in use?

- Do local regulations and site conditions support photovoltaics on your roof?

- If you don't want PV on your roof, will it work as a ground-mounted array?

- Is there a community solar project or option that you can support?

- Is a battery system appropriate for your situation, in terms of need and cost?

- Are you preparing for renewables as you reno-vate? Are you replacing fixtures and bulbs with more efficient ones?

# Pretty Good Renovation

THIS 1,100-SQ. FT. HOUSE in Cape Elizabeth, Maine, was located in an excellent neighborhood and within easy striking distance of oceanfront state parks and the city of Portland. But the one-story house was worn down and simply too small for the blended family of five that lived there. Neither the children nor their parents had the room they needed, and the house suffered other shortcomings ranging from a lack of light to a cramped kitchen stuck in a corner of the house.

With no room to enlarge the footprint on a tight lot (above), the only option was to go up. The completely overhauled home has double the volume (top) of the original plus a new detached garage.

# FLOOR PLANS

## ORIGINAL

FIRST FLOOR

SECOND FLOOR

An open circulation plan on the first floor makes even a modestly sized living room seem spacious. Removing a massive brick chimney from the center of the house also helped.

LOCATION: Cape Elizabeth, Maine; Climate Zone 6A

DESIGNER: Michael Maines Residential Design

BUILDER: Kolbert Building

LIVING AREA: 2,200 sq. ft.

NUMBER OF BEDROOMS/BATHROOMS: 4/2.75

FOUNDATION: Full basement

FOUNDATION INSULATION: R-12 interior polyiso

SUBSLAB INSULATION: None

WALL CONSTRUCTION: Double-stud (10 in. thick)

ABOVE-GRADE WALL INSULATION: Dense-pack cellulose, R-36

ATTIC FLOOR INSULATION: Blown-in cellulose, R-60

AIR LEAKAGE: Not tested

SPACE HEAT: Hydronic baseboard, high-efficiency gas boiler

DOMESTIC HOT WATER: Heat-pump water heater

MECHANICAL VENTILATION: Exhaust only, bathroom fans

PV SYSTEM CAPACITY: None

The lot was tight and left little to no room for expansion outward (so tight, in fact, that designer Michael Maines was forced to erase the rake overhangs he had drawn for the roof because they intruded a few inches into the required setback). So, the plan was to go up, not out, doubling the volume while leaving the footprint essentially the same.

If lot size was an issue, so was the budget, prompting Maines and builder Dan Kolbert to look for any possible way to cut costs. The foundation was in good condition and so was most of the first-floor framing, so those elements could stay. Kolbert removed the existing rafters to beef up the framing for the new second story, but they worked with as much of the first-floor framing as they could, including some existing window rough openings.

One of the principal problems that Maines was trying to solve was a lack of what architect Sarah Susanka calls "away space," a room or part of the house where a parent or child might find a little peace and quiet. A new second story with enough bedroom space for everyone was a big start, but on the first floor Maines also looked for ways to make rooms do double or triple duty. One trick he's learned is to allow adjacent areas to share space with each other. The living room is relatively small, for example, but it doesn't feel that way because it's open to the dining room. Removing a massive brick fireplace in the center of the house helped, too. Circulation in the downstairs is now unimpeded, although someone could still turn the family room into a private space simply by rolling the doors closed. "That's one thing that makes the house feel bigger," Maines says, "there are no dead ends on the main level."

In planning the renovation, Maines worked through a list of family objectives. They included a more func-

**New bedrooms on the second floor were on the family's wish list, along with more interior light and more closet and storage space.**

## Penny Wise, Pound Foolish?

With an ultra-tight construction budget, Michael Maines and Dan Kolbert decided to save as much of the existing one-story house as they could before adding a new second floor. That meant the foundation and most of the first-floor walls stayed put. In hindsight, that was a mistake, Kolbert says. They spent a lot of time trying to get the second-floor deck leveled, and retaining some of the first-floor window openings limited choices for new windows. Says Maines: "Now I tell clients that no matter how much we demo, in the end we're going to wish we had done more. It's always a challenge to know how much demolition is enough. We try to save what we reasonably can and usually end up wishing we had done a little more demolition."

**TOP** Also on the list of needed updates was a more functional kitchen. A large window over the sink, bright cabinetry, and a generous central island made for a good start.

**LOWER LEFT** In addition to a renovated bathroom on the first floor, Michael Maines added two new baths on the second floor.

**LOWER RIGHT** A central brick fireplace and chimney in the middle of the original house was replaced by this nicely detailed stairway to a new second floor.

The private patio at the rear of the house is accessed via a door in what was originally the kitchen and is now the dining room.

tional kitchen, additional bedrooms, more interior light, more closet and storage space, and a new front entry. Maines also added a new, two-car garage, connecting it to the house with a roof and open breezeway. Those changes transformed the appearance of the house. Maines and Kolbert teamed up to improve its energy performance just as dramatically by insisting on some construction details—double-stud walls, high-quality windows, and lots of insulation. The payoff was a house that is double in volume but consumes no more energy than the original.

## WHAT MAKES THIS A PRETTY GOOD HOUSE?

- Used existing foundation and left footprint unchanged.

- Doubled volume of house without increasing energy use.

- High performance without foam: double-stud exterior walls with dense-pack cellulose insulation, cellulose attic insulation.

- Efficient floor plan puts four bedrooms and two and three-quarter bathrooms in 2,200 sq. ft. of floor area.

- Adds a flex room that could be a fifth bedroom or second living area.

# CHAPTER TEN

# VERIFICATION AND CLIENT EDUCATION

**Come on in, your home is complete, like Meadow View House shown here. Once construction is complete, it's time to learn how to live in, operate, care for, and maintain your brand new PGH.**

In this final chapter, we introduce you to two critically important subjects that will help ensure your house works effectively on completion and continues to perform well in the future. The first is verification. All the smart design in the world means nothing if, during construction, someone doesn't verify that systems and components were installed and operate correctly. The other is client education. When the house is completed, the owner should be taught how to operate and maintain it.

## It Don't Mean a Thing without...Verification

The first question: What are we verifying? As we discussed in Chapter 2, an energy model is a critical first step in designing for energy efficiency. It also gives benchmarks for evaluation during and after construction. Energy-modeling software can vary, depending on what you are looking to achieve. Code compli-

There are many parts and components of a home that are hidden inside the walls. It's important to verify that those pieces are installed correctly prior to covering them with insulation and drywall. A detailed inspection will also include photos of where those components are located for easier access in the event that something needs to be serviced or repaired.

# Independent Verification

For a HERS (Home Energy Rating System) rater, the following site visit inspections are part of a project. You may need more (but rarely fewer) check-ins to make sure your goals are being met. At the final inspection, a HERS rater will include the homeowner(s), so they can learn how to maintain and operate their homes.

- Inspection of sub-slab insulation before the foundation slab is poured.
- Inspection of air-sealing details before the insulation is installed. This may include window and door installations, exterior or interior air-barrier inspections, sealing of penetrations through air barriers, and blower-door testing.
- Insulation inspection prior to drywall installation.

- Post-drywall air sealing prior to final attic insulation installation. This may be the first time you can get a preliminary blower-door test, depending on how you have chosen to build your envelope (see "Where's the air barrier?" on p. 104).
- Final testing: This is when the last blower-door test is done to verify that the building has met code or target program requirements. It is also when we collect data on the equipment that has been installed, from appliances to heating and ventilation units. HERS raters will test systems for duct leakage and proper ventilation rates on range hoods, bath fans, and ERVs. They will also check combustion appliance zones for safety and will collect data on window ratings, appliance ratings, and HVAC commissioning.

ance, in some areas, will ask for a ResCheck energy model that proves your design will meet the current energy code. Most PGH designers, on the other hand, will use something more in depth that may tell you the overall energy usage, or help evaluate the ability of your wall system to resist moisture damage. We

also are seeing performance modeling that can predict the carbon footprint of our buildings or supply information on the toxicity of products.

"Commissioning" your PGH happens during construction and once the house is completed. (Commissioning is just a fancy word for checking that equipment is

# The Blower-Door Test

Our book is peppered with references to a *blower-door test,* an essential step in evaluating both new and existing homes. The test measures how airtight the building enclosure is.

A blower door is basically a fan attached to various gauges. The fan fits into an adjustable screen that covers an exterior door opening, sealing it in place. After closing and latching the other exterior doors and windows and plugging vent holes, the fan is turned on. Typically, the fan depressurizes the building (think sucking on a straw), to pull closed any backdraft dampers (among other reasons).

There are two specialized devices that then record data. One is an anemometer, measuring the difference in pressure between inside and outside of the blower door, and the other is a manometer, measuring the rate of airflow.

The standard pressure difference is 50 pascals. This is about the pressure that a 20 mph (32kph) wind would create. When the pressure gauge hits that number, the airflow is recorded from the manometer, in cubic feet per minute (cfm).

That number by itself is useful, especially if you're doing multiple tests on the same building. But the same number in a very small house means a very different draftiness than in a huge house. Typically, we take into account the volume of the house to derive a number called ACH50 (air changes per hour at 50 pascals). This shows us how many times per hour the entire volume of air is replaced via outdoor air entering the building through leaks.

The blower door can diagnose as well as measure. With the house under pressure, it is easy to find leaks. An infrared camera can show hot and cold spots, a smoke stick can show air movement, and even your hands are sensitive enough to feel the drafts. You can (and we often do) use a strong fan to do this, and ignore the measurement part, but it's useful to see the immediate effect of plugging holes on the airtightness.

OK, you ask, so what's the magic Pretty Good Number? That's a matter of some debate. When we talked about it in our Discussion Group, we picked 1.0 ACH50, but that was mostly because it was easy to remember. Chasing airtightness is fun, and many contractors like to brag about getting to 0.5 ACH50 and lower, but whether it is worth the time and materials to get much below 2.0 is open for debate. The latest International Energy Conservation Code (IECC 2021) mandates blower-door test results of 3.0 or below. As a comparison, the threshold for Passive House certification is below 0.6 ASCH50 (although, nerd alert, they measure volume slightly differently).

**BELOW LEFT** Blower-door testing is a critical step in verifying that a PGH has reached its air-sealing goals as specified in the energy model. The blower door has an expandable frame that fits tightly in a door opening.

**BELOW RIGHT** The gauge (like this DG700) reads the flow across the fan (red hose) and the pressure inside as it relates to the pressure outdoors (green hose). The test measures the amount of air leakage in the building enclosure.

operating normally.) There are many systems and components that need to be tested, verified, and evaluated to ensure that everything works as well in practice as it did in theory. Who does this will depend on the project and the specific areas of expertise required, so this could be a design team member, a contractor, a subcontractor, an independent energy consultant—or even the owner.

The commissioning team will likely visit the site several times during construction or arrange for the builder to take photos of critical details before they're covered by subsequent work. A great team that is well versed in the importance of air sealing and insulation will do this as they go along, so that verification happens as work progresses. Having checklists can be a great help as well.

---

## *The final step in verification is you, the owner.*

---

Doing a blower-door test to see if you met your final air-infiltration goal from your energy model is an important step in making sure you will be comfortable in your home. In some areas, final blower-door testing is required, while certification programs may require several blower-door tests. Blower-door guided air sealing is a great way to guard against surprises at the final blower-door test.

We have discussed in previous chapters the importance of commissioning your mechanical systems (see p. 191), but there are other systems in your home. The entire building envelope, in fact, is a system. If you have joined the online building-science community, you may have seen PGH enthusiasts demonstrating how they test their enclosures for water and air leakage at critical locations like corners and windows. There are many ways to evaluate how your new home will meet the targets established during design.

The final step in verification is you, the owner.

# PGH Home Ownership 101

After months of planning, execution, and working with a top-notch team, your dream has come to life. You feel confident that all the choices you've made, easy and hard, have resulted in a beautiful, efficient, safe, comfortable, and durable home. Your builder hands you the house keys and walks out the door. Looking around your wonderful space, you heave a sigh of relief and satisfaction. And then some doubts creep in. "But what about the ventilation?" you ask yourself. "Didn't my design team say I had to have ventilation? Aren't ERVs and heat pumps the same thing? And what does ERV stand for again?"

So, you shrug and spend the next few weeks, months, or more trying to figure out how to operate and live in this new-fangled home, or, worse, not realizing that you don't really know how it works at all.

No house, not even a PGH, is maintenance-free, and that's why it's so important that you have the information you need to properly maintain systems after construction is complete. In an ideal world, every mechanical room would have an owner's manual to help you do this, similar to what you get when you purchase a car. This guide would help you understand your home and the maintenance schedule required for every component, system, or product. Many conscientious builders include this as part of their contract, but if not, we suggest that you compile the material yourself or delegate someone else on the team. We also strongly recommend that you work with local installers who are available to service systems should you ever need it.

Even if you have received a hefty binder full of user's manuals, other how-tos, and an exhaustive contact list of contacts, there is no substitute for in-person explanations, demonstrations, and practice runs for all occupants. All this client education may feel like a lot for the project team to cover in a single walk-

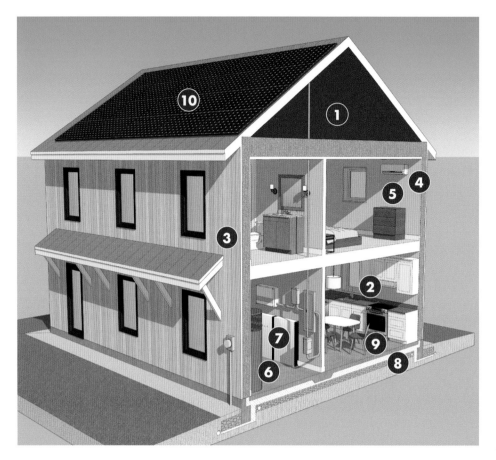

1 A well-insulated and air-sealed attic will drastically reduce the amount of energy needed to heat and cool your PGH, as well as keep moisture out of the attic.

2 Mechanical ventilation like HRVs, range hoods, and bathroom fans can provide fresh air for your PGH, but they can also cause negative pressure that creates comfort and durability issues.

3 Framing techniques, like those shown in Chapter 4, allow for more space for insulation.

4 Air sealing helps reduce costs but can increase negative pressures created by your ventilation systems.

5 Air-source heat pumps provide energy-efficient heating and cooling, but they need to be properly located and maintained for optimal comfort.

6 Heat-pump water heaters are two to three times more efficient than standard electric water heaters, but they can reduce temperatures in the area where they are housed and make noise when the compressor is running.

7 Energy storage is a great add-on system but still remains pricy.

8 Always insulate foundation walls and below the slab.

9 Energy-saving appliances and LED lights help reduce electrical consumption.

10 Solar panels for on-site energy production are a great add-on that is becoming more cost-effective.

through session, so everyone should be prepared to give it the time it deserves—which means don't schedule it for late in the afternoon after a grueling day. The time you invest will be well spent. When you learn how to use and maintain your new systems and monitor your home for safety and comfort, your wallet will thank you and you'll feel more content with your new home. And a well-educated homeowner will also make for restful nights for the design and construction team.

Once you've learned all the ins and outs of your new house, be sure to demonstrate your Pretty Good, high-performance house to friends, neighbors, and family, because educating others in person is a great way to spread knowledge of this better way to build. And once someone experiences a high-performance house, it's hard to settle for standard housing, so con-

sider this a way of making your own contribution to what we hope will be a snowball effect in the world of homebuilding.

# The Educated Walkthrough

Energy modeling makes certain assumptions about how occupants will use a building based on average behaviors, such as setting the thermostat for certain temperatures or closing windows when outdoor humidity is high. But occupants don't always behave in average ways, so it's important to learn how to operate your PGH.

The PGH community is proud of our open sharing platform. It's an opportunity for us as a community to grow and share our knowledge. It's also a great way to connect owners who are thinking about building with owners and professionals who can answer their questions and share their experiences.

uHoo, one of the many indoor air quality monitors available on the market today, tracks indoor temperature, humidity, air pressure, $CO_2$, volatile organic compounds, fine particulates, carbon monoxide, and nitrogen dioxide.

Let's start with the one thing that no one seems to notice unless there's something wrong with it: air. We spend 90% of our time indoors, yet homeowner education on heating, ventilation, air conditioning, and dehumidification (HVAC + D) is often bafflingly neglected. We'd like to remedy that.

## TRACK YOUR SYSTEMS

To fully understand how healthy your home is, you should monitor a few things. We often recommend humidity sensors to make sure your indoor moisture levels don't get too high. You can start with a simple $10 unit or select one that also measures $CO_2$, fine particulates, and VOCs. There is still some debate on how accurate these devices are, but at the very least they can detect changes from the norm. That's an indication to dig deeper into what's going on in your home.

Indoor air quality can affect each occupant differently, so we recommend using an IAQ monitor. If you notice a health issue that seems to correlate with a spike on your monitor, no matter what the number reads, you can increase the rate of ventilation, open a window, or do additional testing. Temperature, humidity, and carbon monoxide are relatively easy to monitor. And regular monitoring, combined with your own powers of observation, can really help you maintain both your home's durability and your own health and comfort.

## BEATING THE BEASTLY CARBON BROTHERS: CARBON MONOXIDE AND CARBON DIOXIDE

Carbon monoxide (CO) and carbon dioxide ($CO_2$) in the interior environment are irritating at best and fatal at worst. In simple terms, CO is a harmful gas produced by combustion, while $CO_2$ is what we exhale.

**Carbon monoxide (CO)** Even in a PGH, you can have combustion appliances that produce CO, like a wood stove, gas range, furnace, or water heater. No matter what kind you have, you need to install a CO monitor. Homeowners should learn about their combustion appliances and the effect a ventilation system may have on them. But knowing how to operate and maintain your combustion appliances is not enough. As current building codes require, install CO alarms. They should not be installed directly over a stove or fireplace, of course, and because CO is slightly lighter than air, make sure they're at least 5 ft. above the floor or on the ceiling. These should be low-level CO alarms with audible and visual alarms that go off before they register 35 ppm (parts per million).

Even short-term exposure to low levels of carbon monoxide (under 35 ppm) can cause fatigue, chest pain, shortness of breath, memory loss, flu-like symptoms, and more. Long-term exposure can cause even more serious conditions—and high-level exposure to CO can be deadly. Unlike a gas leak, CO is tasteless,

colorless, and odorless, so unless you have a reliable monitor, you may not even know when you have a CO problem.

**Carbon dioxide (CO$_2$)** CO$_2$ can also be irritating and dangerous. If you have ever been in a poorly ventilated conference room after lunch, you've probably felt an almost overwhelming desire to take a nap, thanks to the overabundance of CO$_2$ in the air from all those people having the nerve to exhale as frequently as they inhale. CO$_2$ is relatively harmless in small quantities. It is most commonly produced in our interior environment by the air we breathe out,

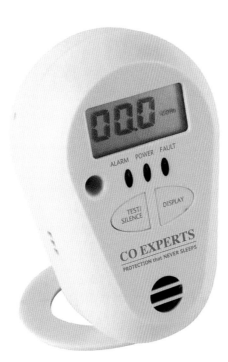

This ultra-low level carbon monoxide alarm is designed to start reading at 5 ppm or 10 ppm depending on your specific health risk needs. Continued exposure to carbon monoxide can have serious impacts on your health.

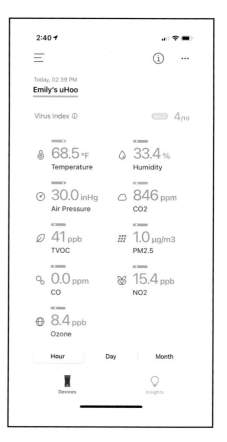

This is an output from the uHoo energy model shown on p. 229. Although modern science disagrees where the ranges should fall between acceptable, elevated, and extreme, the display can indicate a change in the environment that warrants investigation or action. This monitor was located in a home office with the door closed. In the afternoons, the occupant would become tired and unfocused. As you can see from the chart, CO$_2$ was reading yellow, which is considered elevated. If the numbers are green, they are considered good. If they are red, they are considered very poor.

although it can also be created by combustion during cooking, automobiles in attached garages, and other sources. It can shoot up without good ventilation and lead to stale air, which, in turn, makes for low productivity, poor sleep, headaches, and other ills.

Some of the simple IAQ monitors can detect a spike in $CO_2$ and let you know you need to open a window or increase the mechanical ventilation. You might see a spike in $CO_2$ in a bedroom with the door closed or in a home office where you spend a considerable portion of your day, and the simple solution in the short term is to open a window. The best long-term plan is to provide each space with proper ventilation.

## TAMING THE INTERIOR MOISTURE MONSTER

Water is one of the biggest potential risks to a building, but it doesn't only come from leaks in the structure; it also can come from the humidity produced *inside*. You should run bathroom exhaust fan(s) for three times the length of time of the shower you've

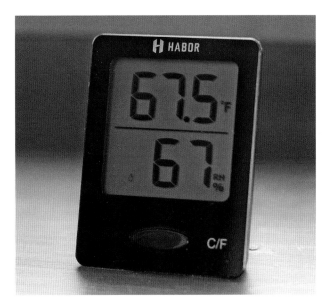

Simple and inexpensive indoor temperature and humidity monitors are available at many retail locations.

taken, your range hood during and after cooking, and your ventilation system at times during the day when the most people are home. It is especially important if you have teenagers—you know, those notoriously

# Theory vs. Practice

Emily remembers speaking with a client once during the design phase of her high-performance home to go over the planned mechanical systems, including heat pumps and an ERV. Fast forward many months, and Emily had occasion to talk with the homeowner again just after she'd moved in. It was apparent that there was a big difference between learning in theory and learning in practice.

As the energy professional on the team, it fell to Emily to follow up with the client to ensure she knew how to use all of the systems backwards and forwards. So Emily and her team got to work. First, they covered how to clean the heat-pump filters and how important it is do so frequently during the first few months to help remove construction dust.

Then they went over how the heat pump functions and how to set the thermostat, which is located on the wall unit and not on the remote control. Once they finished with the heat pump, Emily walked her client through all the ins and outs of how to use the ERV in all seasons, and when an occupant might be experiencing health-related issues. Before she left, they also talked about the environment inside her home, including potential interior humidity and pollutant issues.

The next day Emily got an email from the client, who reported that she could tell there was high humidity in the bathroom where the laundry was located, because she'd seen condensation on the window and now knew what that meant, thanks to their discussion. It turned out the dryer vent was not connected, a budding moisture as well as health risk.

long shower-takers who never seem to remember to turn on the exhaust fan.

An inexpensive temperature and humidity sensor is the key to ensuring that indoor humidity stays within a healthful range: typically, between 30% and 60%, depending on the time of the year and the climate zone. If you don't know what your interior moisture level is, you can easily overlook the issues it might be creating and misinterpret what you're seeing. When you see condensation on your windows, for example, you might assume that there's a problem with the windows themselves, but this isn't necessarily the case, especially in a new home. Although a seal failure in a window could cause condensation on the interior, exterior, or in between the panes of glass, condensation on the interior of a window typically is a sign that indoor humidity is too high. When it gets to the point where you notice surface mold, more damage could be happening somewhere else, even though it can't be seen.

## TURN UP THE TEMPERATURE—OR DON'T

Temperature and humidity are directly related. The warmer the air, the more moisture it can hold. The cooler the air, the less moisture it can hold. What might this look like in our homes? When we keep our bedrooms really cool at night, for example, and then breathe warm, humid air into the space when we sleep, we can cause condensation to collect on the coldest surface in our room, which usually means the windows or the back wall of the closet.

Our comfort is often directly related to the temperature *and* the humidity of our environment. In warm climates, where the cooling system runs more frequently than the heating system, if you maintain optimal humidity levels in the house, you can run the AC system at a higher temperature (say 80°F) and be even more comfortable than if you kept the temperature at 70°F but disregarded the humidity level. (Read more on dehumidification in Chapter 8.) Other benefits to having lower humidity levels and warmer air is that

you'll use less energy to keep comfortable, saving you money, and it can also help prevent mold and mildew.

In almost every climate zone in the U.S., we handle excessive indoor moisture through ventilation and dehumidification. Air conditioners rarely provide the necessary dehumidification, so a separate dehumidifier is usually needed. In the Northeast, we mainly use dehumidifiers in basements during the shoulder seasons when the humidity is high but the temperature is low. In winter months, when the exterior humidity is lower outside than in, we can use ventilation to help solve our interior moisture loads.

## RUN YOUR VENTILATION

Now that we've covered some of the things that affect our interior environment, let's talk about how to properly operate and maintain your ventilation system.

There are three types of ventilation systems you may have in your home:

- **Exhaust ventilation**, typically your bath fans and kitchen range hoods.

- **Balanced ventilation**, like an ERV or HRV.

- **Makeup air**, used to provide fresh air for an appliance, range hood, or wood stove.

You may have one or more of these systems, so it is critical to know how to use them properly in both summer and winter. In terms of indoor air quality, the worst thing you can do is not use your ventilation systems, especially while cooking and showering. In a PGH, fresh air for occupants is a must, so once the ventilation system is installed, you need to regularly check the systems each season, adjust them as needed, and replace or clean the filters. When you do this, you'll not only maintain your equipment warranty in good standing, but you'll also protect yourself and all other occupants from the airborne contaminants we discussed earlier.

This is the guts of an energy-recovery ventilator. It's found in the basement or mechanical space and is connected directly to the outdoors. The ERV draws air in from outside and expels stale air from inside. It supplies fresh air to areas like bedrooms and living spaces while drawing air out of bathrooms, laundry areas, and near the kitchen.

The ERV is adjusted at a central wall control. This unit from Broan is shown in continuous, low-level ventilation mode. It reads the indoor humidity at 56%, which can easily be changed on the touch screen control.

The same Broan ERV also has what they call "boost mode" and is operated by a control located in bathrooms and kitchens to increase the ERV from continuous low-level ventilation to maximum ventilation.

# Keep Your HRV/ERV in Fighting Trim

HRVs and ERVs are typically programmed for wintertime conditions. This means that the unit assumes the humidity is lower outside than inside. Unfortunately, in summer and in hot, humid climates, if you increase the ventilation, you'll bring in more warm, moist air to the cool, dry interior of the home, making it feel clammy, uncomfortable, and possibly leading to moisture damage.

If you don't understand how to use your ERV, problems can develop. For example, there is a setting on most ventilation units to increase airflow if the relative humidity is higher than the setpoint you entered. This only works when the outdoor humidity is lower than the indoor humidity. Unfortunately, most ventilation systems cannot dehumidify; in addition, they cannot add humidity in the wintertime if your indoor air is too dry. HRVs only increase or decrease the amount of air entering and exiting the home. ERVs can transfer moisture between the outgoing and incoming air. They can only maintain that humidity, not make it higher, or in the case of humid exteriors, make it lower.

Even if you live in a temperate climate and leave the windows open, turning off the ventilation system isn't recommended. All too often it gets forgotten and isn't turned back on when you need it.

Exhaust-only ventilation, like the bath fan shown here, exhausts moisture and stale air. That air is replaced by leaks in the building envelope from outdoors. The tighter the home, the harder it is to pull in fresh air from the outdoors, often causing pressure differences between the inside and outside of the home. If you have a really tight PGH, or large ventilation hood, you may also need to provide makeup air.

A balanced ventilation system supplies fresh air and exhausts stale air in equal amounts, eliminating pressure imbalances between indoors and outdoors. These systems are more challenging to design and install than exhaust-only ventilation systems and are not designed to replace spot ventilation in the bathroom and kitchen.

## FILTRATION

Filters are commonly found in a balanced ventilation system (ERV or HRV) and forced-air heating and cooling systems. Filters also can be found in a range hood or the indoor unit of a mini-split heat pump. Some homes also have stand-alone filtration systems, which are used to further filter the air inside the home and provide additional filtering for people who are especially sensitive to contaminants or dust. Typically, VOC filters contain charcoal, while particulate filters help with pollen or dust allergies. We strongly encourage you to stay away from ozone-generating and ionizing systems: They irritate and inflame the respiratory system and may have other harmful health impacts.

And last but not least, you may have a filter on your water system, especially if you're on a well. The filter may treat water for the whole house or just the kitchen sink, capturing anything from particulates to chlorine.

Regular maintenance is key to maintaining equipment warranties. This includes cleaning the filters, replacing them, and in some cases, using different ones. Your owner's manual should include a recommended maintenance schedule and specify which filters to use. It is all too easy to damage a system by using the wrong parts, so be careful when you replace a filter to use the right type and size. And, most importantly, if the system is not designed to run with higher MERV filters, such as HEPA-level filtration, don't install them. This can cause a reduction in airflow, reduce air quality, and overwork the equipment, leading to early equipment failures and voided warranties.

However, in some areas, like those prone to wildfires, outdoor air may sometimes be of lower quality than indoor air. Very few homes need HEPA-level filtration, but many may need higher MERV filters to handle different levels of particulate matter found in outdoor environments during short periods at certain times of the year. These short periods of dangerously

# MERV Filters

MERV (minimum efficiency reporting value) ratings are a way to evaluate how well a filter captures particles between 0.3 and 10 microns. The higher the number, the smaller the particles it can capture.

Sonia Barrantes, a mechanical engineer in Maine, believes that an ERV needs only a MERV 8 filter (which captures 84% of particles 3 to 10 microns in size), which is simply to protect the core from things like dust. "There's no point in higher filtration here in Maine because the outside air is fresh," she says. "And the air being replaced is leaving, it's not recirculating back into the home. Indoor air, however, needs to be filtered before it is reintroduced into the space." For this you need a better-quality filter, like MERV 12 (which captures 80% of particles 1.0 to 3.0 microns and 90% of particles 3.0 to 10.0 microns). Rarely will a home need high-efficiency particulate air (HEPA) filters. HEPA filters capture 99.97% of dust, mold, bacteria, and particles down to a size of 0.3 microns.

According to our Energy Vanguard principal Allison Bailes III, "One of the biggest issues [homeowners need to] understand is that if a ventilation system isn't sized for better-quality filters, you're going to end up with problems, because the better filters are more resistive. Contractors often are the ones doing the design, [but] they're not the ones who should be doing the design in most cases. There are some good contractors who know what they're doing and can design systems well, but so many design for the standard one-inch MERV 2 filters. And later on, some homeowner is going to buy the one-inch MERV 13 filter and put it in there and cause problems."

contaminated air may be handled with a more effective filter for a short period of time. It is critically important to monitor the system and replace the filters with the proper ones as the outdoor air quality improves. In areas where the air quality is poor for longer periods of time (in polluted cities, for example), systems will be designed for higher filtration. The owner's manual will list what filters are appropriate for yours.

As a new PGH owner, check your filters regularly for the first full year during each season and as often thereafter as recommended in the manufacturer's specifications. The first year is critical for understanding how each season affects your home and how to adjust the frequency of filter replacement. Filters may not need to be changed every three months if they are not dirty, for instance, but may need to be changed every month, or even every week, during certain times of the year. And remember that no matter how hard we try, construction dust will be present in every new home, even if you spent hours cleaning at the end of the project, so changing your filters more often for the first few months may be necessary.

## HEATING, COOLING, AND REFUSING TO TOUCH THE THERMOSTAT

The most complex equipment tends to be in the HVAC system (heating, cooling, dehumidification, and ventilation); see Chapter 8. In a PGH, the heating and ventilation strategies are likely to be completely different from the ones in any home you have lived in before. In what are currently seen as "conventional" homes with traditional heating systems, if you turn down the heating system at night 5 to 8 degrees, you'll save money. In low-load homes (homes that need less heat to maintain the temperature you want, like PGHs), heating systems typically use lower temperatures to maintain the comfort and take a considerable amount of time and energy to raise the temperature that same 5 to 8 degrees. Low-temperature

**LEFT** Air-source ductless mini-splits come with a remote that controls many functions, including switching from heating to cooling modes, direction of airflow, temperature, and fan speed. The temperature sensor is located on the indoor unit itself, not the remote.

**ABOVE** Ductless air-source heat pumps have filters located in the wall units. They are simple to access, and easy to wash off in the sink. This extra level of filtration protects the unit and cuts down on the amount of dust floating around in your home. Be sure to check and clean filters regularly.

systems are often "set it and forget it," which may take some getting used to for most new owners.

Take, for example, air-source heat pumps. Home owners are typically unaware that the thermostat is on the unit, not in the remote. Warm air tends to rise, so when the unit is installed higher on the wall, the temperature setpoint will need to be higher for the room to maintain a comfortable temperature for those seated several feet below the unit. It's counterintuitive to any owner who has lived with a traditional heating system in which the thermostat is often located on the wall no higher than 5 ft. above the floor. It may also be hard for new owners to get their head around the fact that the remote control now reads 72°F or 74°F when they've never turned their wall thermostats above 68°F. What is commonly misunderstood is that low-temperature heating systems, like heat pumps,

may only produce slightly warmer air than the thermostat setting to maintain the 68°F temperature you want while seated on the sofa. This is yet another example of why it's critical that the project team educates you on how your particular systems work. Don't be afraid to call the contractor if you're freezing in your brand-new, high-performance home simply because you don't know how to use the system.

Oil combustion systems like boilers need to be cleaned, tuned, and evaluated every year. Gas combustion systems are much cleaner, but still need periodic maintenance and cleaning over several years. Electric systems, like heat pumps, also need regular maintenance. You don't want to pay higher electric bills because you didn't get the outdoor unit inspected and missed that a mouse had turned your compressor into a hotel room for the winter.

ABOVE Air-source heat pumps have external units that need to be serviced every few years to keep the unit free of dust as well as critters that like to build their nests in the warm environment.

RIGHT All-electric homes need properly sized electrical equipment that can handle current and future needs.

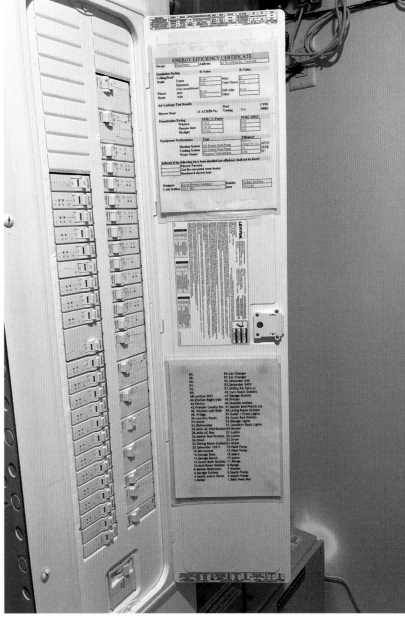

But no matter how you heat or cool your home, when you practice regular system maintenance as specified in your owner's manual, this will mean fewer repairs and a longer system life span. Cool? We thought so.

## ELECTRICAL SYSTEMS, APPLIANCES, AND BEYOND

Typically, when you get a surprisingly high power bill, you try to figure out why. We recommend doing an annual energy assessment so you can learn how you are using energy at different times of the year. Electricity costs may rise sharply in some months because of peak-pricing policies. But doing a yearly evaluation may lead to simple energy-saving solutions, like replacing an appliance with a more

energy-efficient one or catching a failure in a system that is suddenly drawing a bigger amount of energy. It is also a great way to check whether your home is meeting your target PGH goals, especially if you have adopted the motto "Electrify Everything." As we move toward using electric cars, induction ranges, electric heating systems, and photovoltaic systems to power our homes, it's even more important to understand how electricity is being used.

**Solar electrical systems** Maintaining your photovoltaic system is usually easy. If you live in a dusty area, you may need to clean off the panels periodically. If you have a Wi-Fi-connected system, we suggest you regularly check your power production. You need to maintain your system if your home is completely off-grid, of course, but it is always a good practice to do this with grid-tied systems, too, to ensure that your production is equal to your credits or to pinpoint a failure in the system. The type of system you have will determine whether the output can be measured for each separate panel or the system as a whole. If you notice a dip in production, this could be a clue to a failure of a component or an obstruction that is casting a shadow on one or more panels.

**Appliances** There are so many different types of appliances it is beyond the scope of this book to discuss them all, but just make sure that all of the appliance manuals are included in the owner's manual. Replace them when you get new appliances and carefully read the operation and maintenance sections. Having your water tested may also be critical to the long life of appliances that use water, as certain minerals and sediments found in water supplies can be detrimental to appliances like dishwashers, faucets, shower heads, and water heaters.

# But Everyone Wants a Checklist

Because no house is maintenance-free, even a PGH needs well-organized, complete documentation on both its mechanical systems and its structure. So, if you think *owner's manual* is another term for the junk drawer where a random assortment of dog-eared appliance manuals lives, think again. An owner's manual should be a comprehensive collection of resources from your house plans to a detailed maintenance schedule and everything in between.

Construction contracts come with warranty periods for workmanship, materials, equipment, and systems.

# An Owner's Manual from the Pros

HELM Construction Solutions in Vermont has spent years developing and revising its own version of the owner's manual, and generously answered the following question: "What's the purpose of the manual?"

*It's a marketing tool. Something with your logo, a way to present a gift, and a binder at the end of a project. A way to set up an exit interview and figure out what you could have done better throughout the process and what went well. It can change a difficult experience into a glowing review for you and future referrals.*

*But in practical terms, it's a place to put before-and-after photos so a client can find plumbing in the walls and floors, for example.*

*It's a great place to do a written explanation of the systems. What they have, how to use them, and where to find the information on operation.*

*It's a location for maintenance schedules and reminders that not operating the systems properly voids warranties and can lead to major issues.*

*It's a link to the schedules, house plans, cut sheets, and specifications.*

*And it has lists of whom to contact in the event of an issue or to set up maintenance. It can be the general contractor or the subcontractors, depending on your preference, and a list of the vendors for each product or system."*

For more information on putting together an owner's manual of your own, go to https://www.efficiencyvermont.com/trade-partners/technical-resources and scroll down to "Other References."

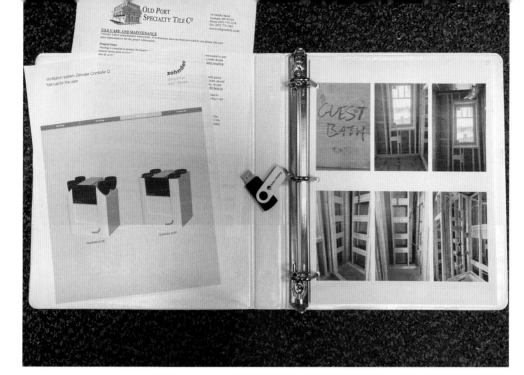

A great owner's manual will have photos of what is inside your walls, behind the drywall, along with user manuals for any equipment you own and a list of specifications for the products you selected.

Mark these dates on a master calendar to help you keep track of when equipment or appliances need maintenance or replacement. You'll also need to know who to call if there are problems, so the warranty section should be followed by a complete list of these contacts. This list should include materials and their vendors, too. If you (and future) homeowners have complete information, you'll know where to find kitchen tile to replace a cracked one, for example.

As a PGH owner, you can manage many home-maintenance tasks perfectly well on your own, as long as you have enough information and a system in place to ensure they get done in a timely way. So instead of calling the builder every time you have a question, you can simply look up an item in the owner's manual. But the best, most comprehensive information in the world is useless unless you can find it, so, elementary as it may sound, the owner's manual should be kept in an easily accessible place, and everyone in the house should know where it is.

Maintaining the various systems in your home may seem mundane, but this will help keep utility bills low, reduce the likelihood of damage, improve safety, provide good air quality, and keep you comfortable.

We would say that's a win-win all round.

## THINGS TO CONSIDER

- Systems and component verification happens throughout construction and is an important aspect of meeting your PGH goals.

- Create an owner's manual for all the systems and components of your home.

- Spend time walking through every system with your team at the end of the project to fully understand how to operate and maintain your home.

- Keep track of temperature, humidity, CO, and $CO_2$. Sudden changes may indicate a problem.

- Run your ventilation system.

- Check, replace, or clean your filters on a schedule recommended by the manufacturer.

- Know how to operate your heating and cooling systems.

- Do a yearly energy assessment.

- Update your owner's manual when you change a system or component.

- Get an energy audit before any renovations. Perform blower-door tests before, during, and after any work involving air sealing.

# Pretty Good Garage

This detached garage was part of a major renovation to a 200-year-old Cape-style home in Brunswick, Maine. It was designed by Michael Maines to complement the house without looking artificially old and without overwhelming the house in scale.

A GARAGE CAN BE MUCH MORE than a secondary structure for stowing a couple of cars and a lawn-mower. Case in point is this detached garage next to a 19th-century Cape near Bowdoin College in Bruns-wick, Maine. It fills a number of practical needs while meeting the aesthetic goals of its owners and fitting comfortably into a neighborhood of similar homes. In the process, it demonstrates that Pretty Good House principles work for outbuildings as well as they do for houses.

The 672-sq.-ft. structure grew out of a renovation of the nearly 200-year-old house on the property. That project included the transformation of a tiny attached garage into a sunlit family room and making a number of other changes and updates.

Although the house dates from the 1800s, the owners have modern tastes. Renovated interior spaces show a mix of traditional and stylish, contemporary materials and detailing that reflects the interior design back-ground of one of the owners. When designer Michael Maines turned his attention to the garage, he looked

Although the house is two centuries old, the owners' tastes lean toward contemporary styling, as reflected in the reworked kitchen designed by Balance Design Studio principal Catherine Weiland.

for a way to complement the house without over-whelming it, and without making it look artificially old.

If sizing a PGH hinges on simplicity and careful planning for how space will be used, the same can be true with an auxiliary building. Functionally, this garage is not any larger than it needs to be. The one-car family needed no more than a single bay for a motorized vehicle, but did need some lockable space for bicycles, kayaks, and other outdoor gear. The side of the garage facing the house is open storage that can handle the multiple cords of wood they'll need to keep two wood stoves going during the winter. And it will save the owners the trouble of scraping ice off their previously open-air wood piles. Upstairs, there's additional storage.

"We wanted storage for wood, and we wanted storage for our stuff," says owner Kevin Cashman. "We did go back and forth between a two-car garage and one-bay, and we ended up with this. We think it's pretty cool."

A cornerstone of Pretty Good House thinking is to build only as much space as you need—and that applies to garages and outbuildings as well as principal dwellings. The garage has a single locked bay and outdoor parking for the family's lone car.

To Builder Ben Hemberger of Benjamin & Co., the scale of the building is especially attractive. Unlike some of the oversized houses he's worked on, this one has low roof lines and trim that you can reach up and touch. The exterior is clad in white cedar harvested and milled in Maine. Hemberger's timber-framing experience is visible in the exposed joinery at the corners of the building. Maines chose rough hemlock for the exterior posts and, at Hemberger's suggestion, stained them a gray-green to complement the color of the cedar.

In all, it's not your typical lumberyard garage package, says Maines. The shape is respectful of the early New England home it's built for, adding to it without overwhelming it. "As simple as it is," he says, "it's one of my favorite projects."

The builder drew on his background in timber framing for detailing in the exposed posts and beams at the corners of the garage. The rough hemlock is stained a color that complements the white cedar siding.

## WHY THIS GARAGE IS PRETTY GOOD

- No larger than necessary.

- Uses locally sourced and naturally durable materials.

- A pleasing design that complements the house and the neighborhood.

- Uncomplicated shape simplifies construction: Form follows function.

## Aesthetics Matter

The central part of the garage is built on a concrete foundation—stem walls that go below the frost line with a slab poured on top of them. The wings on either side are not fully enclosed and are built on concrete piers. Designer Michael Maines could have reduced the carbon footprint of the building by using helical piers (a.k.a. piles) instead of concrete in those locations. That's a consideration worth making. Helical piles, which are essentially metal pipes that are driven into the ground hydraulically, are installed quickly and economically, and they would have been more than adequate to support their intended loads. But they would have looked out of place, even spindly, in this neighborhood of traditional older homes. To Maines, the modest tradeoff in carbon emissions to go with concrete was worth their more robust appearance. "A building has to be loved," he said. "I think this was worth it."

Wood storage for the family's two wood stoves is under cover but within easy access from the house. There's enough room for the multiple cords of wood the family will use over the course of the winter and for next year's wood to be drying.

Siding for the garage is white cedar, cut and milled in Maine. The wood is naturally durable and will weather to a muted gray over time.

LOCATION: Brunswick, Maine; Climate Zone 6A

DESIGNER: Michael Maines

BUILDER: Benjamin & Co.

AREA: 672 sq. ft total, 264 sq. ft. enclosed

FOUNDATION: Concrete stem walls and slab, concrete piers

FOUNDATION INSULATION: None

WALL CONSTRUCTION: 2x4 on 24-in. centers

ABOVE-GRADE WALL INSULATION: None

ATTIC FLOOR INSULATION: None

SPACE HEAT: None

# IN CLOSING

CONGRATULATIONS! You made it to the end of the book. We know that there is a lot to take in, a lot to worry about. As we sometimes say, half-jokingly, developing an interest in building science is a good way to never sleep well again. It's possible to overthink details, but underthinking is more likely to get you in trouble.

We hope that the book has been more reassuring than worrisome. Our goal has been to demystify high-performance building and make it approachable for people with the desire but not the experience. In fact, we have so much faith in the abilities of our readers that we have gone ahead and prepared ready-for-download Pretty Good House certificates! Download from www.prettygoodhouse.org in your choice of simple or fancy logo, as shown below. Proudly display the certificate in your own Pretty Good House, and welcome to the club.

**DAN KOLBERT** has been a building contractor in Portland, Maine, for 20 years and a carpenter for 35.

**EMILY MOTTRAM** is an architect and principal of Mottram Architecture. She is a building-science educator, co-host on "The BS & Beer Show," and host of a monthly podcast "E3: Energy and Efficiency with Emily," focusing on building science, architecture, and female entrepreneurship.

**MICHAEL MAINES** designs homes and renovations that meet Pretty Good House principles. He shares building-science knowledge through writing and "The BS & Beer Show."

**CHRIS BRILEY** is a principal architect and certified passive house consultant at BRIBURN (Portland, Maine), where he practices "architecture for life" specializing in sustainable design.

**SCOTT GIBSON,** author of the ten case studies in this book, is a contributing writer for Green Building Advisor and *Fine Homebuilding* magazine.

# GLOSSARY

**Advanced framing**   A framing method that seeks to minimize structurally unnecessary framing.

**Air changes per hour (ACH)**   How many times per hour an amount equal to the entire volume of air in a house is replaced, either from drafts or ventilation.

**Air control layer**   A continuous layer of material or materials that prevents air from moving either from interior or exterior. It can be anywhere in the assembly, and even move from one place to another, as long as continuity is maintained.

**Air leakage (windows)**   Rate of air movement through a window, as determined by the U.S. DOE, as an optional rating for the NFRC label.

**Air-source heat pump**   Electric heating and/or cooling equipment that uses the outside air as its heat source.

**Blower-door test**   A building diagnostic test that puts a house under pressure and measures the rate of air leakage.

**Building envelope**   The exterior surface area of a building: roof, walls, and under the slab or foundation.

**Capture area**   The volume that a range hood can effectively ventilate air from.

**Carbon accounting**   Quantifying the energy required to manufacture and deliver a building material and its components.

**Carbon footprint**   How much energy and resources a person or group of people consumes, translated into greenhouse gas units.

**Carbon load**   The entire amount of $CO_2$ or equivalents required to manufacture and maintain an item, assembly, building, etc.

**Carbon sequestration**   Storing $CO_2$ to remove it from the atmosphere, either through plant growth or mechanical means.

**Climate zones**   Divisions showing rough gradations in climate. The continental U.S. ranges from 1 (tip of Florida) to 7 (northern Maine, Canadian border at the Great Lakes) and is divided by both temperature and moisture.

**$CO_2$ equivalent**   A unit measuring the climactic damage of various gases, using the potency of $CO_2$ over a specified time span (usually 100 years) as the standard.

**Commissioning**   Ensuring that systems (mechanical, ventilation, etc.) operate as designed, usually prior to occupancy.

**Condensation Resistance (CR)**   A measure of how likely condensation is to occur on a window, on a 0-100 scale.

**Conditioned (space)**   The area inside a house that is heated, cooled, or otherwise treated by mechanical equipment. Should align with the insulated space.

**Control layer**   A material (membrane, film, tape, insulation, etc.) used to control the intrusion or movement of water, air, vapor, or heat.

**Daylighting**   The strategic use of windows and/or shades to bring natural light into a building to avoid the need for artificial light.

**Design pressure**   A structural rating of a window or other building component, with specific air and water leakage at a given wind speed.

**Design temperature**   The temperature used in a certain location to design heating or cooling systems, based on average low or high temperatures over a previous period.

**Embodied carbon**   The energy used in the manufacture and installation of an item, assembly, or building. Differs from carbon load in that it does not measure ongoing use and maintenance.

**Energy modeling**   Software used to calculate the energy used in a house for basic occupancy, based on plans, wall sections, levels of insulation, etc.

**Energy-recovery ventilator (ERV)**   Also called an enthalpy-recovery ventilator, a balanced ventilation system that allows exhaust air to transfer some of its conditioning (heat and moisture) to incoming air.

**Exfiltration**   The effect of pressure on a building forcing conditioned air out; opposite of infiltration.

**Frost wall**   A foundation system where the walls only extend to frost line (depth dependent on location). Instead of a full basement, there is either a crawlspace or a slab on grade.

**Global warming potential (GWP)**   *See* $CO_2$ equivalent.

**Ground-source heat pump**   Electric heating and/or cooling equipment that uses the ground (typically either trenches or a pond) as its heat source.

**Heat-recovery ventilator (HRV)**   A balanced ventilation system that allows exhaust air to transfer some of its heat energy to incoming air.

**HEPA**   High-Efficiency Particulate Air filters; able to remove over 99.95% of particles 3 microns in diameter or larger.

**HERS**   Home Energy Rating System, a scoring system designed to assess a home's energy efficiency. A net-zero home would have a HERS score of 0, a home built to the 2006 IECC (energy code) would be 100.

**Indoor air quality (IAQ)**   The measure of various pollutants and particulates in the air inside a home.

**Insulated concrete form (ICF)**   A wall system typically used for foundation walls, made of stacking hollow blocks of rigid insulation, filled with concrete.

**LED**   Light Emitting Diode; very efficient lighting, able to be used in a variety of forms and hues. Produces very little waste heat.

**LEED**   Leadership in Energy and Environmental Design; a building rating system developed by the U.S. Green Building Council. It rates residential, commercial, and institutional buildings on a variety of factors, from energy efficiency to access to public transit, shopping, health care, etc.

**Lumen**   A unit of measurement for light intensity, standardized across light technologies.

**Mechanical system**   The equipment used to produce and deliver conditioned air and water in a home. Includes heating, cooling, hot water, dehumidification, and ventilation.

**MERV**   Minimum Efficiency Reporting Value; a standardized measurement for air filtration. Measures how effectively a filter captures particles from 0.3 to 10 micrometers; a higher number captures more but also obstructs airflow more.

**Net zero, net-zero energy home**   A home that produces (through renewable technology like photovoltaic panels) as much energy as is consumed over the course of an entire year.

**Operational carbon**   The energy used once a building is occupied, to heat, cool, light, power, etc.

**Outsulation**   A continuous layer of insulation applied to the exterior of a building's framing or sheathing.

**Passive House**   Also called PassivHaus, a program originally developed in Germany to build ultra-low load houses. Buildings are certified by running multiple factors through their proprietary software, PHPP.

**Permeability**   A measure of how much and how fast water vapor can pass through a material.

**Photovoltaic (PV) solar panels**   Glass panels, typically mounted on roofs or on ground-mounted racks, that convert sunlight into DC power via semiconductors.

**Rain (or weather) control layer**   *See* Water-resistant barrier.

**Rainscreen**   A space created behind a building's cladding (siding) to allow any bulk water from the exterior (typically rain) or water vapor from the interior to drain or evaporate.

**Relative humidity**   The percentage of humidity in the air relative to how much it could contain at current temperature.

**R-value**   How much a given material slows the transfer of heat from the warm side to the cold side; higher numbers mean greater resistance. The inverse of U-factor.

**Solar gain**   The heat energy introduced into a building through windows or from the absorption of heat radiation by the building's materials.

**Solar Heat Gain Coefficient (SHGC)**   How much solar energy, in the form of radiation, gets through a window or other glazing, on a 0-1.0 scale. Lower SHGC means less energy is getting through.

**Stack effect**   The movement of warm air upward in a building, caused by both drafts and by the relative buoyancy of warm air.

**Thermal break**   An interruption of heat transfer from the interior to exterior, usually by creating a space and insulating it.

**Thermal bridging**   A direct heat-conductive pathway from inside to outside, typically created by framing members.

**Thermal control layer**   Material used to maintain the temperature difference between inside and outside. A building will often have multiple insulation types depending on location.

**U-factor**   How much a given material slows the transfer of heat from the warm side to the cold side; lower numbers mean greater resistance. The inverse of R-value.

**Vapor control layer**   A membrane or film (including paint) used to slow down the passage of moisture through a wall or roof assembly. It can be used to control interior or exterior humidity, or allow passage in both directions, depending on conditions.

**Visible Transmittance (VT or VLT)**   How much light gets through glass, on a 0-1.0 scale, with 0 being opaque and 1.0 being perfectly clear.

**VOCs**   Volatile Organic Compounds; the carbon gases emitted by various compounds, typically by exposure to air or sunlight.

**Water-resistant barrier (WRB)**   A membrane or film that keeps bulk water (typically rain) from infiltrating into a framing assembly; also called weather-resistant barrier or, previously, housewrap.

# CREDITS

*Note. For each entry, photographer (or illustrator) is listed first, followed by architect, designer, and/or builder as appropriate.*

### TITLE PAGE

François Gagné; BRIBURN; Emerald Builders

### INTRODUCTION

p. 2 Michael Maines

pp. 4, 7, 8 Dan Kolbert; Kaplan Thompson Architects

### CHAPTER 1

p. 10 Robert Swinburne; architect Robert Swinburne

p. 11 Claudia Uribe; Brillhart Architecture

p. 12 (left) Malcolm Taylor; Malcolm Taylor Design

p. 12 (right) Amadeus Leitner, courtesy NEEDBASED, Inc.

pp. 13, 14 (bottom) courtesy U.S. Department of Energy

p. 14 (top) courtesy USDA Agricultural Research Service

p. 16 (top) Mario Ferro (based on original drawing by Michael Maines)

p. 16 (bottom) Jesse Schwartzberg, courtesy Black Mountain Architecture

p. 18 Ann Kearsley Design

p. 19 original drawing by Robert Morrison, PE

pp. 24-29 Patrick Heageny; architect Thomas Bateman Hood; builder Carl Seville

### CHAPTER 2

p. 30 Adapted from U.S. Census Bureau

p. 31 courtesy The Taunton Press

p. 33 Adapted from Dr. Allison Bailes, III

p. 34 courtesy Michael Maines

p. 35 (top) Dan Kolbert

p. 35 (bottom) Ben Morton; designer Joe Waltman; builder Ben Morton

p. 36 courtesy Woodhull of Maine

p. 37 Scott Gibson, *Fine Homebuilding*

p. 38 (top) Robert Swinburne

p. 38 (bottom) courtesy BRIBURN

p. 39 Adapted from ATTOM Data Solutions

p. 41 courtesy Tedd Benson, Bensonwood

pp. 42-47 Irvin Serrano; architect Harry Hepburn, BRIBURN; builder Benjamin & Co.

### CHAPTER 3

pp. 48, 53 (top left), 54 (bottom), 64, 65 (left) Michael David Wilson; Mottram Architecture

p. 49 (top left) Emily Mottram

pp. 49 (top right), 68, 69 Dylan Kinsey; Kinsey Construction

p. 49 (bottom) Michael David Wilson; Progressive Path Bldg.

p. 50 (left) ncob photo; BRIBURN

p. 50 (right) Robert Swinburne

p. 51 Dan Kolbert; Kolbert Building

p. 52 Michael David Wilson

pp. 53 (top right), 72 (bottom) Michael Eric Berube; Mottram Architecture

pp. 53 (bottom), 56 Erin Little; Michael Maines Residential Design

p. 54 (top) Michael Maines

p. 55 Robert Swinburne

p. 57 Erin Little; BRIBURN

p. 59 (left) Emily Mottram

p. 59 (right) Scott Gibson; Michel Maines Residential Design; Kolbert Building

p. 60 (left) François Gagné; BRIBURN; Emerald Builders

p. 60 (right) John Gruen; designer/builder Rafe Churchill

p. 61 (top) Dylan Kinsey; architect Robert Swinburne; builder Dylan Kinsey

pp. 61 (bottom left, bottom right), 62 Robert Swinburne

pp. 63, 70 Irvin Serrano; BRIBURN

p. 65 (right) Trent Bell; Kaplan Thompson Architects

pp. 66, 73 (top), 74 Dan Kolbert

p. 71 (top left) Jamie Salomon; BrightBuilt Home

p. 71 (top right) Emily Mottram; Mottram Architecture

p. 71 (bottom) Lars Blackmore; Unity Homes

p. 72 (top) Mottram Architecture

p. 73 (bottom) Jamie Salomon; Unity Homes

p. 75 (top) Sandy Agrafiotis; BrightBuilt Home

p. 75 (bottom) Bill Spohn

pp. 76-83 Michael David Wilson; Mottram Architecture; builder Patrice Cappelletti

### CHAPTER 4

pp. 85 (left), 89, 90 (top), 91 (top), 92 (top), 98, 100-101, 102 (top), 106 Chris Briley

p. 85 (right) Patrick McCombe, *Fine Homebuilding*

pp. 88, 95 Dan Kolbert

pp. 90 (bottom), 91 (bottom), 92 (bottom), 94, 96, 102 (bottom), 103, 105 BRIBURN

p. 93 Irvin Serrano; BRIBURN

pp. 97, 107 courtesy Maine Passive House

p. 99 Robert Swinburne

p. 108, 111 (top) Robert Swinburne; Mindel and Morse Builders

pp. 109, 110, 111 (bottom) Lindsay Selin; Robert Swinburne; Mindel and Morse Builders

**CHAPTER 5**

pp. 112, 122, 124, 125, 126 Chris Briley

p. 113 BRIBURN

p. 114 (left) courtesy Dörken Systems Inc.

pp. 114 (right), 115 Dan Kolbert

p. 118 Mario Ferro

p. 120 (left) courtesy Maine Passive House

p. 120 (right) Andy Engel, *Fine Homebuilding*

p. 121 Robert Swinburne

p. 123 Dan Thornton, *Fine Homebuilding*

pp. 127-131 Jim Raycroft; Rachel White, Byggmeister Design-Build

**CHAPTER 6**

pp. 132, 135 (bottom right) Lynn Dube, courtesy Maine Build Studio

pp. 133 (left) 143 (top left), 146 Michael Maines

pp. 133 (right), 135 (left), 139 (top), 144 Mario Ferro

p. 134 (top left) courtesy Birdsmouth Design-Build

p. 134 (top right) Pamela Cook, courtesy River Architects

p. 134 (bottom) Brian Vanden Brink; GO Logic

p. 135 (top right) Steve Demetrick; architect Steven Baczek

p. 136 (left) Russell Chapman, courtesy Sierra Pacific

pp. 136 (center, right), 137 (center) Zoe Konstantino, courtesy Performance Building Supply

p. 137 (left) courtesy Pinnacle Window Solutions

p. 137 (right) courtesy Alpen

p. 139 (bottom) Michael Eric Berube; Mottram Architecture

p. 140 (left) Dylan Kinsey; architect Robert Swinburne; builder Dylan Kinsey

p. 140 (right) Emily Mottram

p. 141 courtesy NFRC

p. 143 (top right) ncob photo

p. 143 (bottom) Zoe Konstantino

p. 145 courtesy Robert Swinburne

p. 147 (top) Randy Ashey Photography, courtesy Fine Lines Construction

p. 147 (bottom) courtesy foursevenfive.com

p. 148 Toby Welles, *Fine Homebuilding*

pp. 149-153 François Gagné; BRIBURN; designer Stephen Peck; Emerald Builders

**CHAPTER 7**

pp. 154, 158, 160 (top), 161, 164, 174 Dan Kolbert

p. 155 adapted from 2030 Inc./Architecture 2030

p. 156 Ace McArleton, New Frameworks

p. 159 courtesy Building Science Corporation

pp. 160 (bottom), 176 Ben Bogie

p. 162 courtesy David Murakami Wood, Wolfe Island Passive House

p. 163 BRIBURN; builder Benjamin & Co.

p. 169 (top) Dan Thornton, *Fine Homebuilding*

p. 169 (bottom) BRIBURN

p. 170 Irvin Serrano; BRIBURN; Taggart Construction

p. 172 Michael David Wilson; Mottram Architecture

p. 173 BRIBURN

pp. 178-183 Michael David Wilson; Mottram Architecture; Stacy Brothers General Contractors

**CHAPTER 8**

pp. 184, 187, 194, 195, 198, 200 Dan Kolbert

p. 185 Erin Little; Michael Maines Residential Design

p. 189 Tim Biebel, *Fine Homebuilding*

p. 193 (top) ncob photo

p. 193 (bottom) Chris Battaglia; Michael Maines Residential Design

p. 196 Michael Maines

p. 197 Mario Ferro

p. 199 Andy Engel, *Fine Homebuilding*

pp. 202-207 Kat Alves; architect Jeff Adams; Atmosphere Design Build

**CHAPTER 9**

pp. 208, 212 Michael Maines

p. 209 Cari Balbo

p. 211 David Warfel

p. 213 courtesy U.S. Environmental Protection Agency, Energy Star program

pp. 214, 216, 218 (bottom) Dan Kolbert

p. 215 Michael David Wilson; Mottram Architecture

p. 217 Robert Swinburne

pp. 218 (top), 220-23 Erin Little; Michael Maines Residential Design; Kolbert Building

**CHAPTER 10**

p. 224 Kat Alves; architect Jeff Adams; Atmosphere Design Build

pp. 225, 226, 229 (right), 230 (right), 231, 233, 236 Emily Mottram

p. 228, 234 (top), 243 (bottom) Michael Maines

p. 229 (left), 234 (bottom), 237 (right), 239 Dan Kolbert

p. 230 (left) courtesy CO Experts

p. 237 (left) Michael Eric Berube

pp. 240-242; 243 (top) Erin Little; Michael Maines Residential Design; builder Benjamin & Co.

# INDEX

## A

Advanced framing. *See* Framing, efficient
Air barriers, 104-106
    pencil test for, 104, 105
    at roof-to-wall connections, 106, 107
Air conditioning, 190-92
    and dehumidification, 192-93
Air control layer, 104, 105, 106, 112, 125
Air leakage, 141
    measuring, 107
Air sealing, 103-107
Air-source heat pumps, 186-88
    ductless vs. ducted, 186, 187
    maintaining, 236, 237
Aluminum, recyclability of, 164
Appliances, Energy Star rating for, 213
    maintenance, 238
Architects, and PGH design, 18
Attics, vs. cathedral ceilings, 93-94

## B

Basements, disadvised, 57-58, 59
Bath fans, 196
Battery system, for energy storage, 214-16
Benson, Tedd, and open building, 40-41
Biophilic design, 65, 76-81
Blower-door tests, 106, 107, 225, 226, 227
Builders, and PGH, 20, 21-22
Building envelope, 84-107
    roof assemblies, 93-95
    wall assemblies, 88-92
Building materials, buying local, 164-65
    health and environmental impacts of, 166-69
    recycled, 163-65
    resource efficiency of, 157-63
    *See also* individual materials

Building regulations, 22-23
Building Science Corporation, 86-87
Building Science Discussion Group, 3

## C

Carbon accounting, 33
Carbon dioxide, monitoring, 230-31
Carbon monoxide monitors, 230
Carbon sequestration, 156-57
Cathedral ceilings, 93-94, 103
Caulk, PGH options for, 177
Client education, 227-39
Climate change, 15
Climate zones, 12-15
    maps of, 13, 14
Commissioning, 191, 225, 227
Composite materials, recyclability of, 164
Concrete, PGH options for, 168, 169
Condensation resistance, 141
Control layers, 112-126

## D

Daylighting, 210
    strategies for, 52-55
Decking, PGH options for, 171-73
Design pressure, 141
Design, biophilic, 65, 76-81
Design, of PGH
    considerations for
        beauty, 60-62
        budget, 67-69
        comfort, 62-63
        emotional response, 64-65
        functionality, 50
        house form, 59-60, 61
        location, 48-49
        orientation, 50
        security, 64
        site, 49
        size, 50
    guidelines for, 58, 70
Design/build teams, services of, 21
Designers, and PGH design, 18, 20

Doors, exterior, 142-45
    flashing, 146
    materials for, 142-44
    parts of, 144
    styles of, 144-45
Double-stud construction, 37, 47, 91-92, 100, 102

## E

Economics, of PGH, 30-41
    builder's perspective, 37-38
    and building complexity, 35
    costs vs. benefits, 33, 35-36
    designer's perspective, 38-40
    and house site, 36
    and house size, 36
Electrical energy, 208-209
    producing your own, 213-14
    reducing demand for, 209, 212-13
    storing, 214-16
Electrical grid, on-grid vs. off-grid, 23
Embodied carbon, 155-57
Energy considerations, for PGH, 208
Energy modeling, 31, 34 224-25
Energy Star rating, 213
Energy-recovery ventilators, 198, 233
Engineered lumber,
    cross-laminated timber, 162, 163
    I-joists, 161
    laminated veneer lumber, 161

## F

Filtration systems, 234-35
    MERV filters, 235
Financing
    calculating payback, 32
    first vs. on-going costs, 31
Flooring, salvaged, 150
Forest Stewardship Council (FSC), certification by, 157
Formal spaces, disadvised, 58
Foundation walls, insulating, 96-98
Foundations, waterproofing membranes for, 113-14

Framing
    efficient, 157-63
    roof, 93-95
    wall, 88-92
Frost-protected foundation walls, 98, 99
Furnaces, 189-90

**G**

Glazing. *See* Windows
Green Building Advisor, 162
Ground-source heat pumps, 188
Guest rooms, disadvised, 57

**H**

Heat transfer, 84-85
Heat-recovery ventilators, 197-98, 233
Holladay, Martin, and Green Building Advisor, 162
Hot water systems, 199-201
    heat-pump water heater, 200
    hot water heater (tanked), 201
    tankless on-demand, 201
House plans, predesigned, 71-72, 75
Humidity sensors, for PGH, 229

**I**

I-joist rafters, for roof framing, 94
Indoor air quality (IAQ), 183, 193-94
    ASHRAE standard for, 194
    Monitors for, 229
    toxins and, 165-69
Infrastructure constraints, and PGH, 23
Insulated concrete forms (ICFs), 96
Insulation
    as control layer, 118, 120-21
        with unvented roofs, 122, 123-25
    cellulose, 85, 173
    costs vs. benefits of, 33, 35
    fiberboard, 176
    fiberglass, 173-74
    mineral wool, 175
    PGH options for, 173-77
    polyisocyanurate, 175-76

recommended amounts for, 85-87
    rigid expanded polystyrene, 175
    rigid extruded polystyrene, 174-75
    spray foam, 120-21, 176-77
Integrated design, 27
International Code Council (ICC), 12, 22
International Residential Code (IRC), 22

**L**

Landscape architects, and PGH design, 18, 19, 52
Larsen trusses, 37, 38, 89, 91, 101, 121
LEED rating, 3, 6, 20, 26, 167
Lighting
    LEDs, 210-11, 212
    for a PGH, 211
    types of, 210

**M**

Mechanical design, 19
Mechanical systems, 184-201
    cooling equipment for, 190-92
    designing and commissioning, 191
    heating equipment for, 184-90
    heating equipment for, compared, 190
    hot water, 199-201
    maintaining, 235-37
Microclimates, 15
Mini-splits, 207
    *See also* Air-source heat pumps
Modular construction, 74, 75
Mortgages, "green," 16
Mortgages, Energy Efficient Mortgage (EEM), 31

**N**

National Fenestration Rating Council (NFRC), window-performance ratings of, 141
Net zero, defined, 213

**O**

Offset framing, for roof framing, 94
Open building, concept of, 40-41
Orientation, house, 50-52
    and window placement, 135
    principles of, 50
Outsulation
    roof, 95, 122, 124
    wall, 89, 90, 100, 101, 121, 122
Owner's manual, for PGH, 238-39

**P**

Paint, PGH options for, 177
Panelized construction, 73, 75
Passive House, 3, 20, 34, 87, 91, 103, 104, 136, 142, 226
Perm ratings, explained, 117
Phantom loads, 213
Photovoltaic (PV) panels, 213-14
    Ground-mounted, 216-17
Plant Hardiness Zone Map, 13, 14
Pressure-treated wood, options for, 173
Pretty Good House
    case studies, 24-29, 42-47, 76-81, 108-11, 127-31, 149-53, 178-83, 202-207, 218-23, 240-43
    design of, 48-75
    economics of, 30-41
    and home-rating systems, 3
    and house size, 30-31, 55-56
    integrated design approach for, 65-67
    and location, 48-49
    origins of, 3
    original, 3,4, 6-9
    owner education for, 227-39
    owner's manual for, 238-39
    predesigned vs. custom designed, 71-75
    as a system, 228
Project team, 15-22
    build team, role of, 20, 21-22
    client, role of 16-17
    design team, role of, 17-20

# R

Radiant heat, 188-89
Rain control layer, 112-16
    *See also* Water-resistant barriers
Rainscreens, 115-16
Range hoods, 194-96
    puffer test for, 195
Renovations, Pretty Good, 5, 127-131,
        218-23
    efficient framing for, 159
Resilience, concept of, 33
Resource efficiency, 157-63
Roofs. *See also* Building envelope;
        Framing
R-value
    explained, 86
    and thermal bridging, 87-89

# S

Sheathing, 110
    as vapor control layer, 118, 121
Siding, PGH options for, 169-71
Site planning, 49-52
Skylights, 146-47
Solar electrical systems, maintaining,
        238
Solar heat gain coefficient, 141
Solar power, community solar project
        for, 216
    *See also* Photovoltaic (PV) panels
Solar tubes, 148
Sorption, and solar drive, 116
Steel, recyclability of, 163-64
Strapping, for roof framing, 94, 95

# T

Temperature and humidity sensors,
        232
Thermal bridging, 87-88, 93-94, 99
    at floor-to-wall connections, 101-
        102
    at wall-to-foundation connections,
        100-101
    at wall-to-roof connections, 102-
        103
Thermal control layer, 113
    *See also* Insulation
Trim, PGH options for, 169-71

Truss-joist rafters, for roof framing, 94

# U

U-factor, 141
    explained, 86
    vs. R-value, 140
Universal design, 59

# V

Vapor control layer, 104, 116-26
    in roof assemblies, 122, 126
    in wall assemblies, 118-22
Vapor retarders, classified, 117-18
Vapor-open assemblies
    roof, 122, 124, 125, 126
    wall, 118, 121, 122
Vapor-variable membranes, 118-20
    with vented roofs, 122, 123, 124
Ventilation, 193-98, 232
    whole house, 196-98
Verification, and PGH, 224-26
    site-visit inspections, 225
    *See also* Blower-door test
Visible transmittance, 141
Volatile organic compounds (VOCs),
        165

# W

Walls, and thermal bridging, 88-92
    *See also* Building envelope;
            Double-stud construction;
            Larsen trusses
Water-resistant barriers, 119
Weather control layer. *See* Rain con-
        trol layer
Wind power, 216-17
Windows
    dual-pane vs. triple-pane, 142
    flashing, 146
    frame materials for, 136-38
    and house orientation, 135
    layout of, 133-35
    performance values of, 138, 141
    terminology for, 133
    types of, 138-40
Wood stoves, 185